PENGUIN BOOKS

A SHINING AFFLICTION

Annie G. Rogers, Ph.D., is the professor of psychoanalysis and clinical psychology at Hampshire College, as well as being on the faculty of the Lacanian School of Psychoanalysis in San Francisco. She is the winner of a Fulbright Fellowship in Ireland, a Radcliffe Fellowship at Harvard University, and a Whiting Foundation Fellowship at Hampshire College. She is the author of *A Shining Affliction, The Unsayable: The Hidden Language of Trauma*, and many other works, both fiction and nonfiction.

A SHINING
AFFLICTION

❋

*A Story of Harm and
Healing in Psychotherapy*

ANNIE G. ROGERS, PH.D.

life

PENGUIN BOOKS
An imprint of Penguin Random House LLC
penguinrandomhouse.com

THE LIBRARY OF CONGRESS HAS CATALOGED THE HARDCOVER EDITION AS FOLLOWS:
Rogers, Annie G.
A shining affliction/Annie G. Rogers.
p.   cm.
ISBN 9780670857272 (hardcover)
ISBN 9780140240122 (paperback)
1. Abused children—Rehabilitation—Case studies.
2. Child psychotherapy—Case studies.
3. Psychotherapist and patient—Case studies.
4. Rogers, Annie G.—mental health.
I. Title.
RJ507.A29R64   1995
618.92'858223'0092—dc20   94-45171

Printed in the United States of America

Set in Garamond 3 LT Pro
Designed by Sabrina Bowers

For Mary Mullens Rogers
and Meg Turner

The oldest meanings of the word affliction *include a vision or spiritual sight that follows upon a time of darkness and torment.*

Author's Note

The names of all the major characters and many of the minor characters in this book have been changed to protect their identity. I have also changed the time and place in which the events took place and created different physical descriptions of all the major characters except Blumenfeld. Some names in the acknowledgments are also fictitious. In particular, while there is an actual child known in this story as Ben, I have changed his name, some details of his history, and added characteristics to my portrait of him to protect his confidentiality.

Contents

A SHINING
AFFLICTION

I

THE OTHER SIDE
OF SILENCE

*If we had a keen vision and feeling of all ordinary
human life, it would be like hearing the grass grow
and the squirrel's heart beat and we should die of
that roar which lies on the other side of silence.*
— GEORGE ELIOT, *Middlemarch*

Why is it that angels like disguise?
— SOPHY BURNHAM, *A Book of Angels*

1

Light filters down among the stacks inside the library's cool vault. Dust motes swirl in the air, tiny particles of color in the muted light. I hold a stone in my hands, small, with a little dip in the very center, little dipper of a stone, cooler than the air and my hands—so I warm it before dropping it into the pocket of my skirt. I begin to sort through my pile of references, assorted scraps of paper. In the vaulted air a little circle of dust motes spins in the cool light, whirled high in space. I follow it around a corner and down a row marked PA2065. Before me stands a child (in a university library?) directly under the circling light, a child of perhaps five or six, no more, straining to see the titles above her eye level. She glances at me and gestures toward a black volume two shelves over her head. Amused, I hand her the book, a heavy volume with a title in Latin, complete with gilded pages. The child sits down in the aisle, immediately bent over this book. I remember her clearly: a child with light hair, impossibly at ease with herself, wearing a gray-and-red dress. I step over her legs, then turn to look back. Her eyes are on me, radiant, and a light moves over her whole face and lights up the library's cool vault. I have never seen such intelligence and love in a child's face. Searching everywhere for my thoughts, for the words that would accompany me into speech with her, I drop my piles of pages, look up to meet those eyes again. There, where she was, the spinning light of dust motes in the all-colored air moves up to the ceiling, and up through the ceiling.

I pound up the marble stairs, my feet a thunder and drumming in my ears, to the reading room above—about where she stood—but nothing. Heads bent over books . . . A young man, chewing a pencil, looks out into the August heat and haze. I rush outside, to look for her across the courtyard. The dry hot air takes the slow hiss of sprinklers back and forth over triangles of grass, water over the golden crisscrossing walks.

I tell you, this light stays. I can't separate the light from the silence—it burnishes my skin, a memory like a photograph—and leaves in my ears a roar of silence, deafening. You could say, "The child did not exist, or if she did, she did not vanish as you imagine." And perhaps this is so. On the other hand, some angels yearn to be recognized, but can't bear to be exposed too long in the light they themselves cast over the human world.

2

Less than a week later, I walk down a dimly lit hallway in Glenwood, a residential and day treatment center for emotionally disturbed children just outside Chicago. This is to be my first psychotherapy session with the first child I will treat, the beginning of my one-year doctoral clinical internship. I extend my hand in a nonverbal invitation to a five-year-old, tense little boy with dark eyes and straight brown bangs. He follows me down to the playroom, without accepting my hand, without looking at me. I open the door and we enter.

Ben stands in the center of this small room, his back to me. He is a stranger to me and I no less a stranger to him. I sit down and wait for him to make the first move which will conduct this overture, our beginning.

He stands very still, alone, silent—then explodes into action. He runs once around the room, touching things deftly in his flight—the desk, the chair, the chalkboard, puppet box, toy shelves, sink. He jerks toys from the shelves, throwing them on the floor.

"I want to play with this and this and this," he says, pulling down clay, a puppet, Tinkertoys and a box of train tracks. He squats down on the floor and begins to put the tracks together. Without looking at me, he speaks again: "There's gonna be a big fire. There's gonna be a big explosion!"

He switches the focus abruptly, but continues to tell me about the same thing: "You and I, we go camping. I get lost in the woods. There is a big fire."

He dumps out the Tinkertoys and quickly sifts through a box

of small plastic figures, pulling out six soldiers, then places them in a circle all around him. "They will protect me." He wraps his arms around his bare knees and sits perfectly still. Silence wraps itself around us.

"The woods are burning down, but you are safe now?" I ask. These are my first words to him.

He glances at me briefly, and, as if to show me how unsafe he really is, he says, "I am sick. They took me to a hospital. You are the nurse and you will give me a shot." He pulls two pillows under his head and lies down among the Tinkertoys and railroad tracks. He extends a fistful of long Tinkertoy pieces to me.

"These will be the shots. I have to get all of 'em." He looks away and a small shudder passes through his body. I see his fear and his bravery at once. I take one "shot" from him.

"Perhaps one shot will make you better." I roll up his sleeve and rub a spot on his arm. He watches me intently.

"It will sting just for a moment, then it will be over and you will sleep," I say. I touch the Tinkertoy to his arm. Ben winces, then closes his eyes and "sleeps," as I suggested.

Abruptly, he sits up and begins to pull more toys from the shelves.

"I am going to play store. We need this and this and this!"

He runs around the room again, picking up chalk, a cup, even the sign on the door. His words come out with quick breaths; his breathing carries the sound of fear. "I have my baby dragons, too, and baby Superman, and they are all very sick," he tells me. "Make them be well," he adds, without looking at me.

He rushes to the light switch before I can answer and turns the light off. Blackness. No text on child therapy has prepared me to work in the dark.

"How can I make them well, Ben?" I ask. But he ignores my question.

"I will sleep in the store alone. I am not afraid," he says.

Blackness and silence. I wait, not knowing what to do. "Turn on the light. It's morning now," he shouts. I grope for the light.

Ben sits up, blinking. "I had a bad dream."

"A bad dream?" I ask, feeling stupid, not in any way prepared for this child.

He nods and moves toward the pile of assorted toys he calls "the store," trying to line up the toys in rows, but he is unable to focus at all now. He runs back and forth across the small room, and then, suddenly, at the other end of the room, he flicks out the light.

"It is night now. You are my mommy now and I am your son, OK? So don't leave me alone at night." Then silence as he settles down to sleep.

"No, I won't leave you alone," I reiterate.

"Goodnight, Mommy."

"Goodnight, Ben."

The stillness lasts several minutes, then Ben switches on the light again. I glance at my watch. Our time is almost up.

"Morning again," he announces. "Now I will be the teacher." He moves toward my desk and uses the paper and crayons lying there.

"This is how to make an eight, little boy," he says. He draws a clumsy 8 in red crayon. "No, not like that, like this!"

I tell him our time for today is almost up, but that I will see him two times a week and he will come again and play as he likes. I ask him to help me put away the toys before we leave. Ben throws them at the toy shelves haphazardly.

"Where is my class?"

I touch his arms lightly. "You're worried about where your class is," I say. "You don't want to stay and clean up now."

He pauses and nods.

"Today, you can go, but tomorrow we'll clean up together, all right?"

He does not answer. He backs away from my touch until he reaches the door, then turns and runs.

I sit alone in the playroom, trying to "see" clearly what this child has shown me, what he was telling me in his play. When a child does not know and cannot describe, in words or in play, what has happened to him, it dominates his life. I knew this from the beginning of my work with Ben.

What did he show me in one hour? Running, being lost, and fire. Fear of being left alone, being controlled, or being touched.

It's a confused story Ben enacts—a story line without a clear sequence or plot, a jumble of scenes—in the woods, in a hospital, in a room at night where he tries to sleep alone. He throws toys and runs around the playroom; his feelings shift quickly. Fear is uppermost among the feelings that come into the room. But there is bravery too, almost a stoicism about taking all the shots. The plot of his story shifts as rapidly as his emotions, and it's hard for me to follow; I stumble after, learning in darkness that he is searching for a mother to stay with him at night, and for a nurse who can make him "better." I know this only as I begin to respond and play my part with him. In the process of playing with Ben, following the pace and rhythm of his play, I feel he is running from haunting memories.

Ben sits inside his circle of soldiers and tells me a story about the danger he feels with the woods burning all around him. There is a story behind this one, a room beyond this room, but neither he nor I know this consciously. In this beginning we are strangers to one another, telling stories and acting on a stage neither of us has constructed alone. Ben is a little boy who has come to be with me in this small room. He is my patient and I am his therapist. Yet from the beginning, different as we may be, we are engaged in a powerful human drama, a drama that neither one of us can play out (or even imagine) alone.

And what have I shown Ben? That I will wait for him to make a beginning. That I will play a part in the play that he began. And that I am willing to work in the dark.

After seeing Ben, I am curious to look at his record. My child psychopathology professor advised us to see a child at least once without any preconception from a record that might constrain a therapeutic alliance. Now, I walk down the hall and return with a heavy, thick file labeled BENJAMIN BRINKER. In it Ben is diagnosed with "oppositional personality disorder," and is described as being extremely bright. He was once misdiagnosed as autistic. Ben was born a bit prematurely, and has two older siblings, both in foster care. He has a history of rocking, head-banging and biting which began in his first year of life. Ben was abandoned by his natural mother at six weeks of age, then placed with a foster family. He was removed from the first foster family at eighteen months after evidence of severe neglect, and placed with another set of foster parents, Charles and Kate Brinker, who just recently adopted him. The file provides no details about the period of "severe neglect."

At eighteen months Ben spoke few words, engaged in head-banging and rocking, and cried and stiffened when held. He did not use full sentences until he was three, and completed toilet training at five, just prior to his placement in the day treatment program at Glenwood.

I read his medical record too. Ben has been hospitalized several times in his short life, at eighteen months and at twenty-four months for severe diarrhea, at three years for neurological tests, and in his fourth year to regulate his medications.

I stop reading and become aware of my breathing, shallow and tight to contain the sorrow which has swept me. I wonder how I will affect Ben and how he might affect me as I swivel my chair to take in a slow panorama of the small white room: toy shelves, a desk and chair, one other chair, more toy shelves, a bottle, a yellow puppet, clay, dolls, dollhouse, chalk and board, paints, building blocks, a blanket, and above the desk, a calendar.

After seeing Ben, I meet with my on-site supervisor, Mary Louise Sweeney, a woman with many years of experience with children. My responsibilities at Glenwood will include psychological testing and team meetings with other staff, as well as individual cases. I have negotiated thirty minutes of writing time after each session with a child. All of my work will be tape-recorded for supervisory purposes. I have already requested additional psychoanalytic supervision and will meet my second supervisor, Dr. Rachael Sachs, later in the week. Mary Louise and I set up my schedule together.

I have made a good choice to come to Glenwood; I feel a renewal of the certainty I felt on my first visit. That day I met the director, Dr. Wilson, a middle-aged man who gave me a tour of the school building and cottages in the company of a large dog of uncertain breed. Everywhere we went, inside and out, he had strategically placed water bowls for the dog's comfort. Those bowls mitigate the institutional nature of this respected residential and day treatment center for seriously disturbed children. In comparison with the other internships I considered, where I would have little choice about my supervision and virtually no writing time, I have definitely fallen into the right rabbit hole.

3

At the end of the first week, I drive to supervision in the hazy heat of the late afternoon, alert and prickly with anticipation, an odd contrast of feelings and weather. Crossing to the revolving doors of the Chicago Psychoanalytic Institute, I pass a man pushing a broom who looks up, but not at me. I follow his eyes to the other side of the parking lot where a teenage girl with short red hair clings to her father's arm, pulling him back toward a car. Grimly, he pulls her in the opposite direction. I am enchanted by her refusal to go into the building, to see a doctor here—but the strength of her misery and the embarrassment of her father's predicament make me hurry along, well ahead of them.

I push through the doors, carrying a briefcase of the tapes and notes from my initial sessions with each of the children I have seen this week. I sit in the private waiting room just outside the office of Dr. Rachael Sachs, an eighty-four-year-old pioneer in the psychoanalytic treatment of children. A consultant at Glenwood, she has already agreed to supervise my work. There, in this tiny space, I find a pile of children's books and outdated magazines, with a painting of a Renaissance angel in one of them. It is uncannily quiet. I sit for several moments before I notice a buzzer with a little note typed beneath it that reads, "Please ring when you arrive for your appointment." I have arrived for an appointment, but I am not a patient. No, I am not. Should I ring or not? I decide to ring. I press the buzzer and hear nothing, and no one comes to answer. Should I ring again? I think not.

Three blocks from this building, in my neighborhood library, I

discovered Freud at thirteen. The dense language of psychoanalysis confused me initially, but, not one to be put off, I discovered a
way out of my confusion after reading Chaim Potok's *The Chosen*,
in which Danny, a boy of fourteen, reads Freud. I read Freud as
Danny did. I lined up a series of books on a library table: an English translation of Freud, Webster's English Dictionary, a German
dictionary, a psychiatric dictionary, and my notebook, in which I
assembled a glossary of terms and kept a running log of my questions and observations. After several months I began to know my
way around in Freud's cases. I can still see myself pushing back my
braids as I hovered over "Dora"—then flying to the other end of
the table to look up *tussis nervosa* in my psychiatric dictionary—
while all about me old men sat reading books and newspapers
calmly. In this way, I began to explore a new landscape: the geog-
raphy of psychic life. And from there I moved on to the library at
this Psychoanalytic Institute as an undergraduate, using a professor's library card to get in. I read Jung and Erikson and Winnicott
and other psychoanalysts. It was the thrill of entering another language, another country, that held me dancing at my library table
Saturday mornings during all the years of my adolescence and
early twenties. Now, as a graduate student, I feel as though I have
cracked the code, I know the woros, I discern the meanings behind
the words—this I believe. I have graduated from a library table of
Freud's densely written early cases to my own cases and my own
words.

Words are angels, messengers—but suddenly, in this airless
room, I have no words, no message, nothing to bring here.

A man pushes his broom, a sweep of sound—a look, unspoken,
toward a girl clinging to her father's arm—she skids along the
pavement, dragging her feet—and I rush ahead of my own fear of
seeing patients. The sky above us is an unbroken white-blue, the
blue of impenetrable secrets. The terror of what I am doing suddenly takes my breath away, empties my mind of all words, while
the angel in the magazine stares back at me, implacable.

Promptly at 3:00 Rachael Sachs opens the door and invites me into her office. With gray-white hair, she is stooped but tall; she walks with a cane, leaning on the desk corner as she returns to her chair. She wears a blue dress with a tie around the middle, but has no waist to speak of: every contour has grown soft, padded into one bundle. As she settles herself behind her desk, I take the only chair in front of it. She leans down and opens a bottom drawer and takes out a box of hard candy.

"Here, Annie, have a piece of candy. I get sleepy by midafternoon," she says, taking a piece for herself. I feel suddenly like a child in a doctor's office. Then she pulls out a pair of bedroom slippers from another drawer and puts them on, making me more at ease, strangely. Finally she sits back and looks at me, a long look. I know this look—it is the look my mother gave me when she discerned my intentions and feelings before I knew them myself. I want to squirm. Reserve, shyness, good sense perhaps, something in me I can't name, holds back the words I have rehearsed.

"Tell me about this week with the children," she begins, rescuing me from wordlessness.

I haul out my tapes and notes. "You have begun to write about the children already," Rachael notices. "No," she says as I hand her my notes. "Read them aloud to me; let's hear them."

I begin by reading the summary of my first session with Ben, taken from my tape recording and my thoughts in the playroom when I was reading his file. My voice quivers a little as I read. Rachael nods. "Go on, read me everything you have." I read about the other three children I have begun to see. When I finally look up again, she nods and smiles.

"I feel that I have a lot to learn from you" is her startling comment. I must have looked startled too, because she suddenly becomes intent, serious. "Trust yourself a little, trust this beginning," she says. These words, from a woman who has been treating children all her life, are a huge relief to me.

I ask if she still sees children, looking over her orderly office (no toys in sight) and at the inevitable couch. "Yes," she says, "but not young children. I can't pull them out from under the couch or lift them up anymore." She is acknowledging the limitations of her age to me, but also telling me that she once had easy physical contact with the young children she treated.

Looking back at the pages in my lap, I ask her what she thinks of the children I have just presented to her. She tells me her impressions, and I notice that they all take the form of various meanings of the children's play.

"But you have been with these children. What do you think, Annie?" I have already read my notes, so this question catches me off guard.

"I'm not sure I understand your question."

She smiles. "I mean, what do you think of my thoughts about them?"

"Mmmm . . . very psychoanalytic." I laugh.

I know I am going to enjoy her because she is laughing with me now. I tell her I was an English major. I have read much of psychoanalysis, I go on, but I think in plays, stories, sometimes in poetry: more about the details of human experience, less in symbols, abstract meanings, changing structures. They are all familiar to me, but I don't feel I will ever have her authority, her ease of interpretation. Much of the time, I don't know *how* I know what I know. And most of my ideas about the children are different from hers, I explain, in case she didn't notice. Again she smiles, as if to herself. Again that long look—this time a look of pleasure. I have the distinct sense that she is seeing something about me I do not yet know myself.

Rachael does not challenge or contradict me. She sets the tone for all our work together in this moment of respect for our different questions and interpretations of my work. Gradually, over a period of months, I will learn a way of thinking: a psychoanalytic way of thinking grounded in practice, a way to decipher the meanings of children's play and their responses to me—but I will also retain my way of proposing alternative and even contradictory explanations. This experience with Rachael makes me permanently wary of interpretations presented as if they were facts.

I come each week with my own agenda of what I want to present to her, but I never know where this will lead us. I learn that Rachael has some problems with memory and often forgets the details of my cases, so I begin a habit of describing a pattern of play that extends over time, not realizing at first that this will be useful to me, as well as a help to her memory. We meet often at the Psychoanalytic Institute, and sometimes on Saturday mornings in the sunny kitchen of her apartment.

At the close of our first meeting, I ask her about a schedule for our meetings, and about her fee for supervision. She tells me she could arrange to meet with me twice weekly and that there will be no fee. I feel embarrassed. I don't have much money to offer for her services, but I do wish to pay her. She interrupts my protest. "I told you that I have a lot to learn from you," she says again. "I'll tell you what. You write down everything that you are thinking about these children, make it a practice you never shirk, and then bring it to me and we'll talk about it. You write what you really think, and I'll listen, all right?"

If she felt she could *not* learn something from me, would she have charged me? If you take something away from a relationship for yourself, should you not charge? That would put most supervisors out of business! I am living on a tight budget and feel grateful for her offer, but I want to ask her these things. But our time is up, and remembering what W. H. Auden once wrote about his muse—"It is she into whose eyes we look for recognition when we have been found out"—words which might well apply to a psychoanalytic supervisor, I decide not to press her.

And, for a long time, I do write exactly what I think about my own work. Until it begins to touch my own life too closely.

4

Ben walks rapidly down the hall ahead of me, his dark head bobbing up and down with the stiffness of his gait, then turns to walk backwards, regarding me warily. "Would you like to unlock the door?" I ask, offering him my keys. He takes them, unlocks the door and walks inside the playroom. He does not speak. He goes to the blackboard and erases the scribbles another child has made, picks up two puppets, then a ball of clay, examining and discarding each toy. He kneels on the floor and throws the puppets behind him, saying, "We need this one, and this one, and this." He leaves them strewn on the floor and pulls a game off the toy shelves, the game of Sorry.

"I know this game," he says.

"You know that game and you will play it," I state back simply.

He sets up the red and blue players on the game board. I wonder to myself if he knows the rules.

He does not invite me to play, but plays the game aloud. He picks up the top card. "Five," he reads, and moves his blue player in five leaps around the board and into "home." "I am the blue and I am going to win." Then he picks another card, a nine, and moves the red player exactly nine spaces, counting each one aloud. "Three," and the blue player makes three huge leaps into "home." Within eight moves he has "won" the game.

"I won!" he announces to me.

"You made up your own rules so your player would win the game," I clarify.

He looks at me, studying me, then bends and picks up a puppet and throws it into the corner by the sink, and looks at me to see my response.

"You can play by your own rules here," I say, wondering if he thought my comment was an admonition. Then he picks up the puppets one by one and throws them forcefully into the corner, and turns again to look for my reaction.

Is he trying to provoke me? Showing me his anger for my comment? Trying to find my rules and limits? I don't know, but I feel it is important for me not to enter into a power struggle. I want him to experience his *own* control and lack of control and his *own* feelings.

"You wanted to throw all those puppets, and you did!" I say.

I hear screaming in the hall and fast footsteps and then a child's body thuds abruptly against the closed door. Ben startles, and looks directly at me for the first time.

"What's that?" he says.

"That is a little boy who is hurting a lot and he ran into our door."

Ben raises his index finger and absently touches his lower lip, which I see for the first time is cut and slightly swollen. "How did you hurt your lip?" I ask. He looks surprised.

"I hit it," he says.

"How did you hit it, Ben?"

He stands for a moment, his blue eyes unfocused, as if in a trance, then walks over to the paints.

I sit back, literally sitting on my hands to stop myself from interfering with his attempt to set up the paints. He unscrews paint lids, spilling, pours water, spilling, and dribbles color from the brush as he begins to paint.

"There is an apron in the drawer to keep it off your shirt," I tell him. Ben reaches in for the apron, using it only to wipe his hands. He makes several swift strokes with the blue paint, then paints a red splotch over the blue.

I lean over to look and ask, "What is that, Ben?"

"A bird that's got his tail caught on fire." He blots it out in black paint, as if to erase it, and says, "Don't distract me."

"You would like me to be quiet?"

"You're distracting me."

And I was! I sit back in silence as he covers the page with black paint. I wonder how he's come to know a word like *distract* in his five short years. He looks up at me.

"Can I put the clay on the paper and cut through it?"

I rephrase it: "You would like to see how that works?"

He nods and goes to get the clay from the lowest toy shelf, then simply sits on the floor, facing away from me toward the shelves. Very still. He twists around and gives me a single clear bark. At a loss, I inquire back, "Woof?" He gives a small, whimpering series of barks. "The puppy dog is sad?" I guess. He growls and barks loudly. "And the puppy is mad now." He barks more loudly and howls and I see his first smile, showing his straight baby teeth. His eyes do not smile.

He whimpers again, then begins to convey a stuffed bear to the corner by picking it up between his teeth and crawling there on all fours. He crawls back to the toy shelves and sorts through a box of small plastic toys, removing six marbles and putting them on the floor next to the chair where I sit. He bends over and puts a marble in his mouth, then nudges my hand with his nose. I open it and he spits the small wet marble carefully into my hand. In this manner he "gives" me all six marbles. Then he barks for them and I give them back. He repeats the entire process again, then leans up against my leg as he fingers the other toys in the box. He crawls over to the sink and raises himself up, climbing into the chair in front of it, and barks. He looks at the paper towels within his reach, and then at me.

"Oh," I say, "the puppy dog wants *me* to give him towels to wipe the paint off, hmm?"

I give him several wet towels and he wipes his hands. It is time to leave. We both know this. I don't need to say it. In silence I accompany him down the hall to rejoin his class.

Ben has made eloquent statements about himself in play today. First he tries to show me that he has complete control over his invisible game partner, and that he cannot bear to lose. When I see this and comment, "You made up your own rules so your player would win the game," Ben makes an attempt for control again by trying to provoke a reaction from me by throwing the puppets. Or perhaps he is simply frustrated with me. Or he may be showing me his anger at my comment.

But I have observed him in his classroom, in the hall, in the cafeteria, trying to provoke a reaction from others in exactly this way, so this seems to me an explanation worth trusting for a bit. He would walk up to an older boy and kick out, or deliberately knock over his milk, or shout into an adult's shocked face, "Shut up, fuckface!" and nearly always get the same reliable response: someone else would take charge of him, at times physically restraining him as he struggles, biting, banging his head, seemingly impervious to pain. In this "out of control" state, Ben uncannily holds a great deal of power. His attempts to control through lack of control ironically mean that he has to sacrifice the experience of himself—just Ben—and that he cannot freely choose to be himself with other children and with adults.

I want to show Ben that he can have an effect on me, that he can choose to be himself with me, and make things happen between us. Insofar as possible, I want to follow his wants and needs, and not impose restrictions unless he begins to hurt himself or me physically. Behind the overt need to control, Ben is asking a haunting question, one seldom heard by adults: "Can I test the width and breadth of who I am, in my anger, my messiness, my babyishness *and* in my real competence, and will you let me be?" My efforts to read his behavior and let him be, with his reminder, "Don't distract me," pays off in the first physical and emotional contact between us. While Ben is testing my ability to interpret his feelings in his barking, he is also making use of the information I give back to him. Through this process of hearing his feelings named aloud for him, he is able to make himself vulnerable in his gift of six marbles, spat so carefully into my waiting hand, and to lean against me in relief as if to say: "This is who I am when I'm being me."

As I play with Ben, I listen "with a third ear," I listen for what's under the surface of his words and play. This depends upon paying attention to both Ben and myself. I notice and take in his words, the pitch and tone of his voice, his gestures, his movements toward and away from me. I attend to my feelings, and especially to those moments just before and just after I respond to him. In the absence of Ben's response to what I say or do I cannot know if I have heard him. But fortunately he is quite clear. When he is painting and I keep talking to him, for example, he says, "You are distracting me!" In his puppy dog play, he barks and growls, and I guess, "The puppy dog is mad?" This isn't a difficult interpretation, but I watch Ben for his response, and he affirms it, barking and growling louder, then rewarding me with his first smile. Within this circle of attention we surprise one another, and then Ben leans up against my leg and gives me his gift of six wet marbles.

This "clinical" listening I am learning also carries particular risks. Were I to listen to Ben as if I already knew the meaning "behind" his words and actions, looking to find some validation of a scheme I have already become invested in, I would no longer hear him. I would shut him out of the present, and nothing could get through to me then. If I claimed that kind of authority with any consistency, how could he correct me? On the other hand, I cannot abandon the meanings I bring to Ben's play. After all, I spend a great deal of my time, in supervision, thinking about the meanings of his play; it's part of my training to learn how to think symbolically about the ways children play. This training is a foundation for what I do when I am with Ben. But my training isn't the only source of my knowledge.

5

It is evening, my work with the children over for the day. I sit at my desk in a little circle of light, painting and listening to music far into the night, unable to sleep. I begin to paint a flaming bird, red against blue, like Ben's bird. I paint over it in black, swiftly, as he did. This same bird has dealt me some blow, a blow to my right temple, surprisingly hard, and left me stunned so that I can't meet myself, can't or won't make the necessary connections between Ben's bird and mine. Red against blue, my mind blackens it out. A girl is dragged by her father across a parking lot to see a doctor—my mind blackens it out.

In the street, beyond the open shutters, the tall hedge hums in the dark. The air grows chilly. Ben is out there, sleeping too, somewhere in this city. A new silence stings just under my skin. I don't know everything I need to know. Above the hedge, a movement. I go to the window and look out on the silent houses. A little black bird is weeping, weeping and flying frantically over the street. While I grow smaller and smaller, it flies farther and farther away. The little black bird goes on weeping as it wings out over the park and the city, as if a fire burns in its eyes and it has to weep to go on seeing.

6

Ben comes into the playroom the next day dragging a light tan jacket behind him. "Let's play outside today," he suggests, and closes the door. I have no objection. Ben looks around the room and picks up two red batakas, big foam bats with rubber handles. His explanation is straightforward if obscure: "We need these." He hands them to me.

Outside, the trees hold the sound of a thousand seashells, and their leaves flash like sunlight on new coins, golden and green. Ben runs ahead of me into the empty play yard and scoots under the slide.

"We are going camping and I'm the boss," he announces.

"Oh. You want to be able to boss me around?"

And he does, with the injunctions and demands children face daily: "Bring me some wood. No, that's not big enough." "Now it's time to eat. Eat all of it, I said." "Now you go to bed, even if you don't want to."

As I comply, Ben grows interested in other things. "Where did all these acorns come from?" he asks, picking them up by the handful. "I know that squirrel. He gave them to me." "He did?" I inquire, leaning on one elbow in the grass. Ben suddenly stands up and does a little dance of excitement. "I know. Let's play bear cub."

Puzzled, I simply request, "Show me how to play it."

Ben drops to the ground, and in my mind's eye I see him sprout soft brown fur and bear ears.

"I am the baby bear," he tells me. "The mama bear got shot and killed. I got shot, too, and I'm bleeding. I'm lost in a big, big forest and no one can find me."

"And what is my part?" I ask.

But he has already left me. Scampering a few feet across the lawn, he scurries between two large clumps of bushes and is hidden from view. I can hear him whimpering. At first I think we are playing a game. I walk around the bushes, thinking aloud:

"The forest is big and dark. What are those noises? It sounds like someone crying."

I lean down and push the bushes aside, entering a small enclosure on my hands and knees. Ben is lying on his stomach, still whimpering. As I bend and pick him up, I see that his upper lip is red and his cheeks wet. We are not playing a game at all.

I take him in my arms, hold his shuddering little body close against my shirt. "You are hurt and bleeding, bear, and I am going to fix it," I tell him. I lift him out of the bushes and carry him around a tree. We go around several times, his small body tense. He continues to whimper. Then I lay him down on the grass and, taking an invisible needle, begin to sew the visible wound over his heart.

"I am stitching up your gunshot wound so it can stop bleeding, bear," I whisper. Ben looks as if he is in a trance, his eyes unmoving, glazed—but his chin quivers, as if he might begin to cry again.

"Don't leave me," he whispers back.

"No, I'm not going anywhere. The mama bear got shot, but I am here to stay."

He lies perfectly still, then gets up and picks up the two soft batakas by the sliding board. He comes back and lies facedown in the grass with the batakas on either side of his head. He is perfectly still a few feet in front of me in the grass. I wait, not knowing what to say.

He stirs slightly. I sit nearer to him and call his name softly, "Ben." Slowly, he sits up, looking dazed.

"Go hunting and bring us some food. I'm hungry," he says. I

gather three sticks from the bushes, our "fish," I tell him, and build a "fire" out of dried grasses and cook the fish for him. Ben watches me intently. He eats the first two fish, then hesitantly offers me the third. He sits and watches me as I eat it.

"It is nearly time to go back, bear," I tell him, glancing at my watch for the first time. It is, in fact, a bit over time.

"We can play bear cub again?" he asks.

"As often as you want," I answer.

Ben takes my hand and we walk back across the field toward the playground and the classroom building. The high-pitched shouts of children coming out of the building for lunch move toward us, but Ben and I walk along in silence, and their voices bounce back from our silence.

Somewhere, a little black bird flies over the city, weeping.

Ben does not come back to play bear cub with me for a long time. He refuses to see me at all for three weeks. In his play, he has re-enacted his early abandonment, allowed me to play a part in this powerful scene, and invited me into the core of a drama he desperately sought to evade.

Ben makes himself into a baby bear who lost his mother and is mortally wounded, but not dead. But he doesn't simply play in my presence; he invites me into an impromptu and enigmatic drama. While we are playing, this particular drama fills the universe. We play together as the mind plays with dreams—uncovering fragments of knowledge, making them over symbolically, making memory as real as can be borne.

Ben slips into the world of make-believe as many young children do, so graciously and completely that he does not even bother to tell me my part—or perhaps he wants me to figure it out for myself. How he moves into fantasy play becomes a window into what he has suffered. How I enter his play reveals what I have taken in of his suffering. I see him sprout bear ears and soft brown fur as he crouches in the grass. But it is not until I look for him and find him, with real tears on his cheeks, that I know this is real. And because the world of make-believe has become real, all sorts of further transformations are possible for us. Actions become abbreviated and ritualized, and we understand them. My carrying Ben around the tree is a symbolic journey out of the forest. Ben accepts my invisible needle and mime of sewing the wound over his heart. As I transform the play that Ben begins, he in turn is affected by what I do, because my actions and words are truthful responses within the drama we are playing.

But this drama is so distressingly real that Ben backs off from continuing to see me, as if sizing up his risks. I say "as if" because I do not really know why Ben refused to see me for three weeks. The boundaries between pretend and real have been completely blurred for him. He appears to be in a trance during his intense absorption with his feelings. I sense that he is frightened and might need to retreat.

7

When I come to get him in his classroom for the next session, Ben gives me a wary glance.

"No, I don't want to come," he says. I kneel down by his desk to talk this over. He slides out of his desk and backs away, saying, "I don't want to come." When he sees that I am not going to come any closer, he stands and watches me.

"Ben, you don't have to come," I tell him gently, as if speaking to a frightened animal. "You are afraid right now, and you don't have to come with me."

His pupils are dilated; he never takes his eyes from my face.

"I'm still going to keep your time for you, and ask when you want to come back to see me, OK?"

He nods, a slight movement. He returns to his desk only when I move into the doorway.

During the following weeks Ben watches me warily on the playground or in the cafeteria. Walking with another child, I feel his gaze follow me. But he does not respond to my questions about coming to see me, nor does he return my greetings. He continues his self-abusive behavior, and continues to set up power struggles with adults. Walking by his classroom, I often hear his screams as someone restrains him. Again and again I doubt my decision to respect his distance. What five-year-old emotionally disturbed child can make a sound judgment about whether or not he should see a therapist?

I speak with my supervisors about my decision not to push him, and they agree that this is the best course of action. Still, I worry. Sometimes I imagine physically dragging him down the hall to my office. With another child I might have done that, as a sign of my investment and caring. But it seems to me that with Ben this would accomplish nothing. It seems to me that he has stumbled into something very painful in his play and needs a retreat. I do not need to show him that I, as an adult, can force him to do something. This he knows already. This has been his experience many times. I want to show him the respect and trust I really feel for him, while remaining fully available if he wants me.

During this period of waiting I decide to find out all I can about Ben. My supervisor at Glenwood, Mary Louise, suggests that I talk with Ben's parents. His mother welcomes this opportunity and comes to talk with me the following week.

We meet in the playroom, over Styrofoam cups of coffee with little clumps of dried creamer floating around on the surface. Kate Brinker wears a purple dress with dangling purple-and-gold earrings, and she carries a purse that looks like a stage prop—black patent leather, large. Her hair, dyed strawberry blond, curls around a full face. Her lips are outlined in red. I know she is older than I—how much I am not sure—and feel suddenly inexperienced. But Kate's eyes are kind, distinctly kind. She rescues me from my shyness by beginning to speak about Ben and her life with him.

She has an older child, Jacob, as well as Ben, she tells me. Though Ben was recently adopted, it is a difficult commitment she and her husband have made to him. They feel overwhelmed by his behavior. At home Ben hits, kicks, rocks, bangs his head, and continually provokes battles of control. He plays by himself, not with neighborhood children. He sleeps in a "bubble bed" at night, rocking and banging in the privacy of his room. Kate explains that a bubble bed is a convex sheet of plastic that fits over a large crib. Without this protection Ben would wreak havoc on the house and on himself at night. He sounds a lot more disturbed than I realized.

"What was Ben like when you first knew him—as a baby?" I ask.

"Well, he was eighteen months then. They told us he had been neglected."

I remember his records: severe neglect. "What did you know about that?" I ask her.

"Not much. He was just a baby and he needed us, we thought. But when we got him home, that was something else. He just hated to be held or cuddled." Kate pauses, remembering. "Whenever we picked him up, he would cry and squirm, and if we didn't let him go, he'd start to scream. It was pretty awful."

"It must have been. Do you remember how you felt then?"

Kate pulls in her lips, stops breathing. "Hopeless, pretty hopeless. I knew something was very wrong with Ben, but we wanted to do right by him. The social worker told us he'd spent a lot of time in a little room alone in that first foster home. It would take time for Ben to catch up to where he should be. I didn't know what she meant by that. I mean, I didn't know child psychology or anything like that. But we knew something was really wrong. So we took him to doctors. Lots of them." She laughs, a short laugh.

"Finally, when he was just four, he was diagnosed as autistic. Then we took him to the Harrisburg Center for Autistic Children."

"What was that like?" I wonder, putting aside my cup of cold coffee.

"It was a good place, good people there. Those therapists really helped Ben—and us too. They would have him playing alone and then run a soft blanket over his arms and legs. He got to like it. Then, they'd have us stroke him, light, like the blanket. Sometimes he liked that, but sometimes not."

For the first time, tears gleam in her eyes. "Even now, you know, it's hard not to be able to comfort him or really hold him. And he kicks my husband and hits his brother. If I try to hold him, to stop him, he bites. He's made my hand bleed!"

Kate breaks the spell, laughing. "Then they told us he's not autistic, after all. We've been to so many doctors I can't tell you all of them—psychiatrists and psychologists. Ben and I see a psychiatrist every week. A few years ago I hardly knew what a psychiatrist was, and now every week I'm seeing one. And Ben has been hospitalized too, did you know that?"

"Yes, I've read all his records, his medical records too. There is a lot of information there, but a lot is missing. You know more about Ben, you have spent more time with him than anyone. There's so much I need to know from you to help him."

She laughs again, "You treat me like . . ." and stops. "You're so young!" She blushes. "I don't mean to insult you or anything, but you don't sound like the others."

I laugh this time. "I'm twenty-seven."

"You don't look twenty-seven," she counters, "but you do sound like you know what you're doing." We laugh together—as if this is the funniest thing in the world—because so much depends on it.

"What do you need to know?" she asks, serious now.

"When Ben was away from you, when he was hospitalized, what was he like?"

Ben's mother looks down at her hands. "The last time was a real nightmare. I'm not exaggerating. They took him off his Ritalin and Mellaril, and he just went berserk. He scratched his skin raw, he screamed. I begged them to put him back on. He covered his head with bruises from rocking and banging it on the bars of the hospital crib, even with a helmet on him."

"And then? When he came home, what was it like for you?"

"Back to square one—he wouldn't let me touch him, pick him up, and worse, he wouldn't let me out of his sight. So, I couldn't go anywhere. My husband, Charles, felt just overwhelmed, angry, God —we were so tired."

I try to imagine living with Ben. Not one hour here, one hour there, but living with him—twenty-four hours a day. I can't really grasp it.

I look at his mother with more than a little awe. I tell her about playing with Ben, the details of our play, and his refusal to see me now. Kate can hardly believe that he, her Ben, has played with me. Then she grins at me, a wide grin showing her teeth.

"You are going to help him," she says. It is a pronouncement I cannot refuse—I see that right away, but I am not so confident myself. As we leave the playroom, she asks if I would speak with the psychiatrist she and Ben have been seeing now for two years. I readily agree and write down the address and phone number.

The psychiatrist is not encouraging. She thinks that Ben is too disturbed to benefit much from play therapy, but that the medications help—somewhat. What is most essential, she says, is supporting and educating Ben's family. Ben's family, I learn, regularly meets with a social worker at Glenwood. And they use a system of "respite care"—an occasional weekend off from struggling with Ben.

I begin to know other people in Ben's world: the staff at Glenwood, his classroom teacher, and the consulting psychiatrist at Glenwood. Between staff meetings and my regular contacts with Mary Louise on Friday mornings, I am able to find out quite a lot about Ben's day-to-day behavior. What I learn isn't encouraging. Ben hits and kicks the other children in his classroom. He has a very short attention span and reacts with rage in response to the smallest frustration. He has to be restrained several times each day for attempting to hurt himself or the other children. His work in both reading and math is at grade level, however, an amazing accomplishment.

Mary Louise encourages me about my work with Ben and is also very frank about how disturbed his behavior appears. It is a tense, hard period of waiting.

What is clearest to me is that Ben successfully wards off human contact. And attachment. I remember him lying in the grass, the pain of his early abandonment as tangible as the sun and wind on his back. His pain that day had a mysterious quality too. I would wait for him to show me how to approach it.

One day, as I am sitting on the hall bench, talking to another child, Ben walks directly up to me.

"Do you see me today?" he asks.

"No, but I will see you next week, on Monday."

He runs down the hall and comes back. Extending four fingers, he says, "Friday, Saturday, Sunday, Monday. Four days?"

"That's right. In four days I will see you."

He waves goodbye and runs off again.

8

Driving to Glenwood the following Monday morning, I watch clouds darken and rain splash on the windshield. I roll down the car window to breathe in the metallic smell of rain on city streets, and wonder if Ben will or will not come to the playroom.

When I arrive to pick him up in his classroom, Ben is waiting. He walks ahead of me to the playroom and straight through the open door. Immediately he spots a large yellow puppet on the top of the toy shelves. "What's that?" he asks, reaching up to get it.

"That's Tea Bags," I answer, giving him the name of my large furry yellow puppet with a blue nose. Ben puts the puppet on his arm and rubs his face in its soft fur. Then he takes the puppet off and puts it back on the shelf. He looks at the baby bottle.

"What's that? What's that for?" he asks.

"To play with, if you like."

He moves over to the desk, and in a series of swift motions folds a piece of paper into an airplane. He throws it and it careens upward, then crashes into the floor, denting its nose. Ben grunts and stamps his foot. He tears off half of the tablet of paper.

"I'll take this back with me," he announces.

"No, Ben, that stays in the playroom," I tell him. "But you can take a sheet to make another airplane, if you want."

"Two?"

"No, just one."

I have not said no to him before, and I wonder how he will respond. I know that he can fly into rages with very little provocation. But he tears off just one sheet of paper and carefully puts it aside.

"Can I paint?" he asks.

I show him the paints in the top right desk drawer. Ben lines them up on the desk top.

"Do you have any magic paper? Yes, you do!" he answers for me, selecting a piece of purple construction paper from the desk drawer. Stirring the paints, he turns to face me for the first time.

"See how the colors mix? See how it's magic?"

"You think that's magic, hmm?"

"Oh yes. I know!"

He bends and carefully paints several blue squares, then swirls red paint over them. Abruptly he puts the paints aside, getting the blue paint on his hand as he screws the lid on. He squeals and stamps his foot. His face is red with frustration, but he turns to me.

"Will you wash it off for me?" he asks.

I get a sponge, run water over it, and wipe the paint off his hand.

"That's a magic sponge; it's magic, it's magic!" he declares, staring at his hand. "You are the magic lady with the magic sponge."

Ben walks away from me to the toy shelves. He picks up the baby bottle, fills it with water at the sink, then stands and faces me solemnly as he sucks on it. Then he takes a light-blue blanket from the toy shelves.

"We need this," he says, and drops it on the floor. Using the red batakas for a pillow, he lies down on the floor.

"Today, just today, cover me up," he says in a small voice.

"Today I will cover you up," I reply. I cover him up and sit on the rug near him and watch him drink. He sucks intently and does not look at me. In the silence, broken only by his sucking noises, I think of his lost babyhood. Abruptly he sits up.

"I want to leave, I'm missing gym class," he says.

He had been relaxed and comfortable playing baby, sucking on the bottle. I sense a sudden fear and guess he is afraid of being so small and vulnerable.

"I'd like you to stay, Ben. Nothing bad will happen here."

He lies back down, then rolls over to grab a box of small toys. Leaning on his elbow, he searches through the box.

"Where are those marbles?" he asks.

"They were there before and now you can't find them," I say, wondering where they are myself. He puts the box down and reaches for the Tinkertoys. I look at my watch. "In just a few minutes it will be time to go, Ben." He ignores me and dumps out the Tinkertoys, selecting a long piece and two round pieces. He quickly makes a barbell, then walks his fingers up to it.

"This little person is weak. He can't pick it up," and the hand fumbles.

Then the hand walks again. "This big man can lift it!" And he lifts it high above his head.

"Sometimes you are little and weak, and sometimes you are big and strong," I notice.

Ben nods. He folds the blue blanket haphazardly, collects his airplane, his dried painting, his piece of plain white paper, and we go out of the playroom together.

Ben and I do not speak about the three weeks he refused to see me. I do not know with any certainty why he needed time away from me, nor for that matter why he decided to come back. And perhaps he doesn't know himself. I trust his decisions, and do not press him for answers.

During this session and over the next several weeks a clear pattern of playing emerges. Ben comes and chooses to make something, often a painting, and he calls the process magical. At some point during his play he becomes clumsy and extremely frustrated, either with the paints or with some toy he is trying to manipulate, and teeters on the edge of a temper tantrum. Then I intervene, either making a suggestion or removing the source of frustration, and redirect his activity. I am careful not to deprive him of the experience of frustration and of his own solutions, but wait until he is on the edge of losing control. Ben calls whatever I do "magic." Invariably, my intervention calms him down. Then he makes himself more vulnerable. His voice changes, becoming small and sometimes sad, and often he lies on the floor playing baby, as he does in this session.

This is the first time Ben labels his activity or mine "magic." Magic becomes a theme to be replayed in many variations over the year: I am a magical lady, and Ben, too, is a magician. When finally he learns that I am not magical, he makes a wizard's wand and points it at me to reinstate my powers. When gradually he learns that he, too, is not magical, he makes himself into magical beings, such as Superman or Santa Claus.

Like all young magicians, Ben seems to believe that his wishes, his needs, have a special power. And they do—each time I respond to fill his need, whether to provide the satisfaction of painting or the relief of removing a frustration, Ben experiences his magic.

I recognize that it would be easy to let all this magic go to my head and start to believe I know what Ben really needs, or that I can protect him from his pain. Yet I believe deeply that Ben knows what he needs and how to guide me. When I take the magic too seriously, I forget how to follow his cues, and the whole experience of magic is broken. On the other hand, when I hold the magic lightly, I allow Ben to become increasingly open to his feelings, especially his painful feelings.

9

As Ben becomes more open to his feelings, my feelings gather a new force and open too. September's heat has given way to October's golden chill, its shorter days.

I run along the edge of the park near my apartment late in the afternoon, my body loping along at a forty-five-degree angle to my long shadow and the rippling shadows of leaves on the path. The strings on my windbreaker swish back and forth as I run. Crows cry out above. I remember my dreams clearly these days, at least parts of them. I dream of a little black bird with a drop of crimson on its breast, a little bird that goes out walking in the night, its footfalls so loud it sounds like one of those monsters we gleefully frightened ourselves with as children. I dream of a red barn that goes out for a winter night's walk too. It lumbers down to a frozen lake and skates there until the ice begins to break. The barn stands on the shore. The ice breaks and floats in segments that tap together and part in channels of dark running water. Under the water, a girl's face breaks up—I see it in ripples in the dark water as it taps the edge of the ice and disappears. I try to draw this face, and after many nights, finally succeed. I try to guess how old she is, but I can't be sure. I dream of feet that go up rungs. I feel the pressure of each rung on my instep in the dream, but I'm not the one climbing. I see angels climbing up and down wooden ladders, the kind used for painting houses. Among the larger angels, I see the child-angel I thought I saw in the university library two months previously.

Wind pounds the blood in my ears as I run. Gold branches

catch the liquid light's rhythm. Up and down with each footfall the hill rises up to meet me. I could be running like this into infinity, or into my dreams. The horizon doubles, little silver dots of light fall down over the path, and shadows draw me into the recesses of dark trees. Everything seems terribly alive. I listen to surfaces and hear everything roaring with life.

The world is too much alive, too much with me. This experience is not new to me, but I do not speak about it with my friends. I do not allude to it in supervision with Rachael or Mary Louise. I do not mention this world too much alive in my own therapy.

I paint and write and sometimes look sleepy to my friends. We compose ourselves as a study group to prepare for dissertation work. We meet and then go out dancing, or go out for beer and pizza. I fall asleep at the pizza parlor. My friends wake me, give me strong coffee before I climb into my car to drive home after midnight, to dream again and waken early. I write and paint through the early morning hours.

10

Ben meets me in the hall, coming in from outdoors with a red nose. He reaches for my hand and leads me down the hall with his coat still zippered up. When we enter the playroom, he takes off his coat.

"Take off my shirt, too?" he asks.

"If you want to take it off, sure." I am glad to see him.

"No, it's too cold. Take off my shoes?"

"You want them off?"

"Yes," he says, offering me a foot and holding the desk for support.

"Oh, you want them off. But *I* should take them off?"

He nods. I kneel by him and put each foot up on my thigh, untie each shoe, and slide each one off. He pads around the playroom in his socks, looking all around. He turns back to look at me.

"I am five years old. Soon I will be six. January eleventh I will be six. I will learn to write in cursive."

"You will!" I affirm. "Did you know we were born on the same day, Ben?" I ask.

Ben looks at me sharply, raising his eyebrows. "Nope. You are way older than me. You are grown and I'm just coming up."

"That's right. We were born in a different year."

Ben frowns. "Nope. You are older. I know."

He walks up to me. "I know, let's paint." I open the drawer with the paints in it and he pulls them out. He brings water, brushes and paper from the sink.

He tilts his head and asks, "Will you paint with me?"

"You want us to paint together?"

I pull my chair close to where he stands. He paints a long blue strip along the bottom of the page, then turns to me.

"You know what this is gonna be?"

"Nope."

"This is a barn. Will you make it for me?"

"I will do another part. You're doing it fine."

He paints a brown stripe up the page over the top and down the other side. "Will you put a horse in our barn?"

I take the brush and paint in a horse.

"Make some hay for it to eat," Ben says. "Lots. Put some in the barn so he can eat it. Put some extra outside too. A saddle. How 'bout a saddle?"

I add each piece as he requests it. He looks satisfied.

"You paint good," he declares. "When you grow up, you can make art."

"You think so?" Somewhat dismayed, I ask, "You think I am not grown up yet?"

"No. You are all grown. But you are not as old as my mommy."

"Oh?"

"Yes. You are grown up young."

His accuracy stuns me a little. I hand over the paintbrush. He paints a little boy in the corner of the barn, then picks a smaller brush and carefully paints the letters of his name.

"You helped to paint, so you will help to clean up, too!" he announces, grinning.

We stand at the sink running water over the fat bristle brushes. Ben leans over so that he is snug against the sink up to his underarms. "Ooh, look at the colors." He laughs, and then he splashes me, a light splash, but I laugh and splash him back a little. This is the first time he has ever teased me. We lay the brushes on paper towels on the sink to dry.

He puts the paint jars in the drawer and covers them with the apron. "I am putting them to bed. Go to sleep, paints. You wake them up in the morning."

He sits on a plastic chair and slides his shoes back on, then asks me for my assistance with the shoelaces. He picks up his coat in one hand and the painting in the other. He stands in front of the door and looks at me. I open it for him and he walks down the hall a pace ahead of me, dragging the jacket behind him, his entire attention fixed on holding his still damp painting away from his body.

It is mid-October. I have been seeing Ben twice weekly since late August, with the interruption of his retreat. This is a session of many significant firsts. This "hyperactive, oppositional" little boy converses with me and paints in an organized, relaxed manner for nearly thirty minutes! He reaches out for my hand, then gives me his feet twice—to take off his shoes and to lace them up. For the first time, he invites me into his painting, creates the painting through a turn-taking activity. It is Ben who introduces the word *our* to refer to the painting, and it is Ben who teases me about helping to clean up, and then initiates splashing at the sink. I can hardly believe this is the same child who was labeled autistic one year before and now has to be restrained several times each day because it is so unbearable for him to give up control and to cooperate. I mark the difference and feel uneasy with it. I know that this is not an "integrated" picture. I wonder about this.

It seems for all the world as if Ben has put big parentheses around our relationship, or rather, that we play together inside big parentheses. He sounds and looks like a different child with me, but this is not odd; so do all the other children I see, if not quite to such an extent. It is as if Ben has decided that the long sentence of his life can be broken up now, that he can play with me and enjoy it—almost as if he's taking a break between his battles for control in the classroom and his rocking, head-banging nights at home in bed. For my part, playing with Ben brings me unadulterated happiness, a rare thing for anyone.

11

I sit in a seminar room listening to weekly student case presentations. The floorboards in this room are scuffed with desk tracks. We've arranged the desks around a large bare circle. White walls rise around us, fluorescent lights hover overhead, humming tubes of brightness. Three floor-to-ceiling windows stand together along one wall, closed tight. The slanting surface of my wooden desk is scratched with words. Its pencil slot at the top is etched in a line of thick lead, and it has a place for books underneath. I feel as if I could blink my eyes and find myself back in Sister Joel's fifth-grade class.

Today Darrell is presenting a case to us, his friends, his clinical colleagues. Darrell has thick brown hair, horn-rimmed glasses. It is rumored that he obtained perfect 800 scores on all three parts of the Graduate Record Examination. An aura of envy and awe surrounds him. He is never entirely unguarded. This afternoon he wears a tie and suit jacket. I like him, nonetheless. We sometimes play racquetball. Now he presents a woman he calls Mrs. A., his voice dry.

"Mrs. A., a forty-seven-year-old Caucasian woman, sought treatment with me for her adolescent son after he was picked up by the police for illicit drug use." He loosens the knot of his tie and takes off his jacket, as if he is going to let us in on something big. "She appeared for her interview dressed in the fashion of a teenager herself. Although socially poised, engaging, and intelligent, she portrayed herself as helpless and confused when dealing with the demands of handling an adolescent . . ."

This is familiar enough to me: the case presentation, short, evaluative, the summing up of a human life in a few paragraphs. Darrell is treating Mrs. A. and her son, and he isn't getting very far, from what I can tell. He's diagnosed this mother as "borderline" and sees her son as the teenage delinquent victim of a "borderline mother." Now he begins to discuss Mrs. A.'s "rapidly escalating confusion" around her son, and to consider her "seductive and inappropriate manner of relating" toward Darrell. My throat tightens. I am suddenly irritated with Darrell, his seeming smugness, his test scores, his dry voice under the humming lights while others take notes, copying out his words, his brilliance twisted into this jargon.

The professor uses Darrell's case now to talk about "the provocative communications of some patients." We are ready to be launched into another familiar genre—"the countertransference warning." In the face of Mrs. A.'s "provocative communications" Darrell is instructed to hold to a consistent line of "appropriate expectations" and to keep his "boundaries" clear, because Mrs. A. shows a "fragmenting ego structure" and she needs this "structure" to support her son. We scarcely mention her son, but it doesn't seem to matter. I don't think Mrs. A. would recognize herself.

I glance out of the corners of my eyes at my colleagues—a mix of strangers and friends, none of them really close to me. Not one of them seems in the least disturbed by this. Yet who among them would recognize herself or himself described as a case here?

Driving away in the gray, muted green of the early evening, I want to hide myself in the yellow leaves and silent shadows, slink into the dusky edge of myself. Out of sync with the new clinical speech of my friends, I feel like a foreigner in a strange land. I admonish myself not to take it all so seriously. I roll down the window and the night air blasts in, roars in my ears.

12

Ben comes into the playroom and hangs back by the door. He wants to go back to his classroom to get the angel costume he has made for the school play. I tell him, "Yes, sure, go get it." He reappears shortly, carrying a halo covered with tinfoil and a set of tissue-paper wings on wire. Rather than showing them to me, he puts them on my desk and goes past me to the toy shelves. There he turns and shouts:

"I don't want any Thanksgiving turkey!"

Puzzled, I ask simply, "No turkey? Why not, Ben?"

He stares at me intently, his eyebrows knitted in a deep frown, his hands tense, one with a forefinger extended, the other in a tight fist. Why is he so upset, I wonder vaguely. Suddenly he relaxes and smiles and walks right up to me. He carefully lifts the set of wings from my desk top and opens them up. They are a mosaic of brightly colored tissue paper.

"See my pretty wings? I'm gonna be an angel."

"I do see them. And you made them yourself?"

"Yep! Wanna see how I can fly?"

"Show me."

The wire on the wings has a loop for arms, arm holes, but the tissue of the wings themselves is also glued to the same wire frame. In his hurry, Ben pushes his arm straight through the wrong loop and shreds one of the beautiful wings. He tears off the wings, ripping more tissue, and backs into a corner. His face flushes red and he stands there making little grunting noises.

Gently, I tell him, "I know they seem wrecked, but we'll fix them, Ben."

"Shut up!" he shouts.

He suddenly turns toward the wall and kicks it, then bangs his head against it. He grabs my bulletin board, as if to tear it down, and as I reach out to stop him, he lunges for the door. But I have a good grip on one arm. He strikes out with his free hand, screaming and kicking. I quickly pull him down on the rug. I have seen Mary Louise and other Glenwood staff restraining children who are out of control, but they were never alone. Here it is just Ben and myself, and I have been dreading such a situation. Surprisingly, I am not frightened. As I struggle to find a good restraining position, Ben bites himself and me repeatedly. His eyes are dilated with fear, wild. "Let me go!" he shouts. Then he bangs his head against the floor—a hard thud. This effort seems more deliberate, a request to hold him more securely, not to let go. I get him into a position of eye contact and protect his head, as I have seen other staff do. He strains and squirms, screaming as we make eye contact. This is no longer a scream of anger, but a cry of fear and pain. He turns his head and bites my wrist hard. I feel his sharp teeth penetrate and involuntarily shout, "Ouch!" For a moment, I want to turn him over and spank him, but this makes no sense given the state he is in. Ben pauses in his struggle. "I'm sorry I bit you," he says. We are panting from the exertion of the struggle, and when Ben relaxes for a moment to say this, I let go of his arms. He strikes out in hard fists, clearly showing me he still needs restraint. I turn him over on his stomach and pull his shoes off his feet and hold onto his arms. In this position he can struggle, but he can't bite or kick or hit me. But he stops struggling and breaks into convulsive sobbing, then rocks his head from side to side on the rug. The motion seems to calm him a little, and he continues rocking mechanically for a long time. I watch him and wonder how to comfort him. Words seem completely inadequate.

"Ben," I say softly.

He screams and rocks harder, as though to get away from me. I am still, silent.

Finally he stops the rocking motion, and then I release his arms one by one. He puts his hands under his forehead and gently bumps his head against them. His shoulders and neck are still rigid and tense. When he is still, I relax my hold and let go. I sit beside him, one hand on his back. He sits up and looks at me, his eyes red from crying. Someone knocks on the door and I get up to answer it. It is Mary Louise, wondering if we are OK, since I have gone well over the session time. I tell her that Ben is not quite ready to return to class.

As we speak, Ben picks up a handful of blocks and throws them at the wall. I sit near him on the floor again, my heart racing. He raises a block as if to throw it at me and I reach for it. Again we struggle, and again I restrain him. He stops struggling very quickly this time, and lies still. What does he need to hear, I wonder. I speak to him.

"I am bigger than you are, and I am not going to let you hurt yourself or me." He does not scream or cover his ears. "Listen, things didn't go so well today, Ben, but it doesn't really change anything. I still like you. I still care. I still believe you are good, maybe not an angel all the time, but more good than bad. We'll go on, just like before, and you can still be an angel in the school play."

He is very still, and his hands, which still hold his head tightly, slowly relax. His fingers uncurl and he begins to breathe evenly. I stroke his hair and he does not pull away. I sit beside him and he slowly sits up too. He is wet with perspiration.

"Can I make a paper rocket?" he asks.

"No, not right now." I offer him a paper cup and a plastic straw. "C'mon, bear, we're going to get a drink of water and wash up."

He follows me out of the playroom.

After I take Ben to get a drink and then back to his classroom, I return to my office to listen to the tape and write up the session, as is my practice. I complete my notes and stand up. My knees are shaking, so I sit back down.

I close my eyes and see an infant boy alone in a crib in a small locked room, screaming and rocking himself. I wrap my arms around myself and cry, allowing Ben's pain to wash over me in great waves. What was it like to be an infant alone in a crib, locked in a room, with no hope of human comfort? Was he wet or hungry, did he cry? In his rage, did he scream? Did he rock himself to sleep and waken to greater hunger or thirst or rage? Desperate with longing for human contact, his lifeless surroundings wet and now cold, perhaps he screamed through his misery again and slept. No one came. At what point did he become so tortured by the interminable waiting that it was overwhelming? He did not give up. His vital being demanded contact. And now he goes on recreating the torment, trying forever to reinstate the missing response. I am certain that his pain is precisely as serious as it sounds.

There is so much more than control or lack of control at stake here. When Ben was trying on the wings, he already had his hands full of something else; he had his small hands too full even to handle what he was holding. When he teetered on the brink of losing control in previous sessions, he was showing me how hard it was to deal with any frustration he could not solve right away. Perhaps I was not as helpful as I thought by intervening when his frustration seemed too much for him. I will never know. But it seems to me that my responses to Ben were the sort of behavior every mother of young children knows: when a child struggles with his or her feelings up to a point, frustration serves the child well, but beyond that point it leads to loss of control and to overwhelming feelings the child cannot handle.

On this particular day Ben came in already upset: "I don't want any Thanksgiving turkey!" I did not know why he was upset, nor how to respond, so when he dropped the subject abruptly, I went along with him. Then he tried to show me his "goodness," both in the angel costume and in his desire to try the wings on and fly for me. When he tore them in his attempt to show me his goodness, he became furious, and his fury was much too big for him to handle. Had he done anything short of trying to hurt himself or hurt me, I would not have known how to help him contain his rage; I would not have tightly wound my arms about him in full contact with most of his body. Only when I had him in a very secure position could he feel the fullness of his pain. Only then did his sobs break through.

Ben has shown me, very clearly, how he learned to comfort himself when overwhelmed by his feelings: he tunes out human voices and rocks himself, but this comfort is really inadequate. After our first struggle Ben was still very tense and tearful. He could not allow me to leave him. When I moved away from him to speak to Mary Louise, even briefly, he threw the blocks at the wall, and when I did not intervene, he aimed a block at me. The second time our struggle was much shorter, perhaps because he was tired, but also because I had learned a secure position to hold him in and did not have to experiment. Something was missing from the first experience and he needed to repeat the struggle to get it. I do not know what. He brought me an angel costume and then showed me himself at his worst. I tried to put these two parts together for him and to tell him that he wasn't all bad, nor all good. Once he heard me and began to relax, he could also accept my stroking and become really calm.

That night I take home my notes as usual, and several bruises and bite marks to remind me of the fullness of Ben's fury and pain.

13

One of the bites gets infected. By Saturday I am hot with fever.

I lie in bed, propped up on pillows, a glass of 7UP and a plate of saltines on a chair beside me, listening to the faraway sounds of the world: cold wind rattling the glass windows of my back sunporch; children's shouts coming from the back alley; music drifting down from a radio of an upstairs neighbor. I have taken a paintbrush to bed with me, and I brush the soft flat bristles under my nose, back and forth, back and forth—a soft comfort, the motion of childhood. I have no energy to paint, but two pictures come to me, finished already.

A brown oxford shoe and white ankle sock dangle above the floor. The entire picture would include the whole child—in a blue school uniform and white blouse, sitting on a wooden chair—but this is a close-up of just her shoe and sock. I remember sitting on a chair by my bed like this, being punished for some transgression. I remember the hard seat against my bottom and my feet dangling, a stinging on my legs. My shoe was untied and I remember looking down on it, without the will to tie it. I am not subdued—and the rage I feel mixes with a terrible sense of shame. I don't remember anything else.

The second picture is the archangel Michael fighting with the adolescent girl at the Psychoanalytic Institute parking lot. Except that they aren't down on the lot; they fight on a grander plane, up in the dark heavens, turning and rolling out there among bright pinpricks of light. As I see this picture, I feel strong arms about my whole body, wrestling with me—and I know what it is to fight with all my being and have that fury seen and met. I am both maddeningly matched and deeply comforted.

I know what it is to sit with rage and shame, and I know what it is to be met in the strength of my fury. I know that my willingness to see and wrestle with Ben is essential to that relationship. My love and respect for him deepens. He has fought me with all his strength and I have fought back with all my strength. I turn my face into the pillow, into that coolness on my cheek, and finally sleep.

I dream of running down a dark hall. I dream of a hand on my arm, a tight band, and a knot of pain above the band. I dream of my own hands as a child, bitten around the cuticles, ragged, tasting of pencils and blood.

14

When I come to get Ben in his classroom, he rises from his desk and quickly comes right up to me. I see his little body is tense, and give him the key to open the door to my office, a ritual I hope will make me and the room familiar. I have set several animal crackers out on the desk, and Ben says, "For me?" He suddenly breaks into a smile, but his body is still tense. He picks up one cracker and stands several feet away from me.

"What's this?" he asks.

"I believe that one's a rabbit."

He bites the ears off carefully and shows me the cracker.

"Now it's a rabbit without ears," I comment.

A small knowing smile from Ben and another bite which removes the tail.

In this way he eats the rabbit and I comment on each missing part: rabbit without ears, a tail, leg, head, etc.

Ben downs the last bite.

"No rabbit!" I say in mock surprise.

This is a safe activity, a way for us to make contact again. But Ben is also clearly anxious. He fidgets with the drawing paper on my desk and hops from foot to foot. "Can I go to the bathroom?" he asks.

I let him go and wait for him in the playroom. He reappears shortly, but hangs back by the open door, playing with the door-knob, neither in nor out.

"You're a little afraid to be with me in here today," I guess.

Ben smiles, but he is clearly wary. He taps the sign on the door. "What does this say?"

"It says Do Not Disturb. That means don't bother us now," I tell him.

"Don't bother us," he repeats and closes the door and comes in. He walks around me and comes to a standstill by my desk. He offers me an animal cracker—a bear, I notice. He watches solemnly as I eat it. Then he opens a desk drawer and finds a white piece of rolled paper.

"My bones!" he exclaims. "I will be a skel'ton," he decides, on the spot. Then wistfully, "Will you help me?"

"How can I help you, bear?"

"We need to make bones and bones and bones! A mask and feet," he says, his eyebrows raised high in his anticipation.

I assemble paper, tape and scissors for him from a new set of supplies out of his reach. I watch him cut the paper and try to roll it, but it bends and comes unrolled each time he tries to tear off tape and tape it. Struggling with frustration, he whines, "Help me!"

I do not want to make the costume for him; that would only tell him he is incapable. Nor do I want to leave him to struggle alone—that would tell him I am not willing to help. I take the paper and scissors from his hands. I will help, but he will direct and he will help, too.

"Show me how big this bone should be," I say.

Ben marks off the length in the air with his palms open.

"I will hold the paper steady. You cut, all right?" I ask.

In this manner we put the costume together. The last part we cut out are "shoes," pieces of paper which fit neatly over Ben's red sneakers. I ask for a foot and he puts his foot up on my leg and allows me to fasten the shoe with a string around his ankle.

"Boy, they won't even know me!" he declares. I attach the "bones" to his blue turtleneck jersey and brown corduroy pants, as he directs me. He suggests using tacks, but I decline and use paper clips.

"I won't get hurt. I don't ever get hurt," he protests.

I point to the Band-Aid on his forefinger.

"Oh," he allows.

Suddenly he breaks into a wide smile. "Look at me! This is fun today! Let's do this *all* the time!"

"You liked making this costume today, hmm?"

"*We* made it," he corrects me. "And *I* will take it home."

I hand him scraps of paper to throw away and clear off my desk top and we leave together, Ben rustling down the hall in his bones.

Ben is wary, as if he can't quite believe we've both survived the struggle of our previous session. In his play with the animal cracker, he destroys something bit by bit while maintaining contact with me. He has not destroyed the relationship we've built, but he is not really sure of this. His anxiety shows clearly when he goes out to the bathroom and returns but doesn't come into the room. When I explain the DO NOT DISTURB sign to him, I am trying to tell him that it will be all right for him to be alone with me—I don't want any interruptions. Then he comes in, ready to play with me.

Before, Ben moved back and forth between playing baby and being helpless and playing out his need to control. Today he is able to be both helpless and capable, to give directions and to take directions. The kind of costume we made, even its quality, does not matter so much. But the process of finding out how to make it together marks the beginning of a more cooperative relationship.

It is curious to me that Ben (and the other children I see) almost always use the art supplies in the playroom, and that they also draw me into the process of making art, sooner or later. The other therapists and interns hardly use the art supplies. I was an art major originally as an undergraduate, and continue to draw and paint. Ben discovers our pleasure in making things together. He comes back to make costumes and repeat this joy: becoming a clown, Santa, and a reindeer over the next several sessions.

But Ben does not repeat his tantrum—not in this session or ever again. He certainly will be tense, frustrated, disappointed and angry at times, but never again so overwhelmed. At home and at school his self-abusive behavior decreases, but does not disappear altogether.

15

I sit up in bed, my eyes wide open, like one of those dolls I had as a child. Whenever I sat them up, their eyelids flew wide open. My pulse races. Outside it is snowing; I can tell by the light on the shade, the muffling of sounds. I can't remember the dream, but I shake myself from it, and don't want to fall asleep again. I put on slipper-socks and a robe and go into my study. The Christmas paper-whites have bloomed already, though it is only early December. Paper stars above slender green tongues, white rocks in a blue bowl that holds ugly brown bulbs. The scent of their flowering enters every room. At first I did not like their peculiar odor—it made me fearful, a smell of something burned and dampened but still smoldering. But now that I have grown accustomed to it, I don't mind.

The world is quiet and remote tonight. I find myself asking, "Where was he?" I don't know how that question came to me, but there it is—under my nose, so to speak, and I think aloud the longer version of it: "Where *was* Ben when they decided the first foster home was not any good for him?"

I fall asleep and waken in the morning to snow flung over the trees and fence and yard, waken from dreams I don't recall. I remember the smell of paper-whites, a burning smell, and a question. I don't remember it clearly now, but it was about Ben. "Amnesia" goes through my mind—now there's a word! I push away a sense of rising fear with practiced nonchalance and quickly butter my toast.

My mind plays with other words: "memory repression," "psychogenic fugue." I feel muddled with these clinical terms that reveal nothing. I am going to be late if I don't focus and hurry. As I sweep off the car windshield, a line comes to me, whole, like a finished painting—"What you fear most has already happened." I do not apply this line to myself but to Ben, and then I remember my question of the previous night.

That day, and consistently every day for the next two weeks, I call the Division of Children and Family Services about Ben's first foster placement. I get the runaround until finally, one day, a clerk in a record-keeping office gives me the missing information: Ben spent most of his first year and a half alone in a crib, locked in a small windowless room. When a fire broke out in the house, he was discovered there in his crib after the family had been evacuated and the fire extinguished. That was how he was removed from his first foster home.

16

Ben peeks around the door.

"Snow burns!" he declares.

"It's so cold it feels hot?"

"I stuck out my tongue and it burned!" he says, shutting the door behind him.

"Do not bother us, it says. Leave us alone."

He walks once around the room, inspecting the toys, then sits down on the floor and pulls off his shoes. He leans over and sifts through the box of Tinkertoys, pulling out a long red stick. Walking around the playroom, he waves it about in the air. "I'm putting magic back in here!" he tells me.

"Did it go out of here?" I ask.

Ben ignores me and continues waving his stick. At last, satisfied with his task, he comes up to me, looking straight into my eyes.

"Make me into a clown."

"Is a clown magic, Ben?"

He nods.

"Oh, you want magic in this room, and you want magic in here, too," I tell him, tapping his heart.

He nods, his eyes round and serious.

"Make a clown hat, shoes, and buttons and a nose. Can we use that glitter?" he asks, growing visibly excited.

I cut out a red circle and put a piece of tape on it, then hand it to Ben. "Here's your nose."

"And buttons? Black buttons. I'll cut them out," he announces.

They come out in various shapes and sizes, but Ben is happy. "You tape them on," he tells me.

We add a hat, shoes, and a large collar. He turns around for me to tie the collar on. It flaps over his shoulders. As I tie the string, Ben turns slightly. "Will it hurt?" he asks, over his shoulder.

"No, I'll make it loose for you."

When the collar is tied, Ben steps back from me. "Nothing hurts ever. I'm strong."

"I don't believe that nothing hurts ever," I counter.

"Let's make a tree ornament!" he says, ignoring me, and eyeing the container of glitter.

"I don't believe that nothing hurts ever," I repeat.

He frowns at me and hands me his red stick. "Point this at me," he commands.

"Make you magic? A magic happy clown who doesn't ever hurt?"

"Yeah."

He spends the remainder of the session kneeling on my desk chair and gleefully dumping huge quantities of glue over several cut-out circles, then pouring on mounds of glitter. I watch him, a little boy with scratches on his arms, the stubby fingers of his child's hands covered with glue and red-and-green glitter. I see a baby in a crib surrounded by darkness and smoke, fire in the rooms all around him. A smell like the odor of the paper-whites, but stronger. My throat closes and I swallow over and over to keep back my tears.

Ben is talking to me. "Annie, Annie," he says, impatient, as if he has worked hard to get my attention. "What one do you want? What one of my ornaments do you want for keeps?"

I pick out a red one. I try to give Ben a smile, but my tears still swim in my eyes.

He hands it to me. "It's magic," he tells me. "It's magic and it will make you happy again," he assures me.

I don't think that Ben remembers what happened to him at eighteen months. He doesn't remember how he was once in danger, so he places himself in danger over and over again. Nor does he re-member the ways he was hurt, but I wonder about what happened, since he declares again and again that he is never hurt. The need to put himself in situations of danger, coupled with a dangerous oblivion to real possibilities of being hurt, worries me—and the rest of the Glenwood staff, too. Ben runs out in front of cars, dar-ing them to run him down. He picks up sharp objects and gouges his skin, always surprised if he bleeds. He scratches himself. He continues to pick fights with the older boys, who could seriously hurt him but choose not to. I watch him as he is removed from dangers of one sort or another. He cries and struggles, wrestles away from—what?—a memory he doesn't remember?

When I confront him with my disbelief that he can never get hurt, Ben simply ignores me, and when I repeat my disbelief, he retreats into magic. Yet I also sense a readiness to acknowledge small hurts. When I tie his clown collar on, he turns and asks, "Will it hurt?" He was standing with his back to me, and per-haps, without being able to watch me, he felt compelled to ask.

The magic of making costumes is more than a cutting, gluing, stringing-together process for Ben. He tries to come to terms with his fears of being hurt in at least two ways in this session. First, by becoming a magic clown he also becomes free of unhappiness and human pain; and second, when he asks if putting the costume on will hurt, he allows me to see that he can be hurt, and that this sometimes crosses his mind. It is a small acknowledgment with huge implications.

That night I carry home his red glitter ornament, remembering that Ben saw my pain for a moment, and gave me a bit of his magic. I put his ornament on my desk, but I have to throw away the paper-whites—I can't live with that smell for one more night.

17

Mary Louise waves me into the conference room early in the morning. "Annie, I've got a letter about you," she says, laughing. "Go get your cup." She and several other staff members are waiting by the coffeemaker for their morning brew. I retrieve my cup from my office, wondering who has written what to her, completely mystified. I see that the letter is addressed to the director and has already been opened. She shows me the return address, Dr. Michael Connelly and Associates. My heart races, and I want to run from the room, but she is taking the letter out of its envelope. I occupy myself with pouring coffee, shaking slightly. "This is great, Annie. They love your test reports." I turn, spilling my coffee. "They do?" She signals me into her office and reads me the letter, signed by all the members of this group practice.

In addition to seeing children individually, I have been testing children at Glenwood I don't see in treatment. In fact, I have a third supervisor just for this purpose, Dr. Helen Hoeltzman, and I meet with her each week. She is exacting and expert, an intimidating combination, but she is also patient as I score and bring her my reports after administering the Children's Apperception Test (CAT), the Wechsler Children's Intelligence Scale-Revised (WISC-R), the Kaufman Intelligence Test, and the Rorschach. I now take to psychological testing the way I once took to rock collecting as a child—with a sense of curiosity and pleasure bordering on the obsessive. I fall in love with the testing materials: the little red-and-white cubes that belong to the intelligence tests; the storytelling tests of pictures and drawings from another era; and, most of all, the inkblot cards, their sweet cardboard smell and weight in my hands, the blots themselves endlessly interesting. I spend hours doing horizontal thematic analyses on the CAT, transcribing tapes of a child's responses to the inkblots, scoring these responses for form, color, and content. I pore over the intelligence test scoring manuals, and the books and articles about how one interprets the subtests and final test scores.

And then I sit down to write, knowing that this report is about a living child, knowing too that others will use these results to make decisions about this child's life. I give the details and references for the scoring systems I am using, and illustrate my interpretations carefully, as Dr. Hoeltzman teaches me to do. But I also go further: I tape my testing sessions and write dramatically about the testing session itself, bringing the child and myself with the child to life, as I do with my clinical sessions. Then, based on my experience with the child, I raise alternative explanations for various responses to the tests. If a child scores low on one or both intelligence tests but is distracted throughout, I wonder if she or he was anxious, or upset about something alluded to later in the testing period, or afraid of what being tested might mean to important people in her or his life. In my written reports I do make recommendations, but they are offered lightly, in the context in which I know the child, stating clear limits about what I do and do not know about this little person. With Mary Louise's encouragement, I have begun to meet with the children themselves (usually with their own therapist present) to talk about their tests. This, too, is unorthodox.

So I am pleased to know that all my work is being noticed—and by professionals who see test reports all the time. But what Mary Louise does not know, and what I cannot say in this context, is that Dr. Connelly knows me already. He treated me as an adolescent. I was his patient, and now he is reading my test reports. I take my coffee to the playroom and close the door, leaning against it, without turning on the lights. Relief washes over me, making my knees weak. I was afraid he was writing to say I should not be working with these children, something awful, incriminating. I let out a sigh: adolescence isn't so far behind me.

18

When Ben comes to see me, he carries a small stick he found outside. "This is my magic stick!"

He walks into the playroom and waves it around. "I'm putting magic back in here." He seems very tense.

"I want to make something today. Make me a clown. A hat, and buttons, and nose and shoes?"

"Just like the last time, hmm?"

He turns and catches sight of a new game in the room and says, "Let's play that game." He moves toward the toy shelves, and bends over to pick up a small spring lying on the rug. He retrieves the game, a Care Bears game, and sets up the board quickly and accurately. Then he sits back, his feet tucked neatly under him.

"Me be a bear," he says in a small voice. "You want to call me bear?" he asks.

"OK, bear."

Surveying the game board, Ben leans over and gives me some of his stars. I take his cue and in turn give him some of mine. This sets the tone for the game, an arbitrary act of swapping stars that has no part in the rules.

Ben makes bear noises, little grunts, whines, squeals, and growls to communicate his feelings as he spins the spinner. I comment on his feelings each time: "Well, that made the bear happy, didn't it?" or, "Oh, poor bear, you can't move this time." I match his facial expressions as closely as possible. He reaches over and spins the spinner for me at my turn. When it is his turn again, I spin for him. He begins to make a range of noises for *my* side of the game, too, and again I name these feelings aloud: "The mama bear is pretty disappointed about that one," etc.

As I lean over to spin for Ben, he whispers, "Ow!" I look up to see that he has taken the spring and punctured the tip of his finger with it. He sucks on his finger for a moment. Then he looks at me, extending his finger for me to see.

"I poked my finger?" he asks.

I look at his finger, which is not bleeding, and agree with him. He bends over the game again, but does not return to his bear noises. He plays until he wins the game, without much interest, following the conventional rules. He carefully puts the game on the shelf, almost subdued. He goes to my desk and picks up a piece of white paper, folding it quickly into an airplane. He flies it around the room, almost as if it doesn't much interest him—just something to do. He throws it suddenly on the rug, and reaching down into his pocket, pulls out the little metal spring.

"I want to keep this spring," he says provocatively.

"You'd like that, but it can hurt you," I respond, finally getting my cue.

He picks up the airplane on the rug. "Here, Annie, this is a gift, a Christmas gift from me to you," he says, transparently trying to distract me.

I hold out my hand for the spring. Ben folds a new airplane, more carefully this time, and offers it to me.

I accept it, and wait. There is a tension between us, an energy now.

"Can I have this little box?" he asks, holding a discarded animal-cracker box.

I nod and he deftly drops the little spring into it. Clever.

I make my move and take the box from him. "No, you can get hurt with this," I tell him, and remove the spring, giving the box back.

Ben frowns, then opens his empty box. I tuck an animal cracker inside it. "Oh," he says, rolling his eyes, not in the least satisfied. But neither is he very upset with me. He picks up his magic stick and waves it around with a flourish, aims it at me, and trots out of the room, down the hall to rejoin his class.

I watch him go down the hall, then return to the playroom.

I note down today's discoveries: Ben comes in with one reddened ear and scratches on his hands. Not surprisingly, the work of the session has to do with pain. He begins as if no time has passed between the previous session and this one, restoring magic and safety to the playroom with his magic stick. In his playing of the Care Bears game, he sets up much the same process we evolved through making costumes: a pattern of sharing and cooperation. His assortment of bear noises reminds me of his early puppy-dog play, and I name his feelings for him, as I have before. I also match, in my facial expressions and tone of voice, the feelings embodied in his series of growls, whines and squeals, to highlight the feelings themselves, rather than simply comment on them.

All this comes to a sudden end when Ben hurts himself with the sharp end of the spring. The timing of and context for this action are exquisite. Ben sets up a game within a game with his bear noises, and when he sees that I am able to understand his feelings, he punctures his finger. He acknowledges that it hurts by sucking it, and calls it to my attention, asking me to affirm that it is indeed hurt. Then the game within the game seems no longer important and Ben finishes the Care Bears game with little interest in it. Yet something about the real issue of the session, his pain, is left unfinished. Without really thinking about it, I allowed him to keep the spring. He cannot point out my mistake by saying, "Annie, you forgot to take it away from me. Don't you know I could hurt myself again? Don't you know this is pretty important to me right now?" So again he calls it to my attention, pulling it out of his pants pocket, and finally I catch my cue and ask for it. His attempt to bribe me with the gift of a paper airplane is interesting; it is a test, I think, an attempt to see if I am serious about keeping the spring. Though he tries to put it in a box, and frowns when I take it away, and though he is not satisfied with my substitute of the animal cracker, he really does not protest. To allow him to leave with it would have been a betrayal of his trust in me.

Later that day, when I see Rachael, I tell her that I am tremendously relieved to see that some children really do point out mistakes to their therapists. She wants to hear the details, of course, so I tell her the story of my session with Ben. When she finishes laughing, she comments, "It's too bad so few therapists notice these opportunities."

We leave her office together, and in the elevator she introduces me to a gray-suited man. "This is my young colleague, Annie Rogers," she says. I go down the slushy marble steps with the sound of her words singing in my ears.

I sit at a Formica table in a diner a few blocks away, drinking a chocolate malt at five in the evening. This, with a baked potato, is what I call dinner tonight. The woman who serves me knew me in braids. I grew up in this neighborhood. She knows my mother and sister and asks about them. She brings me meatloaf and over-cooked mixed vegetables, though I didn't ask for them and can't pay for them. I protest and she says, "Compliments of the kitchen." The manager knows me too. I pick at this food to please them and suck on the straw of my malt, savoring Rachael's comment and Mary Louise's enthusiasm about the letter this morning.

I watch the snow begin to fall under the streetlight outside the window. I push aside the subtle but ominous feeling that my life is not whole, the increasing sense that the pieces simply don't fit together. I push aside the knowledge that I am leading a double life of sorts: as a promising young woman without a past, or with a past made up to fit a life she wants for herself so badly that anything invented is bound to be a better choice than the actual past. I push aside too the impression that although many people feel close to me, no one has a whole picture of me, and this is bound to catch up with me sooner or later.

19

I sit with my own therapist, Melanie, rubbing a fingertip over the soft sofa's arm, tracing the floral pattern against the dark-green background, going over and over the same pattern. We've been working together for nearly six years, so Melanie is familiar to me. Tall, with auburn hair and high cheekbones, she reminds me a bit of Katharine Hepburn. But today she seems distant to me and we sit through long silences now, pauses that stretch well beyond comfort.

We are talking, ironically enough, about a lack of intimacy: my incapacity to be in the room with her, intact, with all my feelings. We are talking as if I have never been able to be intimate in this way—not with her, nor with anyone else in my life. I know this is not true, but don't know how to convey this without sounding defensive.

I make an attempt to be honest with her: "I feel we're not talking about me—as I know myself." She does not respond. I go on: "When I say something really important to me, it doesn't seem to matter to you." As I speak, her face is closed. My words go out into the air and dissolve, as if I've said nothing—or worse, they hang in the room as if I've said the wrong thing. I keep trying, as if I can find something that will interest Melanie and compel a response. Then I give up, and we sit in silence again. I gaze at the arm of the sofa, stony-faced, tracing my pattern, not beyond such diversions.

"Whether you work to hold in all your feelings, or explode with them and dump them on me, you aren't really ever in contact with me," she says.

I shift in my chair, accused, and search for a way to go on. Over the past months I've learned something new. After she says something like this, if I make up dreams, if I make up events and feelings that fit her impressions of me, then for a few moments something opens up between us, something I think she feels is real, and it moves us forward—into "intimacy." But whatever I make up must contain enough reality so as not to feel utterly false to me. I am becoming a practiced liar.

"I know I am not all here, not really in contact with you. I don't know how to live with this emptiness any longer," I offer.

"To be in the same room with me, that is what is so hard," she says gently. "You are afraid I won't value your feelings."

I nod, confused—because this last part is true.

"You use my feelings to make yours all right, don't you?"

I nod, wondering if maybe this is accurate, if she is on to me.

"You don't want to need me. And now you are afraid because you do need me and your feelings may not matter to me."

My finger is still. I fight back my tears, successfully. In the past she might have moved toward me, even touched me, to comfort me. Over the past several months she has taken a new tack—no touching and lots of silence for me to struggle around in. So I don't expect a response most of the time. Two lines fly through my mind, as if they are spoken to me, but not aloud:

Then, if you speak, you must not show your face,
Or, if you show your face, you must not speak.

These words are Shakespeare's. I make my own translation quickly: "Speak the truth and hide your feelings in response to her nonresponse; or make up what you think she wants to hear, but shut up about what you really feel."

"Where did you go?" Melanie asks after a long silence.

"I was remembering that feeling with my mother, needing her and not wanting to need her," I say, thinking that this will be what she wants me to say, but that it also contains a kind of truth.

For the first time, she leans toward me. "Yes, what do you remember, Annie?"

I describe standing with my head against my mother's leg, not wanting her to go someplace. I fill in the details—how empty it makes me feel, her going *away*, how sad I am, how much I don't want her to leave me. Is it a real memory? I don't know . . . It interests Melanie, I can see that, and this fills me with relief.

But I am afraid of my capacity to make things up, of my own treachery. And keeping up with my own deceptions is not easy.

I appear to have a life with Ben and the children that is more or less continuous with the one I have with Rachael and Helen and Mary Louise. I have another life with my friends who are learning a clinical language and a rule-bound practice that I resist with everything in me. And I have this life, here with Melanie. I have another life of painting and writing, apart from all the others. And there is also the life of my past, the most disconnected one of all. I don't want to make the connections between them.

I gather my coat and briefcase to leave. It doesn't even cross my mind to tell Melanie that the past is becoming increasingly discontinuous, as if someone keeps showing me slides in a carousel that contains frames I recognize, as well as blanks and frames I don't recognize. I have no clear idea of myself in relation to most of these slides. Yet the images fill me with anxiety—or, rather, more accurately, these images, disconnected from me and my life, emanate anxiety from within themselves.

Outside, in the early evening, the wind picks up, rattling ice in the tree at the edge of the parking lot. I rush to my car. This office building is too near school; I am suddenly afraid of being seen. Some locations have become hazardous. I may be seen here—in the wrong light.

20

At Glenwood, with the children, my watchfulness and my fears drop away. I am alive and whole with them. I wave my mittened hand to several of the older girls as I come in the door in the early afternoon, pushing against the wind to get it closed.

I see Ben sitting in the hallway outside his classroom. This will be our final session before Christmas vacation. As I drop off a testing report in the main office, Mary Louise fills me in: Ben spent the morning wrapping presents, he participated in the school Christmas program and spoke to Santa, and then he picked a fight during lunch. As we talk, Ben sits outside on the hall bench, having a short "time out" from his class to regain control. He shouts obscenities and half-heartedly kicks out at any child or adult who goes by, but the after-lunch crowd is thinning out, and he is calming down despite himself. The tears are already dried on his cheeks, I see, leaving little smudges and smears. As I sit down beside him, he stands up and pulls his pants leg up over his knee to show me a Band-Aid.

"Look where I hurt my knee. And that big boy, Rudy, he kicked me right there."

"You must be awfully mad," I say.

He pulls his pants leg down. "I'm littler and he oughta not kick me!" I wonder what led up to the kicking, but do not pursue it. It is a big step for Ben to acknowledge that he is smaller and someone can hurt him. I offer my hand and take him down to the playroom. In the playroom, he turns toward me.

"Make me a Santa Claus hat and a beard," he says.

I have brought a cupcake and some stickers as a Christmas treat, and Ben now catches sight of them. "For me?" he says, his eyebrows arched high. I nod and he dives into the cupcake, eating the icing first. He comes up with his nose and chin covered with red icing and crumbs. I have to laugh, which makes him laugh. He licks most of the icing off, wipes some on his shirt, and finishes the job with the wet paper towel I hand him. The cupcake finished, he comes back to his first objective. "A hat? A beard?" he asks, already reaching for the red paper. He tears off a sheet and I help him roll it into a cone and tape it together. He puts it on his head and, reaching to feel it, raises his hands above his head.

"It don't droop like Santa's," he says, obviously disappointed.

"No, it really doesn't, but it's beautiful and we can pretend," I tell him.

"You got any cotton? Santa has a big white beard."

"No, I don't have cotton here today. But we could go to the nurse and see if she has some," I suggest.

Ben's eyes light up. "No. *I* know what. Cut up this white paper into strips. Hurry up, Annie, help me!"

We cut the paper together and Ben tapes the strips together, then tapes the entire thing to his chin. He snatches up the hat and pulls it down over his ears. He looks exactly like a small gnome with an oversized red hat on.

"Now this is what we do. You lay down over there and go to sleep," he directs me.

"Oh. Then what will happen?"

"You'll see, little boy!" he says, giving me my part.

I close my eyes and hear him running around the room, shouting, "On Dasher, giddyup! Whoa, Rudolph!" I stifle a snicker. Then a quiet little voice near me is saying:

"Open your eyes, little boy."

Ben has arranged a box of crayons, the can of glitter, and a cowboy hat near my feet.

I yawn and stretch, then notice them. "For me? For me?" I ask, just as Ben might say.

I revel in my gifts, but Ben is distracted and withdrawn suddenly. Picking up toy after toy, he asks, "Can I have this?" without looking at me.

"No, all the toys in this room stay here." I don't know why I am saying that, I realize. I don't know what Ben is really asking me. He picks up toys haphazardly and seems not to hear me.

Lifting a baby doll, he asks, "How 'bout this?"

I reach out and turn him toward me, lift his chin so he sees me. "You want something from me. What is it, bear?" I ask him.

"Make me something. Make me an airplane. Write Happy Christmas Ben on it. Make me a jet. No, a sled! Put I Love You on it."

He turns away and begins to look at the toys again. He walks over to the toy shelves and picks up the big furry yellow puppet.

"I could take Tea Bags home with me," he suggests.

I consider this, then think of the other children who play with Tea Bags, and of how much I use that puppet in my work.

"Something from this room. Something to remind you that you're coming back?" I ask.

He nods, placing Tea Bags back on the shelf.

I reach up and take down my calendar. I hold him close and show him the pictures of all the months he has been with me. Fortunately, this calendar includes the first two weeks of January of the next year. I circle the day he will come back to see me. His body relaxes.

"Now make me a airplane, Annie," he says with real enthusiasm. "Write Happy Christmas Ben, I Love You," he says as I fold the paper. I write exactly what he wishes. Ben stands and looks at me, his dark eyes so clear I feel my heart bound. How quickly I have come to love him.

He leaves me and goes slowly down the hall, back to his class.

It is the last time I will see Rachael before Christmas too. I have barely settled myself in the tiny waiting room when she is at the door, inviting me in, ahead of her own schedule.

I follow her into her office, red-cheeked and glad to see her, awake from the cold. Today she makes us tea. She pours water into an electric kettle and asks me if I will kindly crawl behind her desk to plug it in. I find the socket and crawl out again. She opens the bottom drawer and pulls out cookies instead of the hard candy. Placing them on a little paper plate edged with holly, she offers them to me. I feel as if I'm with my grandmother.

She asks me about the children, and I begin to read my notes, as usual. When I finish reading a summary of my session with Ben, she interrupts, "How long has it been, Annie?"

"You mean how long have I been working with him?" She nods. I worry about her memory when she asks questions like these. "A little less than five months," I remind her.

"You have clearly become an expected part of his life," she says. "If Ben doesn't understand time clearly, then he won't understand this break, much less that you will return to him. Yet you managed to get him to understand both these things," she says, smiling.

I tell her how much I felt myself fumbling to understand what was at stake for him in this session. His Santa play brought up the wish for a tangible gift from me. He had eaten the cupcake I gave him, so that was gone, and he had ignored the stickers. I suspect, I tell Rachael, they did not meet his need for continuity—because they were novel, not part of our relationship. She nods. Any of the toys he randomly picked up and asked for were part of our playing together, I explain.

"Would it have been a mistake to give him a toy?" I ask.

"Sometimes that's a mistake, sometimes it isn't," Rachael says. "What do you think?"

I tell her that in that moment I had no understanding of his need, nor of my need to say no to him. It would have been more consistent to continue saying no, but hopelessly obtuse from his point of view. And I didn't want him to take Tea Bags home. That large puppet, made for me personally, had become a cotherapist of sorts, with Ben and with other children as well.

"I don't know if it would have been a mistake. Maybe, if I didn't know what he was trying to ask me, maybe it would have been," I say.

Rachael nods. "Because that would be avoiding his anxiety," she continues. "What made you think of the calendar?"

"Nothing in particular, it was just an inspiration. When I looked up at it, I thought I could let Ben know I was coming back."

Rachael elaborates on what is still inarticulate within me. Ben, especially with his history of abandonment, needs a tangible way to understand time, and the calendar serves both as a concrete way to make time clear and as a bridge of continuity. It has the pictures of the seasons and the months Ben has known me as visible proof of our relationship. It also has a clear starting date. Ben has no real idea of when that will be, but there it is, circled clearly.

Rachael pauses. "You know, you have good instincts, you are good at this," she says quietly.

I know? I don't know. For a moment, I want to cry. I want to cry and fall apart completely with her and then really try to fit all the pieces of my life together again. The very thought frightens me. But Rachael is not my grandmother, and she's not my therapist either.

"This is the child who doesn't get attached?" I ask aloud.

"Well, he is certainly attached to you!" Rachael says. "And all sorts of new experiences can happen within him now."

I take the promise of her prediction into my three-week break.

21

After Mass at midnight, my sister Mary and I drive through the darkened city streets to see the lights. I complain that I am sleepy, but she insists on this ritual, waking me with her wonder and joy. We sing the songs of our childhood and drive slowly up and down the streets. When I finally crawl into bed and close my eyes, the Christmas lights continue to wink and move past me in the dark. I think of Ben lying in his bed. I hope, if he is awake, that he is listening for the sound of reindeer on the roof.

A few days after Christmas, I leave for Boston to attend a research workshop at Harvard, in preparation for my dissertation work. I have spent the last several weeks arranging to go, and now can hardly believe I am going.

In the evening, after my first day in Cambridge, I sit at a desk in the Cronkhite Graduate Center, in a rather musty, hot little room, writing a poem to Ben. I am aware strangely of having lost time throughout the day, so that I can only account for part of the workshop. The poem to Ben comes to me now whole and formed, as if it were written by someone else:

> *What you fear most has already happened.*
> *Come out of your nightmare world, Ben,*
> *for the trees have a thousand leaves*
> *flashing golden and green.*

> *Smell hope on the wind, little boy,*
> *dig out of the black earth*
> *with your small, strong hands*
> *rocks and twigs and magical acorns.*
> *Play for me your forgotten drama—*
> *and look, Ben, outside the glass:*
> *five blooming irises stand tall,*
> *one for each year of your life.*

"What you fear most has already happened," I read aloud, thinking of the mystery of this—how the present moves into the future to repeat the past. I open my window a crack and cold air blows in. Outside, high snowbanks light up the darkness. It is now after 10:00 P.M., but the streets are still filled with people. I put on my coat and boots and go out among them. I can't take my eyes off the women, women of all ages stomping along in long coats, making little white puffs of clouds in the muffled air. Each one seems so alive, riveting in her aliveness. I go along the snowy sidewalks, cleared here and there, treacherous with ice-coated uneven bricks. Clapboard houses perch on the edges of the streets, their porches and windows lit up. I am drawn into their interiors, and I slip into the notion that I actually live here. I live here and I'm walking down to the French bakery to get coffee and a croissant this evening. Time pleats up and suddenly everything looks familiar. I have walked into another life that is my life, as simply as turning a corner. It's an odd feeling I can't shake off.

I go into Harvard Square and think about Carol Gilligan, the writer and researcher I have come here to meet. Her brown eyes light up as she speaks; she tilts her head and looks at me, taking me into some recess within herself, each time I speak.

I go along the sidewalk and down to the river, wearing my headphones and listening to Pachelbel's *Canon* and Mozart's *Requiem*. I take them off to listen to the soft shirr of snow as I walk over the bridge above the river and look down to the boathouses, and across the bridge to the Harvard houses, little squares of yellow light against the snow and dark sky. As I walk back, I look into the dark water. I hear faraway music, a sound of voices singing, close in my ears, in stereo. Disconcerted, I look down and see that I am not wearing my headphones.

22

In the second week in January I see Ben again. I thought of him often while I was away, wondering if he would be able to remember that I was actually coming back to him.

As he walks into the playroom, he wants to transform himself immediately.

"Can I be a horse? A clown? No, let's do something different today!"

"Something new on the first day back, hmm?" I ask.

Ben comes and stands by my desk, but he faces away from me. He begins to roll a small train car back and forth, looking all around the room. Back and forth, back and forth goes the train, faster and faster. Then Ben releases it and it veers through the air, crashing on the floor over by the door. He moves away to the toy shelves and pulls several toys down, assorted puppets and games, and they fall to the floor. He does not examine them further. This reminds me of his distracted play in our very first session. Then he pulls down the ringtoss game and plops himself at my feet. He yanks off the top and throws it aside, his motions tense, clumsy.

"Are you angry with me, Ben?" I wonder aloud.

He sets up the game, ignoring my question. I wait.

"I get the first turn. Move outta the way!" he shouts. Then he looks at me for the first time. "Please," he adds, as if to placate me. I move my chair back slightly.

He stands a few feet from his mark and throws a red ring, misses, and moves closer. He throws more rings and misses. Then he stands right by the peg and hooks the next ring by holding it directly over the peg and carefully releasing it. He gathers up the rings.

"Now you go," he says, handing them to me.

"You want me to play, too?" I ask, wondering where he is leading us. I repeat his positions and toss the rings easily on the peg.

Ben scowls and stamps his foot. "You cheat! That's not fair to stand right there!" he shouts.

"I am playing by your rules and you don't like it," I say slowly. He glares at me.

"It wasn't fair that I came back from vacation a week later than you did," I say softly. "Did you think I wasn't coming back?"

He kneels on the rug and rolls the train back and forth, back and forth, faster and faster, and releases it. It misses my foot by inches. He looks up and smiles.

"And that train almost ran over me for coming back late!" I exclaim.

Ben smiles again, then turns away. He sorts through the toys on the floor and retrieves a large blue plastic key. He turns to me.

"I'm gonna hide this good. You will look for it, OK? Close your eyes," he instructs me.

I close my eyes and hear him rustling around.

"OK. You can peek. You can look!" he says.

I get up and slowly explore the room, commenting, "No, it's not here. Not here." Ben giggles at my efforts, obviously enjoying my search. Slyly, he opens a desk drawer. I look in and see the blue key.

"Silly me. Silly old me. It was right there!" I say. Again Ben giggles.

"Now I will hide it again. Now I will hide it so you'll *never* find her!" he shouts. "Close your eyes."

I close my eyes and hear him scurrying about the room. "Her?" I ask myself. Oh yes, me.

"Open your eyes," Ben says.

This time as I look for the key, looking under the rug, under the desk, opening drawers, I make up a script: "I am Ben looking for Annie. Where is she? She's not here. No, not here either."

Ben joins the game and laughs. "You'll never find her, never, never, never," he taunts.

Then I get angry. "Where is she? She's supposed to be right here!" I shout, slamming things about. I glance at Ben. He is grinning ear to ear.

"Here she is," he says, drawing the blue key out of his pants pocket.

"Oh, there she is. You had her all along!" I tell him.

Ben looks at the key and he looks at me, key to me and back again. I sit down and he comes up to me, just looking. He turns back to the toy shelves and picks up the baby bottle.

"I know. Let's play baby," he says.

"You have only ten minutes left to play baby," I warn him.

He walks over to me and looks at my watch.

"Can I wear that?" he asks.

I put the watch on his wrist and show him where the "long piece" will be when our time is up. He nods and goes to the sink to fill the baby bottle. Carefully he fills it to the brim, then asks for my assistance in putting the nipple back on. He finds a clear space on the rug among the toys and pushes a red bataka under his head for a pillow.

"Cover me up," he asks in a very small voice.

I take the soft blue blanket from the shelf, kneel beside him and tuck it all around him.

"There, the baby will be safe and warm now," I assure him.

He reaches out and snatches up Tea Bags from the floor, pulling the big yellow puppet under his covers, sharing his "pillow" with it.

"Now the baby has company," I comment.

Ben sucks on the bottle and looks at me steadily. Silence and sucking sounds. He pulls the nipple from his mouth and "feeds" Tea Bags, making loud sucking noises for the puppet.

"Is the baby-puppet hungry?" I ask. He nods.

"Is the real baby hungry, too?" I add. Again, the nod.

I get up and find an animal cracker in a box in my desk drawer. I sit next to Ben and offer him the cracker. First he reaches out for it, then pulls his hand back and opens his mouth. I put the animal cracker into his mouth and he chews it, spilling crumbs about.

Then he sits up suddenly.

"I know. Make me into Superman!" he demands, his voice loud and excited.

"Ben, look at the long piece on my watch. Our time is up today," I say.

"No, it isn't," he counters. With that he pulls the winding knob out and sets the watch back to one o'clock, the beginning time for our session. "Now we have lots of time," he says, grinning.

I laugh at him. "No, you are trying to fool me!" I tell him.

"But it could be this time," he offers. I give him my serious look. He sighs and hands me the watch.

"Pick up all the toys? What a mess!" he says, with some exasperation. He begins to pick up the toys, and there are quite a few of them to be put away.

"No, time is really up. I'll get the toys, Ben."

"Just make a big S for my shirt?" he asks, not giving in yet. I open the door and walk out. Halfway down the hall, Ben joins me. He takes my hand. "Superman next time, OK?" he asks.

After our three-week separation, Ben comes back into therapy with his trust in me slightly jarred. He tries to return to the familiar activity of making a costume, but shows me his clumsiness and anger, first with the train car, then with the ringtoss game. When I choose to break the rules of the ringtoss game in the same arbitrary way that he does, Ben reveals his anger. When I tell him it is unfair that I was away longer than he, Ben does not respond verbally. He shows me his anger with the train. When I interpret this, "That train almost ran over me for coming back late!" Ben smiles and confirms my interpretation.

Even after I acknowledge his worry that I wouldn't come back, and his anger, the issue is not settled for Ben. The game with the blue key reverses our roles. Now it is I who will look for something without reward. Ben is delighted with this turn. The second time he hides the key, he reveals his own experience: he slips and calls the key "her," and then he makes "her" impossible to find. Then he shows me his anger more directly, "Now I will hide it so you'll never find her!" When I play Ben looking for Annie and am openly angry that I can't find her, Ben is delighted again. He has the joy of watching me search and get angry, but he also keeps the blue key, symbolic of me. I assure him that he has "had" me all along, and he confirms this interpretation by looking from the key to me.

With the issue of losing and refinding me partly in his grasp, Ben uses the remainder of the session to play baby and simply look at me. It is noteworthy that he adds the puppet, almost in a sibling position, in his baby play. Ben is not so hungry that he can't share, and this large yellow puppet becomes a real character in the therapy after this session. Ben's attempt to extend the time at the end of the session is also a first. He does not seem overwhelmed with leaving me, for his refusal to leave is too full of teasing. But he is concerned about leaving, and his anticipation of his leaving in the sessions which follow this one shows his continuing concern with time and his attempts to cope with it.

I might have easily extended the session into my writing time, and perhaps this is what Ben needed today. But he also seems to be searching for continuity and security—and part of that continuity with me is the reality that we have a regular time to meet and to stop.

This session sets a pattern for the rest of January. For Ben, it is a time of losing and finding; for me, it is a time of taking an active role in interpreting these losses, the searches and the discoveries he makes in his play with me. During this period Ben also anticipates the endings of our sessions with uncanny accuracy.

I walked out of a new life in Cambridge back into what seemed to be, even in the present, even in relationship with the little boy I love, a life of the past. I had the sense of living in the midst of a time already vanishing. This sense made simple things very poignant—the light on my blue coffee cup, the bricks of the Glenwood buildings staccatoed with snow, and the children themselves, their faces, Ben's face.

23

My twenty-eighth birthday is a child's dream. My friends met without me and planned it and I didn't know it was coming: a surprise party with streamers, hats, a cake with sugar-pink roses, noisemakers and balloons.

Patricia brings me to Sarah's on a Sunday afternoon. I am told that we are going for a walk in the park. A gray day, nothing to do but errands and take a break for a walk. But the lights suddenly go on and voices shout, "Happy birthday!" We move the furniture out of Sarah's living room and front sunroom into the back bedroom, and dance until after midnight. My closest friends stay to clean up, and that is the best part of the party. We brew coffee and pick up soggy cups and empty wine bottles and half-finished pieces of cake. We pop balloons and wash and dry the silverware and dishes, keeping a constant stream of banter over the four rooms of Sarah's apartment. We talk to the dog underfoot and speak intimacies in twos and threes and settle finally into the pillows of the couch with fresh coffee.

When I carry my presents out to the car, it is early morning and a few snowflakes swirl down out of the sky. As I drive away with my sister Mary, I see Sarah framed in the light of her doorway and it is like looking at a painting that emanates a mixture of wishes and truths about someone I loved—from a time I can already vividly remember. I wonder if this is a hazard of being a writer: a sense of detachment that sometimes makes the present seem like it is already past.

24

On a warm day in early February, Ben peers around the door to the playroom wearing his red jacket. "Let's go on a treasure hunt *outside* today. Can we?"

"You are wearing your outdoor coat, so you must think I will say yes!" I tell him.

"Yes, yes, yes, yes, you will say yes!" he chirps, hopping up and down with every yes.

"Yes, because it is important to you, and it is warm enough too," I assure him.

Ben takes his coat off and drops it on the floor. "It's like spring. I don't need my coat!" he declares.

I put my coat on and suggest he bring his. Ben picks up the coat and puts the hood on backwards, covering his face, so the coat hangs down in front of his body. Then he bends over and lets it fall to the floor.

"Can we take Tea Bags too?" he asks. I nod and he puts his coat on in the conventional way, and snatches the puppet from the toy shelves. He walks over to me and holds the puppet close to his body.

"Put Tea Bags on your hand?" he asks.

"You want me to carry Tea Bags?"

"Yep!" Ben bends to tie his shoe and stands up. "He's magic!" Ben reminds me.

As we walk down the hall, Ben asks for a bag to collect things. This stumps me for a moment, and then I go into the staff conference room and find one. When I emerge with a large brown paper grocery bag, he gives a little squeal of delight over its size.

Outside, the sun is shining on the cars in the parking lot and a little warm breeze passes over us. Ben unzips his coat and begins to pick up small stones, which he carefully places in the grocery bag. I squat down beside him and put the puppet on my hand.

"How about some treasure for me, too?" I have Tea Bags inquire. Ben looks at the puppet.

"Some for me. Some for you. I'll bring you some shoes, too, for your feet. I got some old boots at home," he answers.

He stands up and looks at me. At eye level, his dark eyes are piercing. "Tea Bags came down to my room today. He said, 'Take me out,' and I did!"

"And here we are," I comment.

Ben looks around him, then motions for me to follow him. "I am taking us to a secret hideout," he whispers.

He leads me over a small hill, around some mud, to a small incline by a large tree just at the edge of the field. He drops his brown bag there and turns to Tea Bags and me.

"There's a monster in that tree. I'll get it," he says. He admonishes me: "No, you and Tea Bags stay back. This is a *dangerous* hunt!"

He picks up a large wooden stake lying on the ground and swings it at the tree. Then he bends down and pulls something toward us, as if hauling something heavy. "That was a big bear!" he exclaims.

Taking a stick, he cuts the bear up into three portions, makes a fire of sticks and weeds, and cooks the bear. After we have all eaten a portion, Ben gets up and motions me to follow. Suddenly he stops in his tracks and points to the side of the building.

"Oh look, there's a little baby bear." Ben runs up to it and bends over it, petting the bear.

"It's got a note on it!" he shouts to me.

I come and take the note from him.

"What does it say?" he asks.

"It says, 'I'm lost. Please take care of me,'" I read aloud.

Ben takes this little bear by the hand and starts back to our camp. On the way, he kneels down by a drainpipe and peers into it.

"I think I see another little bear down there," he tells me.

"Can you call him out?" I ask.

"Here bear, c'mon bear. I won't hurt you," Ben chants.

And sure enough, the bear emerges, another baby bear with another note on it, which I read exactly as before.

When we are assembled back at our "camp," Ben goes out again with the large stake to hunt, motioning me to wait with Tea Bags and the bears.

"I am going to hunt down the mama bear," he announces.

Again he hits the tree and drags something over the grass to me. He looks down at the bear and swings the stake over his head.

"She's still alive!" he says, and he hits her again and again. With the last swipe, a tired, halfhearted swipe, Ben swings at the bear and accidentally (?) grazes my arm. He turns white and drops the stake.

"I'm sorry," he says, subdued.

It was a soft hit and didn't hurt me, but the mangled bear lies at his feet.

"You did not hurt me," I tell him. "I am all right, Ben."

The child looks dazed. He simply stands and stares at me, unseeing, unblinking.

I kneel down beside him. "Look at the bear," I tell him, and he does. "This is the mama bear who left her babies lost in the woods," I explain.

He looks at me with an expression of twisted pain, his features grimaced.

"I killed her?" he asks.

"No, Ben, she left you for reasons all her own."

"I killed her?" he asks again, as if he has not heard me.

I move in front of him. "You hunted her down to hurt her because she left her babies," I say, taking it directly back to his play.

He nods.

"You did not hurt me, just the bad mama bear," I finish.

Again he nods.

"The good mama is still alive, you know?" I ask him. He nods.

"Time to go back?" he asks.

"Yes, it is even a little past that time," I inform him.

"C'mon, bears. I'm taking you home," he calls out.

"Which ones? What if we left them here?" I ask, truly curious.

"All of them. The mama bear and her baby bears," he says, answering my first question.

"What if we left them here at the hideout?"

"Oh, no. Annie, they have to come home with me."

So Ben collects his paper bag, his bears, and the big yellow puppet. He slides the large stake down the drainpipe, far out of reach, and leads me back to his classroom.

The child I usually see right after Ben is sick today, so I will have a longer time than usual to write about my experience with him. I am anxious to write with the details fresh in my mind and return to the playroom with a fresh cup of coffee.

Ben comes to this session in his red jacket, wanting to be outside. He uses the out-of-doors as a stage for his play. The last time we held a session outdoors he reenacted his abandonment in a powerful piece of play. He was the lost and wounded baby bear waiting to be found, fixed, loved. This was early in October. Now it is early February, and he is ready to approach the old abandonment problem from a new angle; he is ready to "attack" it more actively, to grapple with his anger, his fear of his anger, and with something new to Ben: his tenderness.

What are the foundations of this readiness, I wonder. I sit with my empty cup and speculate. Ben has by now established a relationship where he finds anger, bossiness, fear, hunger and joy acceptable. He has established his effectiveness and mine in what he calls "magical" activities. He has experienced a brief loss of me and my return to him. He has taken in enough tenderness from me to extend it to the puppet, who now fully assumes the role of sibling or playmate. Tea Bags is what Winnicott calls a "transitional object." Rachael and I love to consider Tea Bags in this light. I think now of what I will tell her later.

Tea Bags is "magic" and has a relationship with Ben, but Tea Bags also has a relationship with me—I animate the puppet, but Ben treats the puppet as I have treated him. Tea Bags might also be an extension of Ben's body; Ben wants to bring him boots after all, though Tea Bags has no feet. In short, Ben has found a way to put himself into Tea Bags's "skin," to guess what the puppet might want as an extension of what he wants. In this way, he is able to guess what a little lost bear needs and to make a tender response.

In my mind's eye I imagine that I am with Rachael. Already, I imagine, she is hearing me tell her about this session.

But before showing tenderness, Ben creates a scene of hunting and killing, then eating a bear. Here he risks and masters danger, and provides us with food. In a traditionally masculine role, he moves out into the world in his play and conquers something. Then he finds the baby bear, an extension of the baby bear he so recently was, and as I read the "note" he offers me, Ben understands the bear's needs. Anger and need, cruelty and tenderness, become the dialectic of his attempt to master, in his play, the losses of his earliest babyhood. After the first display of tenderness Ben goes out again to hunt, more explicitly, the mama bear, and to beat and kill her. In his final whomp of the mother bear, he makes a slip and grazes my arm with the stake. Such "accidents" (I think Rachael will agree) are significant. Ben looks pale, frightened, and dazed. He does not hear me, as if he were not fully in the present, but so absorbed in his play that he believes in his capacity to kill me as he has just killed the bear. This is too much for Ben.

I can feel Rachael listening to me with that intent look, and so I go on:

Just as I would step in to keep Ben from banging his head, I step in here to stop his overwhelming fear. Might a child feel hate when someone hurts him unbearably, and, in his hate, wish a death? When that child then experiences losses, as Ben experienced two losses in early childhood (his biological mother and his first foster family, I remind Rachael), he may begin to believe that rage kills relationships. My imagined Rachael is with me on this.

"I killed her?" he asks me. When I try to interpret his question as a question about his mother, he does not understand. I return to the metaphors of his play. What he wants to get rid of, kill, is only the bad mother, the one who left him. Attentive now, he listens, hears, nods. What he still has is the good mother, in me, and in others.

Rachael makes some comment here about new introjects, a light comment, one that does not take over my interpretation.

Ben believes in his play so much that it follows him indoors, in the form of an invisible mama bear and two baby bears. This is an act of assimilation; he takes back into himself the bad and the good mama and the lost baby. Interestingly, he also rids himself of the instrument of his cruelty, throwing it down the drainpipe out of reach, the same drainpipe where he knelt and tenderly called one of the baby bears out to him. Rachael likes this interpretation. She is smiling.

My part in the therapy is changing these days too. As I play with Ben, I not only take my cues from what he has said or done, but also help him understand some of the possible meanings of his play by interpreting it for him. In this I am careful, mindful that I may be inaccurate. But these interpretations, if they are accurate, will become an enlarged perspective, to be acted out again and again in his play —until they become more fully Ben's meanings.

Rachael agrees that Ben is now playing out for me the key themes of his early abandonment and trauma: loss and recovery, vulnerability and independence, cruelty and love.

She hands me another piece of candy, and turns on the lamp, as the room has grown dark while we were talking so intently.

25

The playroom is dark. I see that it is after five, and I must have been sitting here for over three hours. I wonder where all this time has flown, as if time could fly up on wings, a winged clock.

I go out into the dusk, to my car, reinventing Rachael again, but now I'm not sure who she is—she could still be Rachael or maybe she's become the old Melanie I loved, or Sarah at my party, or my sister, Mary, or the little girl I saw in the library grown up and now grown old—angels do enjoy their disguises.

There in the car, in the rapidly expanding time of my future, Rachael returns as the one who tucked in the stray strands of my braids with her knotted fingers. I remember how she stroked the bitten-down cuticles of my fingers. I remember, in the rapidly expanding flight from my present, the white spaces in time where she held me, those white spaces that burned her hair white, a fire in her mind, and that's where she got her feathered body too, from the black cormorants who flew around us as time flew ahead of us. Those cormorants took our fearful songs out to sea and dropped them down on jagged rocks so that she and I could be fearless and still full of song. Now she corners me, moving in with her "Ah, ah, ah, I've gotcha!"—making me laugh in that tease that sounds like sneezes, and down we go into that tickling laughter, and I kick against the air and spit out splintered bones of despair. Most nights, I curl up by her side, under the feather comforter and under her wing, and I sleep well, except for the nights when she goes out flying—then nightmares haunt my bed. But sometimes a little circle of dancing light spins over my bed, and I know she is there,

only younger. In the early morning, the wind blows over us and
wraps us in harmonies and blows out the strands of my braids and
blows out the white feathers of her hair, blows us into the far-flung
skies, two minds on fire. If I could get home now, I would find her
there, I'm sure she'll still be there, waiting to chop cabbage heads
and dice little green onions, preparing my past for me in the billowing time of my future, my new life, where I am now going out
into the orchard to gather apples from the eye of green darkness.

It is already dark. Am I still in my car, in the parking lot at
Glenwood?

When I finally get home, I put my briefcase of notes by my
desk, exhausted. I flick on the kitchen light and look at the clock
on the wall. It is now 10:00 P.M. and I cannot account for nearly
eight hours of this day.

26

The snow begins to fall and it falls as if no one can stop it. It covers the back fence. It flings itself outward, like a lost thing, it covers the whole world, erasing time and memory in its great silence.

II

SILENCE

Who, if I cried, would hear me among the angelic orders? And even if one of them suddenly pressed me against his heart, I should fade in the strength of his stronger existence. For beauty's nothing but the beginning of terror we're still just able to bear.
—RAINER MARIA RILKE, *Duino Elegies*, 1

With silence only as their benediction,
God's angels come—
where in the shadow of a great affliction,
The soul sits dumb . . .
—JOHN GREENLEAF WHITTIER, from a letter
to a friend on the death of his sister

But one human heart goes out to another, undeterred by what lies between.
—WILHELM GRIMM, *Dear Mili*

27

In late February, abruptly, I no longer come to see Ben.

28

I cannot stop crying. My face breaks like an egg yolk and sobs shake my whole body. Then the tears turn to streams on my cheeks, and I wonder if they will freeze because my face feels so cold and stiff. But my face breaks again, and the sobbing comes like an invasion. This goes on all day, until by twilight it is difficult to carry on any conversation at all. Sarah and Patricia and my sister, Mary, pack up some of my clothing and drive me to the hospital—not the one I remember—not the old castle on a hill with woods and an apple orchard I knew as an adolescent, but one newly built on the outskirts of the city, a place bearing the same name but not the same place. The old one was condemned.

I glance at the small room with its examination table and strip of paper, its beige metal cabinets, the fake-wood desk. It reeks of antiseptic. A nurse takes my temperature and pushes up my sleeve to wrap my upper arm in a blood-pressure cuff. The tight band on my arm becomes tighter and then the slow hissing release. A little girl in the corner points out my tears and asks why I am crying, but no one knows. My face is frozen again and I wonder if it is possible to build a small fire behind it, behind the bones of my face, to warm it.

Now there is a doctor in the room, just a few years older than I, awkward and gentle. "What brings you into the hospital?" he asks. His tone tells me he has memorized this question.

"A green car," I think to say, and frown, knowing this is not the answer he expects, and when I frown, my face does not move.

"You must have some idea of why you are here. What is it?" he asks, as if I have not answered his question.

I feel suddenly wary. Everything within me is about to be named, boxed, contained and controlled. My hands rest on the arms of a green chair, but I feel as if they could lift up and lift me out of here. But they are still, lifeless. The top of my head lifts off (a strange sensation), and with it my answers to his questions lift and float out of me into the street where they mingle with the smoky breaths of passersby. There is no need to explain anything, I realize.

The earth is covered with snow. It has always been snowing and it will go on snowing for a long time. No wonder I am so cold.

I find myself sitting on a bed in a light-blue gown two sizes too large, with white socks on my feet, not mine. I am shaking violently. A gray blanket is wrapped around my shoulders and a nurse sits in the room with me. She holds me tightly yet softly, and rubs my back. She speaks to me as if she knows me. I tug at the plastic wristband and begin to scratch at the insides of my arms, where my skin is burning despite the extreme cold. A second nurse enters the room and takes my blanket and turns me facedown on the bed and gives me an injection. The liquid burns into me, black dots cover the walls of the room, and then, through the roaring darkness, the longest white silence I can imagine.

Behind the bones of her face, in the caverns of her soul's face, a blue eye is weeping. Tonight one angel will go out into the desert, to search for her among the white bones of rabbits.

In radiant light, he appears in the hospital ward asking for lemonade, of all things! No one hears him, but when the atoms in the room rearrange themselves and he moves among them, she sees his familiar shape. Not many stand over seven feet tall. He moves in close to her with his thoughts, but can't get through, so he rubs his cold hands together as if to light a fire near her, and cries out to see her so broken.

Darkness comes into the room. It presses down and spreads itself flat against her chest. The hammering in her mind goes on and on. Outside, she can see—even through the dense mesh of the window and the static in the air—those strong women folding their ladders and going away. They cannot quench the burning, and in the courtyard below the air fills with a blue haze.

As he speaks to her, she is happy to see his lips moving, although his words make no sound. That he is alive is enough. He has come back to her in that unnoticed way of his, and aligned himself with everything, everyone—touching the afflicted lightly with the length of one dazzling wing.

30

I drop down into my body for a few moments as I stand in the shower, fully clothed. The water pours over my head and whole body. It soothes the burning on my skin and the long burning under my skin.

The light of a soft lamp touches the leaves of the rubber tree in the dayroom. She sits, half in shadow, in the midst of a burning smell—a terrifying smell—once she ran into a creek in the winter to stop it, long ago. The rubber plant sheds a dry shell when a new leaf comes out. One has fallen to the floor, dried, twisted; it's something singed, not burned, and because it's not burned, it is able to cry, to chant, to howl, and to sing—no, it is not burned too badly. The leaf, singing, makes her want to cry.

The water is open and wide, dangerous. That monster-bird, the barn, can't go skating on the lake now. It's not frozen.

Words come into her mind as if from someone lost. They are not really her words, she knows.

On her tongue, a thick glue, and the words, almost hers, yet unspeakable, tumble into her mind—"Please come back, oh PLEASE." A shadow moves. She arches one shoulder and crouches in her chair. A fly lights on her arm. A television blares and buzzes overhead.

32

I slip into my body briefly as my sister tries to take my music tapes and Walkman and headphones out of the wastebasket in my room, where I have just thrown them. She says, "Annie, you're going to want these later. These are important to you." I try again to throw them away. For some reason, I don't want music.

Mary takes my tapes and my art supplies, so that I won't throw them away or destroy them, and hands them to a nurse.

There are others within her. They speak to her as she sits on her bed. They've spoken to her often, but she doesn't remember them. She will remember only a fraction of this.

On her right is a girl with dark-brown hair and bangs, and on her left a blond young woman with two little girls. The brown-haired one says, as if to reassure her, "You will remember almost nothing about this."

Then—confusion—she is different sizes and different people as time runs swiftly backwards—she is lifted up and up, terrified—she is taken into a closet and released and she runs toward one end—she pushes hands away, "No, please no," she cries—she is chased around a basement—the man in these scenes keeps changing.

A voice in her left ear says, "That's because we've disguised him."

They show her more of this on a TV screen and in sharply framed pictures, saying, "Let it unfold."

Later, she remembers only the words "Let it unfold," and "That's because we've disguised him." Nothing else. None of the people.

I drop into my body more often now, coming and going as if in is out, and the way out is back in. Around and around I go, through a swinging door that pushes me into a room, whisks me out, and pushes me back in. I have been making collages, apparently—I suppose because they have taken away all my painting materials. And I see these collages in various stages.

I cut people out of magazines with a child's blunt scissors. Women with long flowing coats, women in dark glasses and hats that shade their faces, women holding rolls of toilet tissue against their cheeks, women standing beside dryers by open windows with birds flying in. I cut out girls too. Girls in baseball hats in the rain, girls climbing up stairs and whispering, girls with schoolbooks in plaid dresses and black Mary Janes. I watch myself carefully cut off their heads.

I see it again after the composition is finished. I notice that the heads of the girls are on the women and the heads of the women are on the girls. You can't tell who is who. You can't tell their ages either. This worries me.

Another time I am the turning pages of *Time* magazine. A voice in my left ear whispers, "That's because we've disguised him." A voice in my right ear is saying, "Let it unfold."

These words, not the voices themselves, but the words, make me afraid. They don't make any sense. I no longer look at magazines or make collages.

35

A body of light comes to her through the walls until a fine membrane of light covers everything, and even in semidarkness this light is blinding. Her own body is another body of light, tapping out messages in freezing and burning codes to unseen presences.

She lies still under the covers, huddled on one side in a little heap, waiting for hands to move her, lift her up, perhaps set her on her feet, get her going. In this white place of great light, she wonders—where are her mother's dark eyes and breasts, her father's light eyes and gentle hands?

The back of her throat closes and it is hard to breathe. Is death a long sleep, not being able to wake up, to move, ever?

Someone is standing over her, "Can you move now? Can you talk to me?"

Over the public address system she hears her own thoughts answering—"No, I don't want to talk," a little pause, then her questions blaring through the hallways, "Am I going to die? Am I dead already?"

Bathed in intense light, with her thoughts heard all over the world, she discovers there is no privacy, not even under her blanket.

36

Dr. Michael Connelly sits on the edge of the bed, holding a chart. He is speaking to my sister about trying more Stelazine, to get me moving again, and perhaps electroshock therapy.

I move into my huddled body, and with a tremendous effort speak one clear word: "No."

The morning sun shines down on the sea, a silver light on the breaking waves, it blinds the young woman sitting on her bed in a dark room. Where do the leaves in the sand come from, she wonders. Brown heart-shaped little leaves, but here there are no trees. She feels she is continually being watched. She turns, turns again—there is no one there.

The night before, she threw up her dinner and coughed up blood, shaking. What is this world she is about to enter?

Looking out to sea, a blinding silver, she shivers. The sun glares down a judgment on her. Little birds of thoughts die in her throat. The sand is soft, pocked with rain, soft under her bare feet, and difficult to walk on. She shuffles along.

Suddenly it is clear to her that someone has died, perhaps someone has been killed. No, someone is about to be murdered.

She enters the sea fully, knowing it is she—the murderer and the one soon to be murdered.

38

I am lifting a spoonful of mashed potatoes to my mouth. A round table. Glaring lights. Others eat too. Patients?

We eat with spoons, not forks, and we are watched. The mashed potatoes are glue and butter, hard to swallow.

I wonder how long I have been here, and who these people are.

I remember something about murder. She? I can't place her. I wave my spoon to the world of the living and speak aloud in tumbling words: I ask her to wake up funny you should ask me it's mirror bright too light I'm afloat like Ivory Soap boat sick? bare bones bare headed bare bum crack open the light is too hot a hat tips up this tastes of glue who is murdered? auk the furnt glue who is gibbled?

She wraps her hands around her head at the table and weeps beneath the weight of it. "How can you talk like that when you know it's my fault?"

A dark-haired girl-woman moves farther out into the sea. The weight of the waves pushes her toward the shore, lifts her up and pushes her and sets her down, hard.

"How can you talk like that?" she cries toward the breaking waves and bobbing head, still sitting at the table while standing on the shore.

The weight of water is heavier now, a stronger push by far, and the waves go over her head. A lighthouse searches the night sky, and there are other islands of thoughts that reach the girl still on the shore. "Will she ever exist beyond arm's reach?" Black cormorants circle overhead. She searches for a face, close in the dark water.

On the shore, she listens to every sound in the perilous night, and quickly goes into a house all lit up. She locks doors, closes windows, even the ones up high. She jumps from a ledge, thumping down to the hard wood floor. There are steps outside, walking, quiet, walking again.

. . .

She is suddenly falling, falling from the sky above the house through the dark, her face up to the stars, her skirt open like a bell. Voices ring out, telling her she will die. They crackle in the cold air, laughing. She falls into snow flat on her back, wearing her snow-blue jacket and snow-blue pants. She rests in the heaviness of her relief, watches the snow fall upward in the night. She moves her arms up and down. She reaches up to draw a little circle above her head.

40

It comes to me like a dream, the image of myself moving along beside myself, trying to steady the me who walks as if moving through water.

I slip into my body, hunched in an impossible position up on a window ledge.

I am standing in a line for bedtime medications. I keep having the sensation that I am falling backwards. It is hard to remain standing.

41

Dr. Michael Connelly is just "Michael" now, a boy of fifteen, sitting in a wheelchair with a bright orange blanket over his knees. He has been working too hard and has a heart problem, a flawed heart. All the nurses have asked him to slow down, and here he is, slowed down and much younger. He will have a second chance now.

She moves through the ward, around and over the patients who wander, who shout, who watch a still point on the horizon of the dayroom. She is thirteen. There is no one she can talk to here. She sees a young man in a wheelchair, a bright blanket on his lap. "Michael," he announces, extending his hand. "The archangel," she finishes, even as he shakes his head no. They play chess by the hour.

42

Dr. Connelly is talking to my sister again, this time in the presence of another doctor I don't recognize. He is telling the doctor that my insurance will soon run out, that he will have no choice but to send me to the State Hospital. I can see that Mary does not want this to happen. Dr. Connelly argues that I am getting worse. He wonders if he should cut back on my medication. I hover above this scene, aware that it is me they are discussing.

I remember another me who played outdoors in the sun with a little boy with brown bangs.

I slam myself into my body so hard it hurts and my skull rings with the impact. "No," I say, "you are not sending me to the State Hospital."

43

I watch her with pity. She has begun to have nightmares and to remember them.

She dreams of a little black bird flying over the hospital, weeping. Frantic flights back and forth.

She is held under water, and memory slips away, like a boat, and still the sensation of being held under water.

She dreams of music that rises and falls, and of trees marching down green hills, their arms outstretched like little children, of fingers entering her most private place.

She lies under a glaring light and cries out, "Don't you remember me, don't you recognize me?"

She wakens bathed in sweat. Sometimes she cries out in her sleep. Sometimes she throws things, when she is awake.

I see that she is terrified of being locked in the "quiet room," a padded room with a little glass rectangle high up in the door. I see that she needs me.

I find myself looking at her hands from above, for hours on end.

I will myself to move them—my hands.

44

Dr. Connelly sits in front of me in a room I vaguely recognize. Soft light and a big rubber tree in the corner. A television perched overhead, now, fortunately, turned off. I am wearing blue jeans and a light-gray sweater and sneakers. I can feel that I am thinner, and my hair is longer, messy.

"Annie, I am going to discharge you today." Relief, followed by fear.

"Do you know what day this is?" Dr. Connelly asks, gently.

I have no idea. Day? Month? "Late February?" I guess.

"No, it's the beginning of April," he tells me.

"What time?" I ask, meaning the year.

He replies, "Oh, it's just after eleven."

My mind whirs in confusion. I remember coming in, the sensation of the top of my head lifting off. A blanket around my shoulders. Cutting out magazine pictures? That is all.

It hits me then—Melanie is gone. I begin to cry, then stop myself with great effort, afraid I won't be able to stop.

I ask, because I have to know: "Melanie. Did I kill her?"

"No," he says, and moves his chair closer. "No, Annie, you did not. But you won't be seeing her any longer."

"Is she dead?" I ask.

"No," he says, and sighs. "But I've spoken to her and she refuses to see you."

I swallow, swallow hard to check my tears.

"Look, Annie, you're not really ready to go home. But your

insurance ran out weeks ago. I can't keep you here any longer. You'll be staying with friends, not by yourself."

"I want to go home," I say.

"I know, and you will in a few weeks or so." He pauses. "Listen, Annie, I want you to stay away from psychotherapy. It could even be dangerous for you."

I look at him, puzzled. I have known this man since I was an adolescent. "What do you mean?"

"What's wrong with you can be changed only with medication and time. By the time you're in your mid-thirties, you'll be out of the woods. For now, just stay on the medication, OK? And stay away from psychotherapy. Promise me?"

I sigh, "All right, I promise." I pause. "Do you remember, or did I imagine this—you reading my test reports?"

He laughs. "Oh yes, I remember them. They were good. Very good. The staff here could hardly grasp that you wrote them so recently. I brought them in one day—to show them who you were, and will be again."

I remember being driven through streets festooned with light green in Sarah's car, with Mary in the backseat.

Yes, it was early spring. I was not going to my apartment, but to the house of friends. I thought I'd be home in just a few days. I could hear snatches of conversation between Mary and Sarah, but I could not follow the drift of it.

Time confused me, the time that had gone by without my living in it, and the gaps in time in this day.

But the interminable winter had come to an end.

45

This April day is cold, cloudy. On either side of the walk up to the house, flowers bloom—brilliant red, yellow and purple—and the light seems to come from within the colors. I bump into the doorjamb coming in. The door opens into a first-floor waiting room. Inside, I find several stuffed green chairs around an old fireplace, books and magazines, a box of stuffed toys, a green plastic alligator that stares out from one side-eye, and a fish tank filled with tiny iridescent fish. It hums at a treble pitch.

Green gauze bandages the bare branches of the trees outside. That green burns into my skin and thrusts a thousand tiny pins beneath its surface.

In less than a week I am already breaking my promise to Dr. Connelly. The need to understand what is happening to me overrode my promise.

The man I am waiting to see is an analyst, Dr. Sam Blumenfeld, someone my friends have unearthed for me after a careful search. Apart from that, I know nothing about him. I called him to ask for an appointment only the day before. Now I wait in the timeless way that one waits for something or someone unknown, to the soft steady ticking of a clock on the mantle, the world's time set against my own, more jarring, inner time.

Dr. Blumenfeld pokes his head around the wall, or perhaps he comes all the way out, but like other things that jump out at me, only his head appears. "Annie," he says, and I follow. I enter a smaller room and take a few steps inside. I turn as I hear him slip a brass latch into place on the door.

He sits down on a black leather chair at the foot of the classic black couch. I choose an identical chair, across from him and at the head of the couch. *His* chair, if I'd thought about it at all, but I did not. The chair holds me, lifts my feet slightly off the ground as I lean back.

My eyes fall to his knees and then to his polished black shoes. The light is dim, with only a single soft lamp lit behind him. The stillness in the room grows full.

A line flies through my mind: "Light blooms from gray darkness." I pause, and ready-made-for-me thoughts continue: "Late in the day I keep the company of a red enamel chair."

These words, disconnected from every other thought coming into my mind, seem unspeakable. I push them away, even as I feel Dr. Blumenfeld lean in a little to listen, as if he is hearing what I have not said, what are not, in all honesty, even my thoughts. I don't look directly at him. On the periphery of my horizon of awareness, I pick up every gesture and every shift of breath. I have learned that this way I know far better what someone is thinking and feeling.

"I took a gun and a knife to my therapist and I threatened to kill her." These words come out of me into the room, the first words I have spoken. They startle me even as I speak them.

"You must have had a very good reason for wanting to do that," Dr. Blumenfeld says calmly, as if this is true.

"I didn't want to. There were voices that told me to do that, and I, I felt compelled to follow them."

Even my straightforward explanation frightens me.

He laughs, a light laugh. "Ah, they must have had a very good reason."

"No!" I say. Yet in the silence that follows, I find that I believe this myself. He sounds as if he is on their side, which is also my side.

I look up. His eyes are blue-gray, almost the lilac color of the sky before it snows. The silence wraps itself around us.

"I can hear you in whole sentences!" I exclaim. "My hearing has been messed up. Sometimes I can't hear people in whole sentences.

In my journal, there are a few lines like that, whole sentences. But they are surrounded by—words that make no sense to me—gibberish!" I spit out the word, hating the sound of it. "And no one in the hospital could understand me when I spoke."

"No one there knew that gibberish is a language too?"

His questions come, like little animals, up into my lap. Tears abruptly fall down my face, and I want to stop them. I have the sense that it is not me who is crying, but I look for a Kleenex.

"I don't have any," he says. "I don't want you to wipe them away. Let the tears be."

I sit and let them drip off into my hands.

After a long time, I begin my story again, from another angle. "The woman who was my therapist, she won't see me, not ever again."

"She has abandoned you," he says simply.

"No, she loved me," I argue, swallowing hard.

"Love? What is love then?" he asks.

The room tilts, as if a huge wave hit us. "I don't know. I don't know what love is, or what is real anymore."

"How could you possibly know?" he asks.

His words come to me like my own unspoken thoughts. I am dizzy, then flooded with relief.

We enter a long silence. He waits, as though he is waiting for himself.

"You are shattered," he says finally. I nod. "When you came into the room, I sensed the little pieces, but I was afraid to address them. I didn't want to injure them with my clumsiness."

"The little pieces," I repeat quietly.

"Yes, the little ones who came to see me."

I suddenly have the sense that I am all there, if in pieces, at least all there.

As I get up to leave, he asks, "When would the little pieces like to come back?"

"Tomorrow?" I ask so softly, he asks me to repeat it.

"Good, tomorrow," he says.

• • •

Sarah is waiting for me. She drives me back to the house where I am staying, the home of a professor and his wife, old friends of mine, and their two teenage sons.

I climb the stairs like a toddler, one foot up followed by the other, holding the banister. The stairs won't hold still in space.

I crawl into bed in my upstairs room and, after days and nights of restless sleep, I sleep soundly.

It is late afternoon when I awaken. The sun has come out. Pepper, the old family dog, a black Lab flecked with gray, whines to go out as soon as I am out of bed. I want to go out too. No one else is home. I'm not sure if I can navigate the neighborhood without getting lost, though I know it well.

But Pepper insists, and I go with him, down the wide, wet board steps. Puddles loom up on the sidewalk. I walk around them, careful not to break them or look into their endless depths. Trees drip on my light jacket. Sunlight beads on the sleeves. As I walk, I repeat over and over, "I don't want to see Dr. Blumenfeld" like a chant, or a prayer for Melanie to return. Yet my shoulders drop down so that my arms swing easily. The breath drops down deep in my body. Without knowing how, I walk with Pepper and find my way home again.

I did not know, after this first meeting, that I had already launched myself into a three-year relationship that would give me new ground to walk upon and the knowledge of a story that had hidden itself from me all my life.

I had just come out of a time of living outside time and memory, living as if in a waking dream. Words still confounded me. It was difficult for me to speak at times.

When I came to Dr. Blumenfeld I was migrating, like birds who hear far below our range of hearing—earthquakes and shifting magma beneath the earth's surface—and feel shifts in the tiniest electromagnetic fields, using this knowledge to orient themselves in flight. I was migrating from a waking dream into the familiarity of "reality." Wordless, yet words dropped into me. Voices came from within and without—as presences, vital and truthful and compelling, and also terrifying at times—and this was not a new experience for me. The physical world around me embodied and spoke to me about a knowledge I was rapidly losing. My senses blurred and sharpened and blurred again.

I could not read whole sentences. The words stood out in short phrases or one by one they dropped into my mind and vanished. The young spring, transparent and translucent, burned under my skin. The spring brought to life the knowledge of feelings— beneath my skin, in my muscles and bones. It was as if my body carried an unspeakable story, and the logic and order of spoken language had become treacherous. The language I knew lived encoded in my body. It held my knowledge and story intact, but I could no longer speak it. This language was not only untranslatable, it never occurred to anyone that it was a language and in need of translation. As if I were an idiot, it was called "gibberish" and "word salad."

Now, as I reentered the English language, beginning to hear in full sentences (yet in a disconnected way), beginning to read again (though only the simplest of children's books), I was disoriented in time and space. The silence of amnesia, like an overnight snow, had fallen and covered over the preceding six weeks. Once again I had lost time in the world. And I was in danger now of losing the language that held an unknown story intact. I was, as Dr. Blumenfeld said, "in pieces."

The Laplanders once traced the landscape in song, followed their songs out into the Arctic and safely back. They did this for centuries before they learned to read. After they began to read, however, they could no longer make their way in the Arctic without getting lost. Without the songs of my voices, and with every step into reading and speaking the English language, following its laws of order and time, I felt increasingly lost. Like an animal who

has wrenched free of a trap and survived, yet goes back to its trap
to find the missing foot, I ached to find a way back to myself.

Dr. Blumenfeld heard the first two lines of my story and identi-
fied it as a story about love and abandonment. He knew that "gibberish" was a language and he trusted my voices. His chair held
me. He listened at the very edge of my own knowledge and then
spoke to me. He welcomed my tears. After seeing him, I could
sleep. His words dropped deep into my body and worked like a
tiny, hidden compass to orient me within myself for the next
twenty-four hours.

46

I see Dr. Blumenfeld each day that week. "Dr. Blumenfeld" seems too pompous a name for such an ordinary looking man. "Sam," his first name, seems too casual. So I shorten his name to "Blumenfeld." In those early sessions, I sit in the same chair and listen to his breathing, in rhythm with my breathing, a quiet ripple. In that dim room, everything in me is attuned to the quality of his silence. I do not speak to him much. The silence opens up, clean and spacious around me. Then suddenly, I feel that we are treading through a thick bog, in danger of being pulled underwater. When I think I will drown in the silence, I find him kneeling next to my chair, speaking soft words.

I know already how to listen to different silences. There is a silence that lies in hiding, waiting for words, but the words of the speaker are carefully censored, for all but the ones the listener waits for go unheeded, denied, into this silence. This silence leaches confidence and vision from the speaker, so that the telling itself becomes unnatural, estranging, annihilating. This silence is a bog, thick. There is no breathing space within it. But there is also a silence that opens out, as a simple wood door opens out on a clean white field, cold, its long slope strewn with stars. This silence breathes and expands. This silence waits for words too, and it welcomes the unexpected ones, the uncanny, disturbing, and surprising ones.

I begin by entering Blumenfeld's silences. I experience both kinds of silences with him, but what I notice most is that his silence breathes and clears an opening for me. It is white, light, a haven from the world—like the ceilings of my childhood.

It is, in fact, up on the ceiling where Galle first came to me. She comes to me now, in Blumenfeld's leisurely silences.

When I first knew her, she was quite small, five years old. She would lie at the bottom of a doorway, not caring if she dirtied her blue school uniform and white blouse. There she would lie, her head almost touching one side of the doorframe, her skinny legs propped up against the other side. There, she lived and played in the white world of ceilings. The center of gravity was somewhere above the ceiling and under her feet, but she was so light, she could leap and fly over doorways, the highest places between the rooms, like a rabbit. She could make that white empty world of ceilings any season, any place, any time. There she rode the high plains of a world of green, golden and purple grasses, of constant wind and endless blue sky, on the back of a lion. She called herself Galle, my middle name, a name no one called me, so that it became fully hers.

I do not tell Blumenfeld about Galle, not then, not ever. Though I do not name her, I must have brought her to him in some way—because with no formal introduction he recognizes her sometime during those first days and begins to call her "little Annie."

He interrupts the silence between us rarely, but when he does, he invariably asks, "What is little Annie wondering about?" Or, "What is little Annie feeling?" Unsure of whom he is addressing, I do not answer.

When I get home, I make whatever little notes I can about my sessions with Blumenfeld, just as I did with Ben and the other children. I need my own words, as one needs to breathe. Sometimes these are just a few words. Still, they are a trace of my inner life and capture a sense of our sessions. In moments of clarity, I fill in what details I can remember.

During those days of silence, I want to tell Blumenfeld an

incomprehensible story, the story of my relationship with my therapist. Often, I feel myself just at the edge of a torrent of words, almost at the bursting point, but I draw back, wondering how I can possibly make myself coherent or credible enough to tell the story I want to tell. I notice what I have not noticed in the preceding weeks and months. I can get lost at times. Whenever I draw, things are not in the proper perspective, or quite in the right places. Whenever I read, there are some sentences I cannot grasp, no matter how hard I try. Yet at other times I seem fully able to draw in perspective, to speak about complex ideas, to read my own and others' words with relative ease. But I do not know how to predict when I will move abruptly in or out of a shared world of "reality," the kind of shared reality that makes telling a story possible.

47

Then suddenly, after a week-long silence, the story I want to tell Blumenfeld presses harder against my ears and comes into my own hearing, and I begin to talk as if I have been talking to him all along.

"In the beginning, when I first met her, Melanie was a student," I tell him, thinking that I should begin at the beginning of that complicated relationship.

"Melanie was your therapist?" Blumenfeld asks.

"Yes, Melanie Sherman." I pause, confused about whether or not he knows her too. "Do you know her?"

"No, I don't know her."

"When I first came to see her, I sat in a wooden chair. She was a student and I sat in a wooden chair in her little office high up in a tower. I wore white shorts, a plaid shirt, and a baseball cap that hid my eyes."

"Oh, do you like baseball?" is his next startling question. I don't know yet that I am in the presence of a baseball wizard, a man who coaches a Little League team in his spare time.

"Yes, I do like baseball. But I wore the cap to protect my eyes, so that I didn't have to look or be looked at. I relied on my peripheral vision to guide my impressions of her. I can follow feelings more accurately that way. I can find out more. Do you know what I mean?"

"It's a way of looking that's less susceptible to deceits?" Blumenfeld asks.

"Yes." I am happy for a moment not to have to explain things, to have to go on and on in some vague hope of being understood.

"Melanie was a student, but she was older, she was, I think, forty-nine."

"And you?"

"Age has always confused me because I am older than I appear, and I am younger and older than my chronological age," I reply.

Blumenfeld laughs. "When you first came into the office, I thought, 'Oh, she is very young, maybe eighteen,' and then when you started to talk, I thought, 'Oh, she could be forty!' and as I started listening to you, I suddenly knew you could be much older and much younger than I first imagined."

"Yes, I was kind of ageless when I came to see Melanie too."

"Don't you mean full of ages?" Blumenfeld asks, laughing.

"Yes, ageful. Like that. But Melanie was older—to me. She was so magical to me. She listened to every word, as you do now. She was such a presence. She wanted so much to learn from me—not just about me, from me."

"So she was really a student. In the very best sense. And then something changed, she stopped wanting to learn from you?" Blumenfeld asks.

"Yes, but how do you know that already?" I ask, not sure what I may have told him.

"Because of the gun and the knife," Blumenfeld says.

"Oh, that." I pause, not wanting to tell that part of the story just yet.

"I loved her so much. I think she loved me. I'm not sure now. Not knowing makes me wonder about everything. Sometimes, when it gets really bad, I wonder if I am imagining you, making you up as I go. I'm still in the hospital and I'm making you up."

My hospital memories are like a dream. I realize now that Dr. Connelly could not have been an adolescent boy and a patient with me. I must have invented him. I am also thinking of Galle and the others I have been told I "made up," and they are as real as Blumenfeld.

"Of course you are making me up as you go, Annie," Blumenfeld says, as if this was some proof of my sanity. He pauses and adds, "I'm making you up as I go too." He pauses again. "But when you are confused about love, everything, everyone, gets caught up in that confusion, doesn't it?"

"Yes. Everyone. In the beginning I was so sure of Melanie's love." I pause, wondering if this is true. "I also tried to warn her not to work with me, as if I knew, maybe I knew already, that she would leave me. But I didn't really know that; we called that particular fear 'transference.'"

"Big words confuse little Annie, don't they?" Blumenfeld asks. I nod, wondering what he is driving at. "Let me say it to you another way," he continues. "Partial truths can be devastating, Annie, and I think you stumbled onto a partial truth and called it transference. And then you could ignore the possibility that you'd discovered some real vulnerability in Melanie."

I am stunned by this response. Little lights flicker off and on in the room. I rush from clarity into confusion.

"Little lights going off and on, faster than fireflies," I comment, half wishing that they would take me to another place, anything and anywhere but here, where truths I can't bear might suddenly overtake me.

Blumenfeld waits for me. Somewhere, outside, a siren goes off, it grows loud and then dim as it moves away into silence.

I glance at Blumenfeld, who is looking off into space.

"What are you thinking?" I ask him.

"I am thinking about the last time I went to a clinical conference. I remember hearing all those big words and thinking that no one was making any sense. I had nothing to say to them. I was thinking about what it was like to look out at a roomful of people at a cocktail hour and not have a thing to say, just looking and listening for someone who might speak my language."

"Did you find someone?" I ask.

"No. I was looking in the wrong place. After that I decided to stop going to clinical conferences," he says, laughing.

I find myself nearer to tears. "I'm afraid to hope. I have a word for it in my language, *leinoch*. Fear-hope. I'm afraid to hope that I am not in a clinical conference with you," and as I finish this last sentence, the tears spill over.

"If you are, Annie, then I've just looked out and I've just this very moment found the one person with whom I can speak," Blumenfeld says softly.

I did not expect this from him. I do not know how to continue for a few moments.

"I am so afraid, because when I first met Melanie, I felt that way about her. She saw my hunger for a mother, my longing and need for a real relationship, and she saw my confusion about love. The first time she touched me—" and here I stop, overwhelmed by the hunger that overtakes me.

"You knew she didn't have any of those ridiculous rules about never touching a patient?" Blumenfeld asks.

I nod, knowing all at once that he, Blumenfeld, doesn't either.

"Yes, I knew that. She brushed a little ant off my collar, and I wanted to run from the room in my hope."

"You were hopeful that she could speak to you like a mother, knowing how to touch you, and when and how not to touch you?"

"Yes. The briefest touch was full of hope. But it felt dangerous, too, to wish for anything by then. Even in the beginning, when she—" and again I stop.

I feel Blumenfeld waiting.

"When she touched me, I knew that she was going to bring herself to me as a mother first, and then as someone learning to be a therapist. Even in the beginning, touch was so full of danger. And I don't know why."

"You really have no idea, Annie?"

"After she touched me that first time, leaving at the end of each session was impossibly hard, because I kept wondering if she would be the same person when I came back."

"Oh, that does help us, doesn't it?" Blumenfeld asks.

"It does?" I ask.

"It helps me, Annie. She was a student. She was learning how to be a therapist. What would she learn that might stop her from speaking to you like a mother and kill your hope in her? If that happened, then she wouldn't be the same person, would she?"

"No, she wouldn't. That is exactly what I was feeling. I didn't know it. Even now, I don't know what to believe. What was real. Will I ever know what was real with Melanie? Will I ever trust myself again?" I pelt him with my questions, and look at him and hold the gaze for the first time, as if searching for something. "I wonder if I will ever be able to trust you."

Then I glance at his desk and see that our time is up. I get up to leave rather suddenly, but turn back at the door. Blumenfeld smiles and tilts his head to one side. "Annie, there are probably reasons not to trust me entirely, and we will find them out as we go, right? Once you find them, then you'll know exactly how much to trust me."

Imagine what it was like for me, coming out of the hospital, unsure of my footing in the world of "reality," to begin to speak to this man, this analyst who had stopped going to clinical conferences because he could not speak to anyone there. In his presence I found words, or rather, words found me. Words that I hoped would unlock an incomprehensible story pressed against my ears and came out into the room. As Blumenfeld spoke to me, my own words made more and more sense. And so, the story I wanted to tell him pressed harder against the limits of what I could know and say.

48

When I come back to see Blumenfeld two days later, I take up my story, as if uninterrupted. I sit down in my black leather chair and look at him and just go on.

"Even in the beginning, I guess I didn't quite trust Melanie. I was terribly anxious. I was always wondering if she would be the same person the next time I returned."

"Sometimes she was not," Blumenfeld comments.

"Sometimes she sort of drew back, into some other relationship with me. I didn't know what was happening. In my fear that she would leave me, I didn't want her to know, I suppose I didn't want to know myself, how much she mattered to me." I look down at Blumenfeld's shoes and past him, at the lamp, trying to find words for what I mean.

"When you doubted her and didn't want to know how much she mattered, then what?" Blumenfeld asks.

"I would do something to see if the relationship would hold."

Blumenfeld laughs. "What would you do, Annie?" he asks.

"Sometimes small things, like coming in wet from swimming and dripping on the floor. Once, I hid under her desk and didn't come out when she called me. That confused her and made her angry. Once I even tried to break one of her windows, when I was really mad at her."

"And did your relationship hold?" Blumenfeld asks.

"I think it did. In the early months, yes it did. She would get upset or get mad, or whatever, and then she'd yell, and later she'd hug me or hold me. I thought that meant that . . . I don't know."

"You thought it meant that she loved you, Annie?" Blumenfeld asks.

I sit shaking my head in disbelief.

"I don't know. I don't know how to tell you," I whisper. Blumenfeld waits, and the story gathers force again within me, and I begin it again:

"On a hot night in August of that first year, one week before Melanie was to go away for two weeks, I sat in my apartment and shivered with a cold that came from within. Do you know the kind of cold I mean?"

Blumenfeld nods.

"My body grew numb piece by piece. Everything I looked at had an eerie sheen of brightness. My ears were filled with a distant roaring, like a train coming from very far away. Whenever I moved, the floor shifted. I got dizzy, and, as the world tilted, I felt more and more unreal. I curled up inside myself. Melanie came to me. I don't know the details of how she found me, only the memory of being pulled away from a small space by a wall and of being held, of gentle words, of rocking, and the smell of a soft shirt. Gradually, I came to life, and as I did, I remember trying to say things, name things . . . that happened to me when I was a little girl. That night Melanie put me to bed and sat beside me until I was nearly asleep. It is a night etched into my memory. If this was not love, I will never know what love is."

The tears course down my face. My hands are numb in my lap. I pause in my story.

Blumenfeld leans forward, into the story. "You do know what love is, Annie," he says.

"I don't know how to tell you what happened after that," I say. "I don't know what went so wrong that everything could end this way."

"This way?" Blumenfeld asks.

"This way, the gun and the knife. Not ever seeing her again. Without any hope of knowing what happened," I tell him.

"Does this ending remind you of anything from the beginning?" Blumenfeld asks.

This is not the question I expected. My mind jumps to the time after Melanie came back from her first vacation—running down a hill in the early autumn, the leaves turning, the light on the leaves and on my skin, the feeling of coming to life, falling deeply in love, with Melanie, with myself, and then the terror of losing all this—of losing life itself.

I look up at Blumenfeld. He says, "What did little Annie know from the beginning?"

"She tried to break Melanie's window and got into a lot of trouble about it. Melanie threatened to stop seeing me."

"Little Annie was mad about that, I bet," Blumenfeld comments. "What did she want from Melanie?"

"Honesty. That's what she wanted. She wanted to be able to be, and to be met in her truths. She was mad at Melanie because Melanie invited us to go to her house, to have dinner and meet her daughter and everything. Melanie was thinking about having us, I mean me, live with her for a while. But she didn't like having me there in her house, she wasn't comfortable, and later, in the very next session, she said that I'd 'seduced' her into letting me come. That made little Annie really mad, because she was lying; it was Melanie's idea. Little Annie tried to break the window. I guess I got confused and started to agree with Melanie and—" I stop. "Oh this sounds so crazy."

"No, you are making fine sense to me," Blumenfeld says. "Did little Annie actually break the window?"

"No, Melanie stopped her. She stopped her and slapped her across the face and said, 'You wanted to get a rise out of me, and you did,' or something like that. And later, Melanie said she was sorry about slapping me, and that I couldn't come to see her, I couldn't come to her office if I ever did that again."

"Little Annie was trying to break out of an impossible trap, wasn't she?" Blumenfeld asks.

"What do you mean?"

"Little Annie wanted a mother all her life, and it looked as if she could have one, and then she was told in effect that she couldn't. What's worse, what she wanted was suddenly all wrong, and she was responsible for it because she somehow 'seduced'"— Blumenfeld's tone is absolutely derisive—"her therapist into giving her the wrong thing." He pauses, as if to let this sink in. "And then you believed Melanie's explanation; you didn't trust little Annie's truths, or her anger, am I right?"

"Yes, you are right. I didn't. After Melanie threatened to stop seeing me, I just wanted to shut her up, so that I could stay."

"Little Annie must have wanted to break a lot of windows after that," Blumenfeld comments wryly.

"She did, but I wouldn't let that happen. Which, I suppose, wasn't the right thing to do, but it seemed like the only thing to do. You can't just go around crashing windows."

I find myself suddenly defensive, as if I am in an argument with him. "I mean, you wouldn't want little Annie breaking your window, would you?"

"Have at!" Blumenfeld says, laughing, and then seeing my fear, he adds, "How will she ever know that she's welcome here, now that she knows how unwelcome she is for wanting to break a window?"

"What do you mean by that?" I ask.

Blumenfeld begins to laugh again, and then stops himself. I sit, rather embarrassed and peeved, looking away from him.

"I'm sorry, Annie. I am enjoying little Annie right now. I'm not laughing at you. Let me try to tell you another way. I have a little granddaughter, and little Annie reminds me of her. The other day my granddaughter wanted to climb up the ladder to the slide alone but she's just too small to manage it by herself, so we had quite a tussle about it. She was right to be so mad at me because of course she wanted to do it alone, but I was also right not to let her go up alone, something she could not possibly grasp. What if I then turned on her and said, 'If you are going to throw a temper tantrum about this matter, then I won't see you again'? She and little Annie would find that outrageous and absurd."

I find myself in tears of rage. I pull my knees up to my chest.

"I loved Melanie, and I hated her!" The tears dissolve into long, low sobs. Blumenfeld moves his chair a little forward.

"Little Annie knew what was going on all the time, didn't she?" he asks. Then he is quiet, but I can hear him breathing more deeply, in rhythm with my crying.

After this session, I sit at my desk, drawing two huge toucans and coloring them in. Galle seems magically joined with "little Annie" and with Blumenfeld's granddaughter. I hum and color the bright toucans and hope that the story I still want to tell Blumenfeld will come into the room with him, clear and bright as my birds.

49

Sarah picks me up early, coffee and donuts in tow—a custom we've created in just a short time—and drives her little green Volkswagen bug from the house where I am living to Blumenfeld's parking lot. The day is bright, new green, flower-filled, and as I leave her, I feel as if I am moving into any ordinary day. It has been months since I've felt the morning opening into an ordinary day. It makes me want to fall down on the sidewalk in gratitude.

Blumenfeld and I settle into our chairs. "The story I keep wanting to find some way to tell you is about what happened to me in early February," I tell him. "But I don't know where to begin, how to get there, even into the beginning."

"The beginning is hiding from you?" His question tickles me.

"No, it's just in more than one place, I think." I pause, realizing for the first time how little Blumenfeld actually knows about me. "One beginning has to do with a little boy I was seeing as a therapist."

I wait for him to respond to this, but Blumenfeld just sits there, waiting for me to go on.

"I was his therapist in a clinical internship." I wait again, and then decide to tackle my doubts head-on.

"I wonder now if that was a mistake, working with such disturbed children. Somehow, I want to say that I was good with them; not just passably good, but really good with them. But I have been diagnosed as so many things, I don't know what to think about myself." I lick my dry lips and continue. "According to my records"——I tell this to Blumenfeld with a mixture of pride and anxiety——"I've been 'schizophrenic' off and on for years. And then they thought maybe 'manic-depressive.' Then they decided I suffered from 'schizo-affective disorder.' Oh, and when everyone wanted to believe nothing was terribly wrong, when I was younger, they said I had something called 'adolescent adjustment reaction.' Now, if anyone wanted to pin me down, they'd probably guess 'multiple personality.'"

I throw out these diagnoses, daring Blumenfeld to take them away from me, or to confirm them. Finally, I look down at my hands. "I probably should not have worked with those children, is that what you are thinking?"

"Is that what *you* had been given to think?" His question is a real question. It catches me off guard and I almost begin to answer him. Then I wonder if he is going to avoid answering all questions, on principle.

"Yes, but you didn't answer my question."

Blumenfeld laughs a huge belly laugh. Then he is somber. "You have a kind of giftedness, Annie, that probably has always been inseparable from your suffering, and we don't know very much about that. I am sure that you were very, very good with those children."

In the three years of my clinical training I heard everything but this, the one thing I needed most to know. Hearing it now from a bona fide analyst, albeit an unconventional one, gives me the courage to talk to him about Ben.

"There was one particular child I loved. Ben is his name. He was neglected and abandoned as a baby. I found that to be with Ben, to play with him and be alive in what we were playing, I had to feel, I had to be with, things inside myself that were, they were . . . well, they were finally unbearable."

"Healing is always two-sided, isn't it?" Blumenfeld asks.

His simple question rings through the recesses of everything I know about relationships. I know, even as I hear this, that his voice will go on asking that question in me—as long as I live.

"In early February, Ben played out killing the mother who left him, and I followed his feelings, which were also my feelings, into his play. He finally knew it was a wish. He welcomed it. And then there was no shame in his play. Something in me opened up, a wish for someone, Melanie I guess, to be with me like that, the way I was with Ben. But I drew back from it, I didn't know . . . That's one part of the beginning."

"Are there other beginnings showing themselves to you?" Blumenfeld asks.

"I don't know how this fits, but I had just come back from Boston. I don't know what going to Boston had to do with everything that happened when I came back. Whenever I travel, which isn't very often, I always get lost—I mean actually lost. Maybe it's my very bad sense of direction that explains it, but it seems like things on the map just don't stay where they should be. So, whenever I went anywhere in the past, I felt afraid. Anyway, this time that didn't happen. I don't know why. I went the second week in January. It was like a homecoming, going into Cambridge—as if I'd lived there all along or something, in this country village on the side streets, in this city bustle in Harvard Square, with the snow piled up high, and students and professors coming and going, breathing white puffs in the cold. I especially liked walking at night, along the side streets, looking into the houses, clapboard, not brick, right on the sidewalk practically. Sometimes there was the smell of a fire, and lights inside, and welcoming porches, and I could imagine living there, as if this place was just waiting for me to find it. No—it was more as if time changed—and I was living in my future. I didn't get lost either."

I pause, remembering, a little astonished that I can talk with such ease today, with such clarity. I do not tell him about the music I heard on the bridge over the river when I was not wearing my headphones.

"As if Cambridge and a whole new life were waiting for you," Blumenfeld muses.

"Yes, it was uncanny, and exciting. And meeting Dr. Carol Gilligan." I pause again. "Do you know her?"

"Another therapist?" Blumenfeld asks.

I smile at this. "No. But she's a rather famous psychologist, and she writes like a poet. Anyway, I wanted to pursue an idea with her about my dissertation. Oh, I guess I didn't ever tell you: I'm a doctoral student."

"You chose to show me your inner life first," Blumenfeld says.

"Yes. So, anyway I went to see what I could find out from Dr. Gilligan, Carol, that is. What I didn't expect was the thread of kinship I felt with her, and she with me, I think. When I left her, she said, "Write, of course write to me. I would like that very much." That was shocking to me, but it wasn't too. Just because of this feeling I had, that we would work together someday, you know."

I pause, not knowing how to go on.

"And then I came back here, and I felt exuberant. I went to see Melanie and told her about my adventures in Cambridge, feeling this exuberance, and then it was like something was wrong with this, and wanting . . . I don't know what."

"You really don't know?" Blumenfeld asks.

"Wanting her to be glad for me, or something." I look down at the knees of my faded blue jeans. "But that day she talked about how disloyal I was being to the woman who was my advisor and who had worked with me for years. I didn't agree with that, I said. My advisor gave me money to go to Cambridge and meet with Carol, after all. But Melanie insisted that it was all part of how I 'acted out repeated patterns of competition,' how I hurt people 'without claiming any real responsibility.' And I believed her about that. I was forever doing things that she and others told me about later. I have never been able to explain that to my own satisfaction."

I look at Blumenfeld's clock and see that I only have about fifteen minutes left.

"Then Melanie said that she knew one of my fantasies was to

have her at my mercy. She said I wanted to try to kill her and watch he beg for her life." I pause, trying to remember, even as I tell this story, if this was ever true, but I really feel it wasn't.

"I felt a lot of anger, even rage, toward her, but that had not been one of my fantasies. I told her that she was trying to impose her thoughts on me, and sometimes I didn't know which thoughts were really my own, and that it wasn't right. She told me I was 'hiding behind a facade of confusion' because I did not want to face my 'oldest demons—rage and hate.' I believed her. I felt so evil and I just started to cry. I asked her again and again, 'How could you go on working with me?' And then she was really gentle. I don't remember her words at all, but I looked at her and I didn't see hate, but I don't know what I did see."

"Fear? Fear that you might leave her?" Blumenfeld asks.

His question startles me. It raises a possibility that I am not prepared to believe. I shake my head, feeling irritable, like an animal trying to shake off flies.

"No, it was I who was afraid. When I came to see her next, I was guarded and distant, I guess to cover that much fear. The long silences pounded in my ears. I was drowning, and I fought the silences with words, while revealing very little of myself. My ears started to roar in the silence. I had experienced this before, and it was not uncommon." I pause, and Blumenfeld nods.

"But this day, in the midst of the roaring I heard a voice say, quite distinctly, 'You have to kill her.' I felt evil and ugly and I wanted to leave then. I told Melanie about the fantasy, forcing myself to expose myself, but I did not tell her about the voice. I didn't want to be accused of disguising my own fantasy as a voice, of not claiming 'responsibility' for it, so I said nothing. I remember her words clearly. 'You need me to help you contain this rage. You need to trust that I wouldn't let you hurt me.' I wanted to believe that very badly. But I needed to know more. I said that I wanted to ask her a question, but I didn't want an answer. 'What would happen if I really tried to kill you?' I asked. And she gave me no answer, as I had requested.

"Did you understand that silence as a letter of invitation?" Blumenfeld asks.

I feel suddenly sick, as if I have been hit very hard in the stomach. "No. Absolutely not. No, she didn't invite anything. No, she wouldn't have done that. No."

Blumenfeld is quiet. Then in almost a whisper, he says, "No, because she loved you?"

These words hit me somewhere deeper than irony could go. I cannot breathe.

Breathless, I sit in the fourth-grade classroom, where time is timeless for Galle and Erin learns fluent French. Erin watches the dust motes light up the air, change color, flicker and stream before the blackboard until the blackboard itself disappears.

I cannot catch my breath, sitting in my little desk, newly arrived from nowhere. I don't know the French lesson we are having, but I do know the language is French. The children themselves are strangers to me—not even one or two look vaguely familiar. I don't know their names, nor the name of my teacher. I cannot catch my breath. Sometimes, in this timeless present, a few words drop down onto my tongue, like a tart lemon drop, mon merle—*and I know the taste of that sound, different from other sounds—* in nomine Patre. *Asked to answer a question, I sit in silence, or reply quietly, "I don't know," a response so expected that I am now seldom required to answer.*

I look up wildly. Blumenfeld's eyes reflect my pain and confusion, and seeing this, I begin to breathe again.

"What happened then, Annie? Where did you go?" he asks. I pause, bringing myself back from the fourth-grade classroom to his office, knowing that time, even here, does not pass by unnoticed. I go back to the story I am trying to tell to him:

"The next day I found that I could barely sit still. Overnight, there was a whole chorus of voices telling me that I must kill Melanie and myself. My skin tingled as if I had been numbed and the feeling was coming back, an extremely painful sensation. My blood was on fire. I was also curiously detached from my body. I paced and paced, rubbing my arms to get rid of the burning. But the burning would not go away. Finally I called Melanie, and she returned my phone call within minutes. I don't remember what I said to her, I don't remember the conversation, just that at the end of it she arranged time in her schedule to see me at three that day. I wanted to tell her about the voices and about my fantasies, to save us, but I did not."

"Your voices and her fantasies" is Blumenfeld's editorial comment.

"No," I say, but I find tears on my face suddenly. "Yes." Sudden blinding clarity. "They became the same thing." I look over at Blumenfeld's desk and see that our time has gone ten minutes over.

Seeing me check the time, Blumenfeld looks too and says, "My next appointment is going to interrupt your story pretty soon."

I feel the strong press to continue telling him this story, the story I need to tell more than anything else in the world, but I also know that my story is being changed even as I tell it, and that I won't be able to keep track of the changes if I go any further, any faster.

"That's probably just as well," I tell him.

"Would you like to wait and see me in another hour?" he asks, perhaps picking up my ambivalence.

"No, my friend Sarah will be waiting for me. I can't drive yet, and it might mess up her whole day."

I leave him, going out into the waiting room to find a young girl there, about twelve, and out into the sunlight where Sarah is waiting for me in her little green bug.

50

Back in the house, on this ordinary day, time pleats up as I walk into the kitchen.

Emily wanders from room to room, followed by the comforting aroma of soup cooking. A tightness gathers within her. In the past she tried to break the tightness by speaking, saying anything at all—but not today. A story had been interrupted in the telling, and she resented it. "No," she thought, "better to wander silent, a ghost-girl among the people inside." She knew that her silence could make everyone uncomfortable, and she hoped Blumenfeld would feel uncomfortable too. But, most of all, she feared her unspoken thoughts. She would now draw them back, make herself a stranger to him. She would stop the process of thinking itself—thinking was too perilous. She might bump into some real meanness within her, some violence waiting to pounce out at her. She might form some awkward words of false accusation and inadvertently hurt Melanie, and thereby hurt herself. But it seemed that she would break herself within herself, wandering around the house without words, planning to withdraw all of her thoughts. And the tightness in her grew. It gathered things to itself, like lint in a dryer—it spelled treachery, knew danger, stood condemned already. The tightness sometimes dared to speak itself, saying, "Tell him everything and it will all begin to make sense," or, "Save yourself. Don't talk! Disappear! Go up in smoke." The leaves themselves spoke to her, rearranging themselves in new patterns, new sentences, and Emily loved the speech of leaves. She'd follow this. Coming out onto the front porch, she wondered—Where was she? Oh, yes, here, in this house and not with her own family, here in her gangly tall body, with her straight brown hair and bangs, thirteen years old and older than anyone she knew. What was going to happen to her? She called herself "muffled and dumb," then decided that the phrase "pensive and a bit depressed" suited her better. But nothing was seriously amiss—she certainly wasn't ready to throw herself over any bridge into the river; she didn't want to wander out to sea. And then suddenly she wasn't there at all.

Sitting on the front porch, I eat a peanut butter and jelly sandwich and an apple, thinking about Blumenfeld, puzzling over him, turning him over like a precious and rare rock plucked from the riverbed of my childhood when I was an avid rock collector. When I described to him how Ben, without shame, played out his wish to kill the mother who had abandoned him, and my own wish to experience this with Melanie, he said, "Healing is always two-sided, isn't it?" How does he know this? Has he ever been "crazy"? How does he know all the things he knows? What suffering has given birth to this kind of knowledge? Am I imagining it all, making it up, creating words he never actually said? Maybe he is a jerk who just sits there, and I make up all the rest, everything. But no, that doesn't seem possible. His "lines" are too unexpected, too good, too far beyond what I could imagine him saying. And, if he is really real, then inside the circle of his trust I can begin to believe that I can travel anywhere—into any question, any feeling, even into the story of my own violence—and come back, somehow whole and intact. I do not want to give up this new hope. In fact, I want to rush into its waiting arms, before I lose every hope of speaking to him.

51

The following morning I see Blumenfeld again, bringing in the last bites of my donut from Sarah, swallowing it down in the first few minutes with him. If I am imagining him, he certainly is an unusual and compelling character! And he looks so ordinary, so conventional. Just by my being in his presence again, the story I was waiting to continue flows from me in a torrent.

"The voices I heard that day, the day I called Melanie and she agreed to see me, were unrelenting," I begin, swallowing the last of my sugary donut.

I look at Blumenfeld. "Even if you are just a figment of my imagination, I have to finish this story today. I have to know what it is about. I don't want to leave and have it interrupted. I couldn't bear that. Do you understand?"

"Yes, I kept interrupting you before, so that I could slow you down, Annie. I wanted to understand everything, but I was really slowing you down a little too much, wasn't I?" Blumenfeld says, and he sits back and settles himself in.

"It was as if I was in a trance that day. I wasn't in a trance really—I was just so detached. I went to a Woolworth's store and bought a toy gun. It became instantly real to me as I carried it to my car. I even drove home and got a kitchen knife before going to see Melanie. As I waited to see her, I wanted someone, anyone, to enter the waiting room so I could tell them to stop me. But no one came, and Melanie finally opened her door and invited me in. In fact, she told me to go in while she got coffee. I sat down on her couch, and put my jacket beside me with the gun in the pocket and the knife under it."

In the telling, my mouth is dry. I lick my lips and continue. As I tell this story, I am back in her office, and all the details, fresh, flood back into my mind, all the feelings flow back into my body. "State-dependent memory," I note to myself, as if sitting in one of my classes. I glance at Blumenfeld, who waits for me to go on.

"At first I could not speak at all. I think she said something like 'What's going on?' When I finally did speak, I told her that I wanted to kill her and to kill her child, her daughter. I did not mention wanting to kill myself, I just put in her child instead of me. She asked me how, and I said, 'With a gun.' She asked if I had one with me, and I said, 'Yes.' 'In your jacket pocket?' she asked, and moved toward me, but I reached into the pocket in a flash. I saw a look of horror come over her when she could not stop me."

I am so wrapped in the details of memory that I do not look at Blumenfeld at all as I speak now. But I watch his gestures carefully and listen to his breathing. He stays perfectly still and his breathing continues in the same even rhythm.

"The voices were strangely quiet after speaking constantly to me for days, and I didn't know what to do next." I lick my lips again, afraid to continue. But the words come fast, and I can't stop talking.

"She was so afraid. She fought for breath and then closed her eyes. I made her sit back in her chair. She did that. She closed her eyes and covered them. I couldn't tell if she was crying or not. She kept asking me why, and I couldn't answer. I felt only hate and detachment. I felt so detached, I couldn't break my staring. I was so powerful and so utterly powerless. She asked if she could get a cigarette. I asked her where they were and told her I'd get them. But I felt too disconnected from my body to walk."

"You were already in pieces," Blumenfeld remarks quietly.

"I begged Melanie not to move. When finally I let her get up, I asked her to move slowly. She turned and looked at me, a look of despair. 'What does it matter now?' she asked me. I stared and watched her light a cigarette with trembling hands and close her eyes again. She gasped for breath and said softly, 'I feel sick.' I wanted desperately to stop what I was doing, but also did not want to turn back from something that had already cost us both so much."

Blumenfeld is quiet, his breathing very steady.

"When Melanie looked up, she said, 'Why, Annie, what have I done that you want to kill me?' I did not answer. She repeated the question several times. I finally said, angrily, 'Don't you know?' 'No, tell me,' she said quietly."

Blumenfeld waits as I pause. I look down on the black arm of the chair where I am sitting and suddenly remember looking down at the floral print on the arm of the sofa in Melanie's office, wondering if she would listen.

"I did not want to begin to talk, words seemed to have no meaning then, words seemed so treacherous to me. But I began to talk. I told her that she had come to me as a mother first, and had in fact promised me she would be a mother to me, and had taken that back. She had loved me and I had loved her, and then she had removed herself, becoming more and more 'professional' and distant. Then, abruptly, she stopped touching me and told me she would never touch me again. Then she pushed and poked at my hate as if there was nothing but hate and evil in me. I said, 'Now you see it. This is it and it's ugly, isn't it?' 'No, it isn't ugly,' she said. I contradicted her, 'Yes it is.' But something shifted inside me suddenly, the first tiny movement. I thought I'd only kill myself. But that would hardly matter to her, it seemed. So I said, 'If I killed your daughter, you would hate me.' 'I don't hate you, Annie,' she said softly. I didn't believe her. 'Look what I'm doing to you. You hate me all right.' 'No, I don't hate you. I love you,' she said."

Here Blumenfeld gasps. I follow, unthinkingly, taking in a great gulp of air, and suddenly find that I am shaking.

"'Shut up!' I shouted at Melanie. 'You are lying to me.' And she was silent. Again she closed her eyes."

I pause, and my voice seems to echo in the dim room. I grasp the arms of the black chair. Blumenfeld's polished shoes are marvelously still.

"She looked up again and asked, 'What about the past six years of work? What about your life?' I thought her questions were only a trick though. I said, 'I don't need you. I can get up and leave. I don't have to wait for you to send me away.' She looked at me again with despair. Then I made my slip: 'I could leave you and it would mean nothing to you.' She looked at me and said, 'Do you want to know what it would mean to me?' I said nothing and she went on. She told me that she had loved me and had never worked so hard to be able to continue to care. I did not move. I did not know what to believe."

"You mean you did not know, of all the things she was telling you, which to believe?" Blumenfeld asks.

"Yes. And there was a long silence after that. She said, 'I really didn't understand you. I really didn't listen to you.' It was the first thing she'd said the whole session that I could believe. I mean I felt this was true, but I didn't know if she meant it."

Blumenfeld lets out a sigh, and goes back to breathing in an even rhythm.

"I told her that I wasn't going to let her abandon me. I wasn't coming back, and the only way to be sure of that was to kill myself. 'There's another alternative, Annie,' she said. 'Put the gun over there, please,' she said. I did not move, and then she added, 'I love you.' I didn't know what to think. I kept looking at her, and then I remembered that she had loved me once. Abruptly, I put the gun aside and showed my knife too. She didn't know I had the knife under my jacket, and I saw another look of horror. I told her that she could hate me and send me away. 'Do I look like I hate you?' she asked me. I looked and I could not tell. She asked me that question again, and I felt tears forming on my cheeks. She sat back and opened her arms, 'Come here,' she said. 'I want to hold you.' It was my turn for shock and fear. I felt a terrible longing and a terrible fear, and utter disbelief. I told her she was setting me up.

I called her a liar. I screamed it at her. She opened her arms and said again, 'I want to hold you, I want to take in some of your hurt.' I screamed at her that she had taken away all touch and now she would offer this to take it away yet again. She told me that she had been wrong and she would not do that again. 'And I won't send you away,' she added. I looked at her, her arms open, her eyes open and full. And I felt deeply confused. 'Are you the same person I saw in the beginning? Are you the same person?' I asked the same question over and over, and she nodded each time. I tried to understand, but could not. I tried to get up and could not."

"So, the little pieces, they recognized her as the mother they knew in the beginning, and still they could do nothing at all?" Blumenfeld asks.

"Yes, nothing at all. And then Melanie said, 'Do you want me to come to you?' I felt a pain from inside my body and screamed, and she gathered me up on the couch and held me close, and still I screamed. I heard her say softly, 'Oh my God.' Then she told me to hold on to her: 'Put your arms around me. Hold on tight, Annie,' as if we were shipwrecked and drowning. I clung to her and cried. It hurt horribly to be held again. I felt her hands stroking my hair and cheek. I buried my face and felt her breast against me. Old anguish, longing. I wondered if I was dreaming. And all this time the voices had been silent. Now there were only the sounds of my crying. Melanie told me that she didn't know how much she had hurt me. She thought it would help not to touch me. She talked for a long time but I don't remember what she said after those first words. I cried and cried, as if I would never stop. Nothing could comfort me then."

I feel my jaw tighten and my face go hard against the impending memory of this. Blumenfeld's breathing slows down.

"I felt afraid that I had forced her into a false choice and said so, but she said no. She asked me to look at her and I couldn't. She lifted my chin and looked at me, as she had done years before. Brief glances, but long enough for me to see her compassion. I think it was real compassion. She leaned over and kissed me gently on the forehead. I was incredulous, stunned. She began to prepare me to leave, asking me if I had friends to stay with. She told me that she wanted me to live and to come back, and again that she loved me. 'We survived this, Annie. You played out your worst fantasy and we survived it. Now there's nothing left but good in you.' I sobbed again, shaking my head no, and heard my teeth chattering in my fear. She said that she would write some things down for me. She would see me the next day and she would call me that night. I got up and put my gun, which for the first time I knew was a toy, and my knife into my backpack."

"No, it was not a toy. It was very real," Blumenfeld reminds me. Again I find that I am shaking.

"Melanie handed me a note. I stuffed it into my pocket without reading it, and began to walk to the door. The air seemed solid, heavy. Walking was very difficult, but I made it out to my car. I sat there and my teeth chattered, my knees shook. And it was so quiet. I waited for a long time, and then I drove home."

A silence grows in the room. I wonder what time it is, but don't look at the clock. Blumenfeld is perfectly still.

"You were trying to heal her, weren't you, Annie?" he asks.

His question seems so unlikely that I ask him to repeat it.

"You were trying to heal her, Annie," he says, stating it as a sentence.

I know that he has caught something, something rare and real, in his fine net. I throw it back into the water and continue as if I have not heard him.

"I knew when she called me that night, and again the next day, that she was very frightened. You see, I know what it feels like to know your life is at stake, and I knew I had made her feel that. I wondered if she would refuse to see me any longer. And ten days after this session, I met with Melanie for the last time. She called me two days before we were to meet and suggested that I bring a friend. I knew then that it would be our last session. In the ten days and nights before this session, I lived in dread, an unspeakable dread haunted by voices. My skin burned so badly at night that I could not sleep. Friends stayed with me. Sarah held me so that I could fall asleep. I kept telling her that Melanie was afraid and that she would abandon me. She kept saying, 'No, you don't know that.'"

"But you knew; your body knew," Blumenfeld says.

"That day Melanie and I were not even alone to say goodbye. She brought her therapist, and I came with Sarah. Melanie looked at me across the waiting room, a long measured look, and I saw that every connection had been severed. Inside her office, she told me that she would not see me again, that I had 'violated and betrayed' her. And I had. I knew that. She said that she had searched for a way to continue to work with me, but she could not work in fear. She said, 'You are dangerous to yourself and to others.' I sat in shame, letting her words pour in."

"As if they were true," Blumenfeld says sadly.

"Yes. And her face was a mask, her eyes hard. Her therapist told me that she was not abandoning me, that I had severed the relationship myself."

"That was the blackest lie of all!" Blumenfeld spits out.

I begin to cry again, and continue, "And then I had nothing left, no pride at all. So I begged her forgiveness, and asked her not to leave me. But she was immovable. So we left one another like that, a severing without any goodbye."

"And then?" Blumenfeld asks.

"Sarah took me to another friend's house nearby. I entered what felt like a waking nightmare. My friends and my sister stayed with me. I don't remember it very clearly. I think sometime in the late afternoon they called a psychiatrist I had seen when I was an adolescent. I knew I had already begun a long journey into oblivion, and I couldn't stop crying. I didn't protest very much when, late in the day, they drove me to a psychiatric hospital. Once I was there, I felt so completely defeated. I remember sitting on a stiff hospital bed in one of those thin hospital gowns after they'd left, tearing at the plastic wristband, just terrified of myself. I wanted to scrape my skin off my arms. And then I did feel hate for Melanie, hate mixed up with longing, longing with the ground of trust ripped away, love itself poisoned by something, something so completely— what? False? One of the nurses tried to rub my back, as if she knew me, and maybe she did, maybe that wasn't even the same night. I am confused about time. But her hands could not ease my anguish. And so I slipped over into madness."

"And you tried so hard to heal Melanie," Blumenfeld says.

"No. I tried to hurt her, to kill her. She was right. Don't you see that I tried to kill her? I was the one who severed the relationship." My body is tense, poised for blows.

"You were trying to bring her a truth—you were trying to show her that all these promises she made to you and withdrew from you were killing you. You brought her the core of yourself, Annie, so that you could heal her and continue your relationship and be free to love again," Blumenfeld says slowly.

A quiet sound, my tears and his breathing together, as the world hangs still. I desperately want to believe him. Then my whole body relaxes in his chair.

"Can I believe you? Can I believe in her first response, when she said she hadn't been listening to me, when she knew it and saw the horror of it, and held me?" I ask.

"Yes, that was her bravest moment with you, and even if she retreated from it later, you can believe in it, Annie."

I look at his desk and see that I have gone just a few minutes over.

As I leave him, I turn and hold his gaze. Standing framed in the doorway, he nods to me, a little nod from this ordinary middle-aged man who must be real after all, because he sees with his heart.

Galle and Erin and Emily, and others, and still others, watch and listen from within and nod too. I feel the fluttering of whispers within, as if a message is being passed down a long passageway. Someone is singing a Gregorian chant as I go out into the sunlight to meet Sarah.

. . .

The poet Pamela Hadas says the self is "any true I" in a story, the true I being the one that can say with conviction, "I am alive," or, with trust in her own vision, "The emperor wears no clothes."

Blumenfeld listens to me as if I am not only creditable, but an extraordinarily trustworthy narrator, a "true I." Since I do not fully credit myself at this time, not knowing what to believe, it is critical that someone else can. I have held a story alone, a story that contains forbidden knowledge, a story I was not able to tell without recourse to madness. But as I bring this story to Blumenfeld, something about the story itself begins to change. As I listen to him, my own words start to surprise me, so that I discover, at the edge of the unspeakable, myself—as a "true I" speaking to him.

Yet in my efforts to defend Melanie, in my repeated denials of her fear, of her invitation to me, of the monstrosity of her abandonment, I seem to be saying to Blumenfeld, "Forgive the teller for giving up her truths." But perhaps because there was no sign of forgiveness, no understanding that might have made forgiveness possible from the person I wanted it from, I also seem to be saying to Blumenfeld, "I alone have escaped to tell you."

And Blumenfeld listens. As he listens not only to what I say, but also to what is yet unspeakable, he alone is able to hold together my "self" and a coherent story—which is, after all, a coherent world, one worth living in. Where we are joined, Blumenfeld and I, is at the tattered edges of my story, the rips and gaps in it. He seems to notice the places where I cannot claim my own most profound experiment in relationship—in this story, the attempt to "heal" my beloved therapist. It will be months and years of telling and retelling this story, playing with Blumenfeld along the tattered edges of it, before I understand my story in a new way.

52

After this session, I lie on the wooden swing on the screened-in front porch of the house where I am staying. The trees, charcoal-penciled against a monstrous drapery of dark clouds, strain in the wind. And then it begins to rain. The swing rocks me to and fro, weightless in cooler and warmer pockets of air. The storm—lightning and thunder playing to a crescendo—breaks overhead. Rain pounds the roof of the house, and the storm within me also breaks upon me. I cry and cry.

Mary comes over for dinner that night, and after dinner we decide to bake a chocolate cake. When we go shopping for the ingredients, and I remind her to get "eight inches of sour cream" for the sour cream fudge frosting, she laughs. "Don't you mean eight ounces?" "Sometimes ounces are inches," I quip. And I laugh with her because I can hear my mistakes with words so clearly. I can play with words, not only with Blumenfeld in his office, but with my sister again.

I dream of Melanie lying on Blumenfeld's couch, or rather floating just inches above his couch, her eyes closed. I can see her dreams in images that appear in cartoon balloons over her head, but I don't hear what she is saying.

I wake up and can't remember any of those images, but I can still hear the timbre of her voice in the room, not her words, just the inflections—the sound of speech before grammar and meaning become clear—the sound of a mother.

I remember myself, or was it someone else?—someone lost, falling in vast darkness, falling in the night sky and landing on her back in snow.

I want Melanie to fling herself into darkness so vast that she won't be able to remember whether it was herself falling or not.

I waken, crying, as I try to invent Melanie—Melanie remembering me.

53

When I return to see Blumenfeld the following week, he gets up to slip the brass latch on his door into place, as he has done each time I've entered the room. This time, I turn and suggest, "No, let's not lock it."

"It's not to lock you in," he replies. "It's to lock out anyone who might intrude."

"No, let's not lock it," I repeat.

"All right. You will be in charge of the lock. If you want it unlocked, fine. If you want to lock it again, that's fine too."

I have brought with me the journal I began keeping when I first met Melanie. Telling the story about the ending of my relationship with her has awakened the necessity to understand what led up to it. The ending still looms incomprehensible before me. I cannot hold onto Blumenfeld's words from our last session. I dreamt about Melanie. And I tried to read my old journal over the weekend by myself.

I hand the volume to Blumenfeld, telling him that I tried to read it but couldn't go on.

"That's right, Annie, there are some things you can't understand by yourself, and it would be dangerous to try."

I do not sit down immediately, as usual. I feel, for the first time, a need to explore my surroundings. I walk slowly around his office, looking at the titles of his books, commenting whenever I come to one that I own: "I have that book too." There are quite a number we have in common.

I come to a bookcase with two doors under it that open when I pull at them. Toys underneath.

"Aha!" I say. "I wondered where you kept your toys."

I continue my tour, and come to a door. I turn and look at Blumenfeld, who nods, so I open it, expecting something interesting, to find only a closet with boxes and a few coats in it.

I sit down. "It's strange not to be seeing a woman, and especially not to be seeing Melanie," I begin, noticing for the first time that Blumenfeld might be my therapist.

"Were you looking for her in those places where you found the toys and the coats?" he asks.

"No, I did not expect to find her really." I sigh. "No, but if you were a woman, if you were a mother, I would want to know where to hide sometimes."

"And you don't because I am a man?" he asks, eyebrows up in surprise.

"Because you are a man, I don't feel the need to hide in the same way. With a woman, I would feel so exposed, as if I had no skin. But I can't go to a woman now, not now."

Blumenfeld nods, as if this makes sense to him.

"I don't know if I should go on seeing you," I tell him, as if this is our first meeting. "I don't know how I will pay you. I don't even know what your fee is!" I'm a bit embarrassed to say this, when I've been seeing him almost daily for two weeks already.

"If you should go on seeing me, then the fee will settle itself. You need not worry about that right now," he says as if his is a leisurely, no-need-to-worry-about-money sort of practice.

I don't know what to make of that. I lean back and the chair lifts me up, a sensation of being taken off the ground. I feel suddenly quite small, and think of Galle, or as Blumenfeld calls her, "little Annie."

"I dreamed that Melanie was in your office," I tell Blumenfeld, and sigh again.

"That does help me," he says, his eyes lighting up. "I had a fantasy that I might see her here."

Startled, I look up at him.

"The little pieces are still attached to her, Annie, and they keep searching for her, don't they?"

A rush of relief. "I'm so glad you don't hate her. I'm so relieved that you haven't made her into a monster. Even my best friends are inclined to do that. I keep looking for her everywhere. She appears in my dreams. I even hear her voice in the room sometimes at night when I wake up—but she's never there."

"The little pieces are the cement of your personality, and you are shattered now. But they are still searching for her, they believe that she is still your therapist. So, you see, I had a fantasy this weekend that I might meet with Melanie. We might speak the same language. But you know her better than I do. Do you think this is something to explore?"

"Yes," I tell him. "But I don't know if she will come here." I shiver. "I can't afford another mistake, another shattering. But I can't afford to feel so cut off and completely betrayed. And I can't go to see another woman."

"So, there is no healing for the Annie who held the gun?" Blumenfeld asks.

"I don't care about her. She should never have done that," I come back angrily.

"She is the core of yourself, Annie. You brought the very core of yourself to your therapist. The Annie who held the gun is a girl who sees with blue lenses, and she was shattered. When you say 'I don't care about her,' I know that even the blue lenses were shattered."

I know what he is saying, and I am also confused. "What do you mean, a girl with blue lenses?"

"You have never read that story?" he says, incredulous.

"No."

"It is about a girl in a psychiatric hospital, and every time a doctor or nurse came into her room, she saw a viper, or a ravenous vulture, or an ugly boar. She saw them as they were, she saw their essences, and she trusted none of them. She had blue lenses, as you do. Then one day a Saint Bernard came into her room."

"Were you the Saint Bernard?" I ask him.

Blumenfeld laughs. "I could be," he said. "If you were lost in such a place, I could probably become one and find you there."

"Yes, I think you probably could," I admit.

I sit in the silence, with this image of him carrying something around his neck into a room, somewhere where I have been.

"When will you call Melanie?" I ask him.

"You will need to call her, Annie," he says.

"Why? She won't listen to me." I feel a rising panic. "She said she would answer no phone calls."

"Because it would be like sneaking in her back door, for me to call. I want you to knock on the front door," Blumenfeld explains.

I protest, angrily. "Don't you understand? She said no to any contact! She threatened to call the police!"

"Don't you need to know," Blumenfeld asks, "if she would do that—in response to something so simple as a phone message?"

"No," I tell him. "I don't want to know anything more than I know now. No. I don't want to know. I already know too much."

"I disagree with you there, Annie," Blumenfeld says softly. "Truths about people are never too much."

Suddenly, I feel he is right. But nothing changes my fear. "I am just too frightened to call."

"The little pieces will know when," he says.

I ask him, "If I call her and ask her to call you, will you let me know right away if she does?"

Blumenfeld smiles. "You may know before I know, but yes." He gets up and goes over to his desk, and writes something down on a scrap of paper. He hands me the paper.

"If you want to call me, at any time, call me. I am giving you my phone number at home. And if you call me in the middle of the night, I will especially like that because I love going to sleep, and I will get to do it twice in one night."

As I leave, he adds, "Annie, about the latch. You never liked it because I was locking Melanie out, wasn't I?"

I smile at him, nod, go out into the waiting room, and out into the warm spring air, where Sarah is waiting for me.

I sit at my desk, push aside art materials, and write in a blue spiral notebook, as if I am sitting in the playroom at Glenwood.

In this session, Blumenfeld and I are introduced again at a deeper level. Although I've told him a most intimate, frightening story about myself, this session feels like a first meeting. I explore the office and raise questions about his fee and about whether or not I should continue to see him. Most crucially, in this session, we begin to move, for the first time, through the space between his fantasies and wishes and mine. We understand one another's words and actions through this unconscious and powerfully deep connection. And, as we begin to understand one another in this way, the logic of both sets of our associations becomes clear. For example, he understands my trouble with the latch (he kept locking Melanie out), as well as my tour of his office and its hidden places (I was looking for Melanie there)—through his own fantasy of meeting with her over the weekend. And he is very accurate in his interpretations. We don't even have to be in the same room to be with one another in this way. I "help him out" with my dream that Melanie comes to his office, a dream I experienced over the weekend when he had his fantasy.

But as soon as I sense the possibility of her presence there, I am troubled that Blumenfeld is not a woman, and tell him this. This is a comfort because I don't feel the need to hide, yet I have sought out the hiding places in his office, as if I wished that I did have to hide. The fact that he is not a woman, and therefore not a mother, is inescapable.

54

I call Melanie and leave a message for her to call Dr. Blumenfeld. He calls me and lets me know that she has spoken to him (that same day), and she has agreed to come and talk to him. Blumenfeld also tells me that she said she had a fantasy of working with me again.

A thin sliver of hope opens up in me, and with my hope— confusion and terror.

I dream of an unknown woman and myself entering a dark little house. We must bend over to enter the doorway. Inside there are several children, crying. She undresses them, and me, now small, and, in terror, I move quietly out of my body and hover above this scene.

I dream of going into a dark corridor with Melanie. It is dimly lit by slits of light from above. Above us a little bird flies back and forth, crying, chirping, desperate to get out.

I wake up trembling, walk down the hallway to the bathroom, and coming back, turn the corner, expecting to see Melanie there. I feel her presence and can't stop trembling. I get up to call Blumenfeld, but the whole room tilts. I crawl back into bed.

• • •

I begin to get lost on my daily walks again. Keeping track of time is confusing. I draw a picture of the garden of the house where I am staying, and nothing is in its proper place.

I have cut down on the Haldol I was taking when I left the hospital. I begin to take the regular dose again, but it does not help the confusion. Twitches and spasms wrench my back. I take more Cogentin to allay the worst of these side effects and pace a path in the rug of my room. I decide nothing could be worse than this and stop taking the Haldol altogether.

I stay in my room more often, reading children's books and trying to draw.

At around three thirty each afternoon Noah comes home from school. This fourteen-year-old boy and I are the same height exactly. Fine-boned and thin, with light-brown hair, we look uncannily like brother and sister. We even have matching blue Patagonia jackets, the same size.

He speaks quickly in long sentences, swallowing some of his words, and I can't follow him always, but I manage to get most of his jokes. We walk to the grocery store to buy bubble gum, we fly stunt kites in the field to the left of the house, we cook dinners together (he's an accomplished cook), and we make chocolate-chip oatmeal cookies, called "cowboy cookies" in his family. And at night, Noah comes to my room in his robe and slippers with two steaming cups of tea and talks to me as I draw.

His ease with me reminds me of Ben, whom I cannot see.

55

When I come to see Blumenfeld the following week (we have set-tled into meeting three times a week), I bring a paper bag with two rabbit ears sticking out.

I lift the stuffed rabbit out of the bag by the ears and put her on my lap. Blumenfeld looks up. "Why have you hidden him in that uncomfortable bag?" he asks.

"Her," I correct him. "There are grown-ups in the waiting room," I explain, hoping he has read *The Little Prince*.

"Oh yes, the grown-ups!" he says. "That reminds me of playing 'The Frog Prince' with a three-year-old, Amanda, on the golf course one day. I was playing the frog, of course, and I was really into it, squatting down and croaking, when suddenly Amanda stopped. She looked sort of tense and embarrassed, as you do right now. I looked up, and there was a whole cluster of golfers watching us. So we waited until the people went away. Amanda felt rather silly about it."

"And you?" I ask him, picturing the whole scene clearly.

"I've had more experience at looking silly. I'm used to it."

We sit in the silence. I notice that my journal is on his desk. "Did you read it?" I ask him.

"I started to read it. There is much to absorb, so it's going to take me a long time. I think you knew even from the earliest time with Melanie that she might abandon you, Annie. I sensed that earlier, and now I'm quite sure of it."

"I don't understand that very well," I tell him. "It's almost as if I went about creating the very thing that I feared the most."

"Yes, in a way that's right, Annie. But you did not create it alone," Blumenfeld comments. Tears bloom in the corners of my eyes. I finger the ears of my rabbit. Despair and longing. "And you, you really get this, you get the whole story in a way I never imagined anyone could or would, but you are not a mother-person. You don't have any breasts!"

"I could try to grow some for you," he says, and I have to laugh. But he is perfectly serious.

The silence grows. Blumenfeld breaks it by asking, "Does your rabbit have a name?"

"Her name is Pimmy," I tell him, and thinking about how he might grow breasts, I add, "Do you think you could nurse her?"

He smiles. "I wouldn't know how to. Pimmy would have to tell me how to hold and nurse her."

Immediately I retreat, wondering if he is afraid of this.

"Do you think Pimmy would talk to me about it?" he asks.

I look at the rabbit. "She isn't verbal."

"That's OK—words get in the way of talking sometimes," Blumenfeld says, stretching out his hands to me.

I give him the rabbit. He puts Pimmy up on his chest, her head on one shoulder, loosely cradling her neck and tail. Had the rabbit wanted to squirm, she could have. Her ears flop back. He says, "She is talking to me, and she says she doesn't want to be fed right now, she just wants to be held and surrounded and not dropped."

The image of the rabbit and a baby girl blurs with my tears. We sit like this for a long time, and then Blumenfeld hands me my rabbit back.

"Oh, by the way, I have figured out the fee, if you want to continue to see me," he says. "My fee is sixty dollars a session. You can pay me whatever you can now, see me as often as you like, and pay me the rest when you are wealthy."

"When I am wealthy?" I ask, astonished.

"When you are wealthy. After you publish. You see, when I started to read your journal it became clear to me that you are a writer, and when you publish, you will probably make a lot of money, and then you can pay me."

"And if I don't publish, or don't get wealthy from it?"

"Then you will owe me nothing beyond what you can pay me now."

"I am a student, so that won't be very much at all! That wouldn't feel fair to me." I hardly know what to make of what he is saying to me.

"Then you can pay me whatever you like afterwards as well. But, Annie, if you do not publish, then you owe me nothing more. This therapy will have been a complete failure."

I get up to leave him, stuffing the rabbit back in the bag.

"Someday, I hope you will carry him proudly," Blumenfeld says.

"Her," I gently correct him, and go out.

Pimmy is the fourth in a series of rabbits I have owned, named after the original rabbit called Pimmy, given to me by my father when I was four. This one was white once, but is gray by now, with a worn green ribbon around her neck. She is the rabbit I brought to Melanie as well, the representative of my smallest self.

I bring the rabbit to Blumenfeld after he has begun to meet with Melanie. She has agreed to meet with him regularly to talk. He does not tell me anything about these talks, but I trust him because he has not dismissed my wish to see her again. I also believe he grasps, without my needing to tell him, what is at stake in this meeting with her.

Blumenfeld plays with me through his story about himself and Amanda playing "The Frog Prince" on the golf course. He seems to be saying that he is older than Amanda, and older than me, and is therefore "used to" feeling silly, but there is no shame in Amanda's embarrassment, nor in mine. And he is transparent, he is trustworthy, because he plays. He has not given in to the constraints of "the grown-ups."

Later that evening I find myself thinking about the fairy tale called "The Frog Prince." A little girl, the youngest of the King's daughters, has lost a golden ball in a deep well. She meets a frog when she is crying about her loss. I remember the first line in the story: "In the old times, when it was still of some use to wish for the thing one wanted . . ." And this line reverberates with my session with Blumenfeld. I find myself in despair about my wish for a mother-person in a therapist. My wish comes to life in Blumenfeld's presence—a man who clearly breaks many conventional rules of analytic practice. He tells me that he has played a frog, and I remember a fairy tale where a frog helps a girl by returning her golden ball from the well. The similarities are striking. It's not for free that the frog retrieves the golden ball; he makes the little girl promise him that she will grant him a wish in return. And Blumenfeld's help isn't free either. In this session, we finally agree upon a fee, though in a most unusual way. But I think his wish, his deepest wish, isn't about money. He risks not getting paid if I don't "get wealthy," after all. I think his real wish is to learn how to become a mother-person, something he has not been able to do. When I tell him, "You don't have any breasts," he says, "I could try to grow some for you."

And he and I are both willing to try this. I hand over my rabbit for him to nurse her, and though he does not know how to nurse her, he does find a way to hold her that brings her to life for me, as a baby girl, as myself. But Blumenfeld is a man; he does not have breasts to feed her, and he hands the rabbit back to me. He also confuses her gender, twice calling her "him." Both times I gently correct him. I not only know the difference between a mother-person and a male analyst, a baby girl and a baby boy, but also know how hard it may be to teach a man how to be a mother. But we are very patient with one another because we both share the same wish.

The following week I begin to drive again. I visit my apartment and relish my solitude. On Friday, I move from the house where I have been staying during the three weeks since my release from the hospital, into my apartment again. On the back sunporch I set up my drawing table and paints.

On Monday morning I discover, by the front door, a shoe box and a manila envelope with a set of paintings. I wonder if I somehow forgot to unpack these things. I look in the envelope and find a series of terrifying images and stuff them quickly back in. I don't remember painting them. I open the shoe box cautiously. In it I find a bar of soap, a can of grape juice, a baby bottle, some cinnamon graham crackers, an enema, pieces of rope, my little gun, and a kitchen knife. I know, instantly, that someone intends for me to take all this to Blumenfeld.

Driving myself to Blumenfeld's office for the first time, then carrying the box, the envelope and my rabbit (in a new red-and-blue gym bag) into the waiting room, I feel removed from myself and a bit groggy. I peek into the envelope and shoe box, and see immediately that some of the paintings are gone and some of the things that were in the box are also missing. When Blumenfeld calls me, I am distracted and a little frightened.

Once inside the cool dimness of his office, however, I relax. I pull the rabbit out of the gym bag and sit back. I find myself thinking thoughts that seem to come from nowhere, unbidden, almost inserted into the stream of my thinking:

Rabbit out of a hat, paintings in blue, blue into red, a red enamel chair and yellow table, low to the ground, the smell of burning, of soap, at the kitchen table my chin comes up to the table, just; I am watching my mother cut vegetables with a knife. Somewhere off to the left of the table Telesporus hovers.

"I've brought some things today," I tell Blumenfeld, ignoring the distinct impression that Telesporus, the tall, blond, Viking-sized angel whom I've known since I was about six, is in this room, behind me and to my left.

"The box, that's not for today," I point out to Blumenfeld. "I just want to put it in your closet now. There are things in it, and there are things missing from it."

Blumenfeld nods.

"Is there any room in your closet?" I ask.

"There will always be room for your things and your missing things in my closet. Why don't you look for a place on the top shelf?"

I get up and open the closet door, stifle the impulse to search the inside for all sorts of missing things, and look up.

"It's too high. I can't see that far up. I mean, I can't reach that far up."

Blumenfeld gets up from his chair slowly and takes the shoe box from my hand. He places it neatly on the top shelf.

I begin: "I don't know where these paintings came from. I must have painted them, but they are strange. And they make me afraid."

Blumenfeld waits, leaning forward, his wrists hanging off the arms of his chair. I notice a painting on the wall at the foot of the couch—a man and a child walking down a road. I notice a set of dictionaries lined up on a low shelf, as if the smallest child had to have easy access to them. Words. Little black squiggles on a page with all their lived meanings, all their long lives, past and future. An avid reader of the *Oxford English Dictionary*, I wonder about the place of these dictionaries in Blumenfeld's life.

I bend down and pick up my envelope of paintings, open it up, peer in, and stop myself.

"I don't understand the paintings," I explain.

"You don't know what they are bringing to you?" Blumenfeld asks.

"Yes. I don't even remember painting them. There were paintings and collages I made in the hospital I don't remember clearly either, but they were much cruder than these, and I think I threw most of them away." I pause, puzzled. "Or someone else threw them away."

I hand four paintings to Blumenfeld, one by one.

The first, all in shades of blue, is of a mother holding a baby, and a second baby, bigger, standing and leaning against the little one. I can tell as I look at my painting that it was painted in different blues on wet paper originally, because all the lines of the figures blur. In the foreground there are a series of delicate blue and purple dry washes.

The second painting is almost all bars—the bars of a crib. You have to look twice to see that there's someone in the crib at all. The painting is done in sepia, black and red, with a bit of blue around the crib itself. "It makes me feel uncannily alone," I tell Blumenfeld.

The third of this series terrifies me—long knives, a small yellow table, a small child; toddler-size, a little red chair, ropes. The colors are sepia, red and black, with just a hint of blue around the red chair. Things float in space, disconnected.

The fourth painting is different from the others: the light in it shifts in different layers. A blond girl rides the back of a great lion, right down the center of the page. Below this pair is darkness, a darkness penetrated by little green faces, howling or screaming, I can't tell. Above them, eerie yellow light, too bright, almost electric, searing, seeps down the page slowly into the upper layer of the dark area.

Blumenfeld looks at me. I feel myself bite my lower lip. I don't say anything.

"You look like you know a lot about these paintings, Annie," he says.

I look away. The silence grows around us. My breathing is fast and shallow. Blumenfeld's breathing, however, is deep and regular, a comforting sound.

I find myself looking at his couch, all black. Up until this time, I've never considered it for my own use. It is just part of the room, like the lamp, the books, the dictionaries. I am suddenly tired, really exhausted, and the couch seems like a possible place to rest, a place to lie down and breathe more freely.

"I'm so tired. I just want to lie down and sleep, forget everything for a while."

"You can lie down, of course," Blumenfeld says. "I suspect

that you really want to lie down and wake up and remember a
little."

As soon as his words come into my ears, I feel washed with relief, but as soon as this little wave washes over me, a second wave
of the fear comes up, much bigger.

"But what if I lie down and I get lost?" Task.

"You won't get very lost because I will be right here."

"What if you aren't? What if I can't find you?"

"I will sit where you can find me right away," he says.

I move to the couch and lie down, putting my rabbit on top of
me, so that she covers my whole chest and belly. My head is slightly
raised. Blumenfeld pulls his chair up to the middle of the couch.
I turn my head slightly to the right and find that I can see his face.

I close my eyes. There is a drifting-out-to-sea feeling, a little
rocking motion. The room is cool and dim.

*The room is cool and blue and dim. I am covered with a light blanket,
lying face up. Blue light surrounds me. There in my crib, I turn, arching
my back, and roll over onto my stomach.* Startled by these impressions,
I open my eyes. I look at Blumenfeld. "This is a very drifting position, like being in a boat," I tell him.

He puts one polished black shoe up on the side of the couch.
"I've got you well anchored. I won't let your boat drift away."

I close my eyes again. The room grows cool, and then cold.

*The blanket has fallen off. My arms and legs are cold. I squirm and
shiver. I feel like crying. Hands pull up the blanket—blue warmth in a
cool blue room.*

I open my eyes and smile at Blumenfeld's polished black shoe.
"Blue," I say aloud.

"Blue was the color of your mother? Of comfort?" I nod. He
continues, "And then, the blue got poisoned, love got mixed in
with something nearly lethal to you."

I nod again. Tears fall suddenly, flowing out of the sides of my
eyes and down into my ears, an odd sensation, but I don't move.
Finally I ask him, "How did you know that?"

He laughs lightly. When I look at him, he is perfectly serious. "From your paintings," he says. "The blue gets mixed in with other colors and with terrifying objects—the chair, the rope, the knife—and then it gets crowded out, almost entirely, but not quite."

When he says this, I remember the blue in each of the paintings—at least a hint of it.

He looks over at his desk. "It's almost time to stop," he says, and I'm surprised. The session has passed by incredibly quickly. Then I smile, remembering that I said those very words to the little boy Ben. I tip my feet over the side of the boat, and the room swirls. I steady myself. Blumenfeld puts his foot back up. The boat holds still. I get up, pack up my rabbit in my gym bag, and leave Blumenfeld without a word.

As I open the door, I look back. I have the impression that Blumenfeld is crying. He is softly weeping, and I can see Telesporus, the great guardian angel of my childhood, bending over him, as if to embrace him.

In the place where there is no memory, words terrify. Thoughts come to me fully formed, as if dropped down into my ordinary stream of consciousness.

In the place where there are no words, images terrify. I find a series of paintings that I don't remember painting.

In the place where there are no images, even fleeting sensory impressions terrify.

Blumenfeld is making room for terror. The things I bring into his office seem disconnected from one another and from me. There is no coherent present or past. In terror, the present as well as the past are obliterated. Yet Blumenfeld makes room for past and present when he says, "There will always be room for your things and your missing things in my closet." I notice that he places my box up on a high shelf, out of my reach. Perhaps he knows I am not ready to talk about these things—the baby bottle, the enema, the grape juice and graham crackers, the gun and knife. Perhaps he senses that I do not want to have them within reach. Or perhaps he is not yet ready to have them within my reach, for reasons of his own that I don't know about.

After he puts my box in his closet and I look at my paintings, I notice his dictionaries. I know that words have a past and a future. Words are essential to a coherent world, and so must be available to the smallest children. I also know that words can be used to deceive, and so I try hard not to lie to Blumenfeld about my confusion, even when I don't want to acknowledge to him or to myself just how confused and terrified I am about missing memories. I have brought Blumenfeld paintings I do not remember painting.

Through this series of paintings which I have discovered by my front door, paintings I treat as my own, I enter memory. Lying down on the couch, the black couch that becomes a boat anchored by Blumenfeld's foot, without any formal trance, I drift into memory. Protected from getting lost by Blumenfeld's near presence and by Telesporus, I slip easily into the colors of memory. The color blue is the color I begin with, and I discover the meanings of the paintings through the words and associations about my mother that Blumenfeld brings back to me: blue—comfort—love—mixed with something almost lethal.

The colors yellow, red, sepia and black also appear and reappear in each painting. Those colors do not enter my associations when I lie down. Impressions about them come to me at the opening of the session. However, these impressions arrive fully formed, as if they are not my thoughts, and I push them aside, with the sense that Telesporus, my protector, has come into the room. I don't reveal any of this directly to Blumenfeld.

As I drift into the blue room of my beginnings, I remain in Blumenfeld's office, in this man's presence. Terror opens out into memory for the first time with Blumenfeld. Memory is room—room in the closet, the cool dim of my beginnings where the love of my mother once was blue, room inside Blumenfeld himself, room for things missing—where there is no memory. And though there is time missing from my life, paintings in a sequence missing, acts I can't remember, I begin to remember the blue love of my mother, anchored in time and space by Blumenfeld's foot on the couch.

58

The sense that once my mother loved me, and that I felt that love as comfort, gives me a ground of safety I have never known before.

I wake up one morning in early May and notice the silence. Sunlight plays on the windowsill and splashes over my blue quilt as the trees move. A rush of wind in my ears followed by silence. This silence, filled with light and bird songs and a new stillness within me, quenches a thirst I didn't know was in me. It has its own shifting textures, as though I am running my hands over white flour, cold water, rough stone. A sense of my own well-being pervades the air, so strange it frightens me. I have experienced reprieves before, however, and I doubt that this will last.

Blumenfeld, I know, is seeing Melanie (for free, since it's at his request, not hers). He tells me nothing about these meetings, except to offer, "Yes, sometimes we do speak the same language."

I go to my office at school, explaining rather awkwardly that I have been "sick," and leaving out every detail.

I run in the park under a canopy of green, see friends I haven't seen since early February, even go out dancing. I arrange my three-day-long comprehensive examinations for the end of the summer.

. . .

I don't know what to do about my clinical internship, although I miss intensely the children I was seeing. I spend a great deal of my time talking with friends, who are students in clinical programs or practicing therapists, about returning to work. Everyone seems cautious. My sister, too, reminds me that only a little more than a month has passed since I was released from the hospital. Mary says, "Annie, all I can say is how frightened we were. You don't remember, but I saw you in it—every familiar gesture of yours disappeared. You didn't recognize us. Your speech was completely incoherent. Medication had no effect at all. The doctors were asking *me* about whether to increase or decrease your medications! So, just take it a little slow, OK?" Seeing my disappointment, she adds, "But, you know me, I always err on the side of caution."

I dream of Ben and of the other children I am not seeing.

Hot drops of wax from red and blue crayons, melted over a candle flame, burn on my child's hands, and cool and harden into dots. I dream of Ben painting—blue over red, he blackens it out—while I paint in every shade of blue imaginable and do not blacken it out.

I dream of a room, half in shadow. A lamp smokes and burns, catches the curtains.

I dream of a twisted, dried leaf that sings to me.

I dream of a sky on fire, and my birthday party. I invite Ben and other children my age. Later, one child's mother finds burn marks on her pelvis and vagina. She shows them to my mother. I go down a flight of stairs, and as I go, my mother keeps hitting me. I am furious and terrified at once. I don't know why she is hitting me.

. . .

My mother has a burn scar from her knees to her neck, and her right ear is half gone and what's left is melted and crumpled into a familiar oddity. I dream of the lace sleeve of her nightgown catching the blue flame of the ring of fire on the stove top, when she was younger than I am now. I see her fear of fire in her dark eyes, and a cigarette, red at the tip, coming toward me. The rim of the sky is on fire and the flames are rising.

"Put out all the fires in all the skies," I whisper to the darkness as I go to sleep each night.

59

Sitting with Blumenfeld one morning, I ask him, wistfully, "Do you think I will ever be cured?" He begins to laugh and then can't stop. As he comes to the end of his fit of laughter, he wipes his eyes and says, "Annie, only hams get cured." I'm not laughing, however.

Soft yellow slits arranged on the rug from the Levolor blinds illuminate rays of dust particles extending from window to floor. I watch the dust motes stream in the dark room. I wonder if they will form a little circle. Would they take me back to the little girl I found in the library?

"If you were cured, Annie, whatever that means, you wouldn't have your blue lenses," Blumenfeld says quietly.

"If I were cured," I counter, "I wouldn't have to worry about going into the hospital again."

"Hospitals are terrible places for those who wear blue lenses, Annie," Blumenfeld says and pauses. "They are terrible places because the people there who don't wear blue lenses want to cure those who do. I don't blame you for not wanting to go back."

"I know that," I say with some exasperation. I wonder if he is being deliberately obtuse. "You are not getting this. I mean that *I* want to be cured. I want to have my life. I don't want to keep losing time. I want time to run forward, and it just doesn't now."

"You want to feel alive and be alive. You want a past that lives in your memory, not in the present," he says.

"Yes. I'm tired of this Rip Van Winkle feeling of waking up from a long sleep over and over again. I've lost time. I've lost so much time that I don't feel my age. I don't want to end up in the hospital once or twice every year. Is this ever going to change for me?"

"I think that it's changed a little already," Blumenfeld says. "Am I right about that?"

I nod. Tears bloom in my eyes, but don't run over. I look down at my hands.

"I don't know if I can go back and work with the children I was seeing," I mumble.

"I'm sorry, I didn't hear you, Annie," Blumenfeld says.

"Ben," I say, and the tears suddenly brim over.

"The little boy you played with, Ben?"

I nod.

"What about Ben?" Blumenfeld asks.

"I don't know if I can go back and work with him. I keep dreaming about him, and about fires."

I see Ben lying before me in the grass just after he has played out his abandonment by the mama bear. Ben, child of my childhood.

"How could you *not* go back to Ben?" Blumenfeld asks, incredulous.

For the first time, it is clear that it would be impossible for me not to go back to Ben, and to the other children I was seeing.

"What about the fires?" I ask Blumenfeld.

"What about them, Annie?"

"Ben was forgotten in a fire when he was a baby, and my mother was almost killed in a fire, and now . . . but I don't know what to tell you about fire."

"You want to understand all these connections before you go back to Ben?" he asks.

I nod.

Blumenfeld finds this hilarious. When he wipes his eyes, he says, "No, Annie, it doesn't work that way. Don't you remember that healing is two-sided? The connections you want to make will be there when you play with Ben again, not now, not before then."

60

I make arrangements to return to my internship. I tell my three supervisors only a very small part of my story—that I have lost an important relationship in my life, and have been through a time of intense grieving. They assume someone has died; they assume I have been depressed. I do not try to dissuade them of these ideas. I have already lost scholarships, fellowships, and clinical opportunities by being honest about my history. I am not naive about truth-telling in a clinical context. I have learned well how important it is to keep the realms of wellness and sickness separate.

I find that each one of my supervisors is excited about my return to Glenwood and trusts my capacity to take up my work with the children again. I feel deceitful about not saying what has happened and wish I could tell them. Rachael and Mary Louise and Helen seem to have an unwavering faith in my work.

I wonder if it would waver, if they knew.

But Blumenfeld does not believe I must be "cured" before going back to work with children.

I dream of Ben crying to me, "Don't you remember me?"

I dream that Blumenfeld and Ben and I are playing catch with a baseball on a wide green field. Telesporus runs and wings his way over home plate with glee, even though we are not running bases. Even in my dream, I notice the silence on the other side of silence that streams over everything—grass, trees, the sound of the ball smacking into leather, dust, light, cloud shadows—a blessing of silence over everything.

III

MESSENGER

Angels are spirits, but it is not because they are spirits that they are Angels. They become Angels when they are sent. For the name Angel refers to their office, not their nature. You ask the name of this nature, it is spirit; you ask its office, it is that of an Angel, which is a messenger.
—SAINT AUGUSTINE, *Confessions*

Every angel is terrifying.
—RAINER MARIA RILKE, *Duino Elegies,* 2

*Between angels, on this earth
absurdly between angels, I
try to navigate*

*in the bluesy middle ground
of desire and withdrawal . . .*
—STEPHEN DUNN,
Between Angels

61

May is the back door into summer's kitchen; the screened door springs back, and summer light splits the green-and-white lino-leum into wedges of sweet watermelon. Scattered bricks by the curb become intricately feathered cardinals and transform themselves back into bricks again; something or someone unknown plays with her senses, and shifts everything back to reality.

The need to write thrums on the back of my hands, and my knuckles jut out white; my fist is a promise to remember, to define the undefinable edge of lost memories. I begin to write whatever comes into my mind, a free stream-of-consciousness writing, a broadening of memory as if in preparation to see Ben again.

What you fear most has already happened. And outside the glass, Ben, five irises. The purple bloom repeats itself too.

The rain begins to fall in thin, lenslike drops, erasing slowly, like snow, the line between the curb and the street—until all the lines of the boundaried world are unrecognizable and all along the wa-ter's edge the long stretch of sea is gray, blue-gray, white-gray, and white out there where the horizon meets the bright rim of the great bowl of ocean that tips over into European things: better tea older houses famous cathedrals she's never seen. The history of the world opens before her eyes, turn the page, witches are burning, turn another page, a peasant girl hears holy voices, fights a war, fears every war, and listens for voices, burning. The rain falls, erasing a summer life of shells and little sea beings, and she casts off her life too, and comes back in the spring when the poppies, too red, hurt her skin, and filigree of green grows fast on the skinny arms of trees, and memory is ripped wide open. She walks carefully around puddles, centuries deep, broken by the rain—the heart breaks too, shattered by arms held out to her, then gone. The rain falls in thin, lenslike drops, a man holds a stuffed rabbit and cradles it, and she is lost to a little boy. Some ordinary human fear of returning unrecognized turns up in her and she turns it over to see that it was minted just recently, nothing to make a stink about, but the terror in her body wasn't minted yesterday, she knows that from the voices falling into her ears all night long. She sleeps without dreaming and dreams without sleeping. Love was snuffed out under burning lights and she has to make it back to him, one little boy, trying alone to put out all the fires in all the skies . . .

62

In early May I mail Ben cards, stickers, notes, and yellow pom-poms to tie on his shoes, aware that these gifts are no real compensation for my long absence.

Before I see any of the children, I meet with Mary Louise late in the afternoon in her sun-drenched little office in the second week of May. I learn that while I was away Ben has reverted to biting himself, scratching himself, head-banging, and striking out at adults and children without provocation in shattering losses of self-control. He has not been formally assigned another therapist, however. It was clear to Mary Louise that he was attached to me, and she guessed that I would be back. (This astonishes me.) Because Ben was unable to be contained in his classroom, he spent a lot of his time alone with someone familiar, often Mary Louise herself, while I was away. Now as I make plans to return, the Glenwood staff, his parents and his psychiatrist, are all considering residential placement at Glenwood for Ben.

I am bereft, hearing this.

On the day of my return Ben has to be held in his seat on the bus as he rides to school. Mary Louise pulls him into her office as he comes in. He continues to cry and struggle, and cannot or will not tell her what happened on the bus. She tells him that I am back, and he begins to calm down.

• • •

In the playroom, my phone rings. Ben is waiting to see me in Mary Louise's office. Walking down the long hallway, every door and turn familiar to me, the light new as the month of May, unexpected as my return, I wonder if Ben will be able to bring himself to see me again. I wonder if I will be met with distance, or angry rejection, or, at best, with ambivalence. I have abandoned him, after all.

When I come into the room, he is standing by Mary Louise's desk in blue shorts and a gray T-shirt. He looks stunned to see me. He rushes to me and winds his arms around my legs. I reach down and lift him up, and he allows this. He wraps his arms around my neck and clings tightly. It is my turn to feel stunned. I do not put him down, but stand and rock him lightly side to side, talking to Mary Louise.

"You're back," Ben finally says, incredulous. "Will you see me today?"

"I will see you right now," I tell him.

I put him down then, and offer my hand. He takes it and we go down the hall together in silence to the playroom. I hand Ben my keys and he selects the right one without hesitation and opens the playroom door.

He goes immediately to Tea Bags and runs his fingers over the soft puppet.

"I visited Tea Bags while you were gone," he says, turning to face me.

"You did?"

"I did. He was all alone," Ben replies.

"Tea Bags was alone and you felt alone, too," I say.

Ben does not reply. He walks slowly around the room, looking, touching the toy shelves, the edge of the sink, my desk, the wall: a brushing, fleeting touch. He finishes his circle at the toy shelves and stands with his back to me. His movements are the same movements of our very first meeting, except this time he makes his circuit slowly, as if he has grown very old, or very sad.

"I missed you," he says in a voice so toneless and so quiet I hardly hear him.

He stands so still, and I do not know how to make an adequate reply.

He turns toward me and his chin trembles, but he does not cry.

"I missed you a whole lot," he says, accusing me, his eyes hard.

It would be easy to comfort him, to reassure him, but he is being so brave and trying so hard to handle this in his own way. I do not want to rob him of his pain to spare myself my own grief.

"I see that you missed me a whole lot," I say softly. "It was a very long time."

Ben breaks our gaze and turns away again. For a moment he does not know what to do.

Then he picks up a little red cowboy hat from the toy shelves and puts it on, and reaches up for the baby bottle. He slowly fills it at the sink and screws the top back on; slowly, he comes up to my desk and sets the baby bottle down on the corner. Pointing to the hat, he says,

"Make me a cowboy hat, just like this one."

"A cowboy hat you can take with you today?"

"Yeah. And you know what? We can play cowboy in here," he says, picking up a little energy in his voice.

He helps me cut paper and tape a hat together, tearing off long strips of tape and biting them apart with his sharp little teeth. As we work together on the hat, he decides he also wants guns, boots and a saddle.

"And you could be my horse," he suggests.

"I could. And you would ride me?"

"I know. Let's play baby horse!" he exclaims, his eyebrows arched high.

Then he coughs and tightens his hold on my desk as the cough shakes his whole body. He stands very still, unblinking and unfocused, as if in a short trance. Then he looks down and pokes one finger at a ball of gray clay. He smashes it down and rolls it into a long piece.

"This is a worm. No, this is a snake. It will bite you," he mutters.

"It will sting me," I say, leaning in to hear him.

"No, it will bite you." And he moves the snake up to my arm, "Hisss, hisss.

"Bite, bite, bite, bite!" he says suddenly, his teeth clenched tightly together.

"Because I left you, this snake is biting me good," I interpret for him.

"It will make you sick?" he asks, pulling the snake back.

"I don't think so."

He demurs, "Animals will be good to you."

"Your snake will not make me sick," I tell him more forcefully. "I am back to stay, Ben."

But as Ben talks to me, he picks up a ball of string and drops it, unwinding it. He continues to unwind it and moves in rapid circles, tangling himself up in it.

"You have got yourself all tangled up," I notice. "Can I help you out?"

"No!" he shouts. "I can do it by myself," he says softly, with dignity.

And slowly, carefully he unravels himself. He comes back to my desk and picks up the baby bottle. Looking at me solemnly, he says, "You could be the baby horse?" very tentatively, in a small voice.

"Me or you?" I ask. "You would sort of like to be my baby horse?" I feel his longing and his fear.

Ben gets down on all fours by my chair and looks up expectantly.

I take my cue and hold the baby bottle for him, and he sucks hard on it, pulling quite a bit, and letting go from time to time to make a whinnying noise. Then he goes back to sucking hard again. Suddenly he lets go of the nipple and looks up at me. I offer the bottle again, but he shakes his head.

"Burp me," he says, a little annoyed that he had to say it. I smile and kneel beside him on the rug, and pat and rub his back until he lets out a soft burp. This takes several minutes. After he burps, he jumps to his feet abruptly and snatches up the hat I've made for him.

"Now I'm the cowboy. Make me some guns!" he demands.

"You'd like me to make you some guns, but our time is about up today." Ben reaches out and picks up the ball of string he had tangled himself in and hands it to me.

"Then you keep this for me. Hide it away in a secret place."

"Where shall I hide it?" I ask.

"In the very back of this drawer. Way back there," he tells me, opening my desk drawer, "so nobody can find it."

"Nobody but you and me?" I ask.

"That's right," he says.

I take his hand and walk back to the classroom with him.

Ben goes into the room and shouts, "Hey, Mrs. Engle, look. Annie's back!" As his teacher continues to speak to another little boy, Ben goes straight up to them and kicks that little boy hard on the leg. His teacher pulls him away and he begins to struggle. I leave him like this.

For all of this regression, the period of our separation and my return shows me things I did not know about Ben's relationship with me. Whatever he experienced during my absence, whatever questions he had about my return, there is one area where he has made a very solid gain; he has become attached, and even ten weeks of separation could not undo that attachment. If anything, the time lost seems to have intensified the quality of our relationship, though I am not sure why. This intensity is clear when Ben clings to me as I hold him. I might have distrusted it entirely had he not shown me, in his play, his hurt and anger as well. It is as if he is working with greater intensity to make up for lost time.

My absence and return impelled Ben forward in ways which

may not have happened otherwise. It is as if this undeniable period of abandonment and this undeniable return have clarified something Ben kept trying to play out with me earlier. But who can ever step into a child's soul and know what he really gained, what ground he actually lost?

Today Ben becomes reacquainted with the playroom, with Tea Bags and the toys and the room itself. He moves close to me, distances, and comes back, reacquainting himself with the possibilities in our relationship, too. Very early in the session, he is able to say directly, "I missed you," but standing some distance away and with his back turned. Then, given his own time, he says, "I missed you a whole lot," showing me his determination not to cry and his anger at my betrayal. Ben controls the experience throughout, literally finding his way back to me in the way he constructs the drama between us. He has a new dignity in this, something almost tangible, something that demands my respect. But he is also vulnerable. When he first makes mention of playing "baby horse," he is seized by a racking cough, which puts him into a very short trancelike state. Perhaps "baby horse" is reminiscent of "baby bear," and Ben is too afraid to approach me in this way. First, he has to show me his anger. This he does, very effectively, with the snake. Again, his dignity is striking. Not long ago he would have been overwhelmed by his rage. He, not the snake, would have bitten me! But the biting snake frightens him, too. He is afraid it will make me sick, and when I explain I am back to stay, he shows me his confusion and fear, tangling himself up in the string. He declines my help forcefully, and with dignity he again finds his way back to me. It has to be on his terms. Only then is he willing to trust me with his "baby horse" wish. Again, I see a new readiness, a new kind of intensity in him. For the first time ever, he cues me to feed him, and then to burp him. Never before in his play did he invite or allow this. At the very end of the session, he again reveals his vulnerability, asking me to hide the string, to keep it in a special place, as though asking me to safeguard the tangled-up, confused Ben.

• • •

The story that continues after I return to Ben astonishes me even now, years later. It remains a mystery to me—how Ben's attachment to me endured that long two-and-a-half-month separation, and how we then proceeded to heal one another in the few months left to us. The dramatic conversation of our playing can't be reduced to the inner life of either one of us as individuals; rather, it contains the overlapping drama between us—the conversation of two playing. We two, Ben and I, are also accompanied in our playing by Blumenfeld, by Rachael, Mary Louise and Helen, and by Telesporus, to mention just a few of the other characters and players.

Later in the day, Ben asks Mary Louise, very anxiously, if he had made me sick. She tells me that she doesn't know exactly why he imagines that, but it is not so unusual for a young child to believe he or she has that kind of power over someone else. I missed this question in his snake play, this fear that he'd sent me away and been the cause of his own suffering. Mary Louise assures Ben that he had not made me sick. Before I leave for the day, I repeat this to him. As he waits outside for his bus, I kneel beside him. "You did not make me sick, Ben. You are magic, but not *that* magic," and he smiles and blushes a little.

63

Returning to Ben, however, awakens an intense and overwhelming wish to see Melanie.

This wish, an unbearable wanting, surfaces and follows me everywhere, including into Blumenfeld's office.

I sit in my chair and pull myself inside myself, closing my eyes. I try to imagine Blumenfeld as a woman, as Melanie herself. I imagine his next words will be hers, and wait for the sound of her voice. But Blumenfeld is strangely quiet this morning.

I open my eyes and tell him, "I miss Melanie. I was sitting here trying to make you into her. It didn't work very well."

"I guess I'm not growing my breasts yet," he replies, flattening his maroon-and-gray-striped tie over his chest.

Suddenly, he irritates me. I say, "No. I don't want *you* with breasts. What I want is to see *her.*"

"I want you to see her too, Annie," Blumenfeld replies. "But I want you not to be blind when you do see her."

"What do you mean? Do you think she would agree to see me again?" I ask, hopeful.

"That's not clear to me yet, but it seems doubtful."

"Has she already decided not to see me again?" I ask. I don't want to know the answer to this, but feel forced to ask it.

"No, but it seems likely she will. She wants to find a better way to say goodbye to you," Blumenfeld says.

"Goodbye? Not see me?" I ask, my throat constricting.

"Are you wondering, Annie, how someone who doesn't see you, really doesn't recognize you, could possibly say goodbye to you?"

Blumenfeld asks this last question very slowly. Word by word, it gathers into a storm within me. In the eye of the storm, where I am not, I find myself coming out of my chair, moving fast across space, and kicking Blumenfeld hard in the shins. I also begin to hit myself in the face, in a frenzy. He holds my arms fast against my sides, and pulls me into his lap. I squirm and slide to the floor. He leans over and crosses my arms, and holds them braced against me. His striped tie hangs down in front of my face. In this position, against his chair and knees, I can't go anywhere. I struggle and then begin to cry.

"Use words, Annie," he says gently.

I cry and struggle.

"Use your words, Annie. What is it?"

But there are no words. Rage and fear break within me and upon me wordlessly. I see a man going away from me, very tall, gray. Blumenfeld is mostly brown, not all gray, and he's behind me, still holding me fast.

I find myself lying on the couch. Blumenfeld is by my side in his chair, one foot up on the couch. I am crying. Slowly, he places his hand, palm down, over my forehead. I close my eyes and sob harder. His hand grows warm, a little blanket of warmth over me. Gradually, my sobs subside and turn into hiccups. He takes his hand away. I lie still for several minutes, then slowly swing my feet to the floor. I can't look at him directly. I glance at the clock and see it is time to leave. I don't know what happened for most of the hour, however.

"I'm sorry I kicked you," I tell him, flushing with embarrassment.

"You were actually very gentle with me, Annie," he says.

I get up to leave, stuffing my rabbit back in its gym bag. I steal a little glance at Blumenfeld. He smiles at me.

"Next time, wear your hiking boots," he says.

"What?" I ask, confused.

"You were very, very gentle with me," he replies. "So next time, wear your hiking boots."

64

After this session, I feel a little dizzy. I drive to a nearby McDonald's and buy myself a Coke and sit outside in the sunlight watching the light play on the chrome of passing cars. I remember Ben's loss of control with me in November the day he tore his paper wings, and in his classroom the other day he kicked and struggled, rather more deliberately. And this was not the first time I found myself, wordless, out of control either. As an adolescent, listening to the voices of the students reciting in Latin class and listening to the voices within me, I threw my books off my desk and screamed, "Shut up!" I pounded my head against the desk top, ending that day's class. The following year, in the hospital, I kicked the one therapist I felt I might be able to trust. I also remember listening to Telesporus, then being thrown violently (by no one, nothing) against the walls of the "quiet room." In each instance, others' words came into me, but I had no words of my own.

Blumenfeld's words were: "Are you wondering, Annie, how someone who doesn't see you, really doesn't recognize you, could possibly say goodbye to you?"

"Are you wondering?" Blumenfeld's phrase goes through my mind like a chant. With his words, I touch my fury again, and it puzzles me. While kicking Blumenfeld in the shins I felt violent—wild thing, unable to stop myself or contain myself—but Blumenfeld himself experienced my kicking as "gentle." Now I see that when his words came into me, carrying some unbearable truth, they conveyed more than a message about Melanie recognizing or not recognizing me as she said goodbye. They must be larger than that. I hold his words beside my need to recognize and be recognized by Ben when I returned to him. A return without such recognition, after all, would not be a return at all. And I remember now, in the session with Blumenfeld, the image of a man with gray hair retreating.

My father's hair was gray. He committed suicide by jumping from the fifth-story window of a psychiatric hospital when I was five years old. I was told, months after his death, that he died of a heart attack, and did not know what really happened until I was fourteen.

I drive back to my apartment to study for my end-of-the-summer examination. I try to copy summaries of research articles onto index cards, but I cannot concentrate. I sit at my desk, close my eyes and enter a scene as if dreaming while awake.

Walking through a dark basement, I know I have never been in this place before. The basement goes on and on and I have no idea how to get out. Windows too high for me to see out. I walk slowly, afraid of the basement smell—musty concrete, damp dirt, wet wood. In one room, washers come up to the top of my head. In another, a huge furnace hisses and thrums. Behind the furnace room, I come upon long lengths of clothesline weighed down by wet clothes and towels that almost brush the floor. Behind the clothes, a door. I turn the knob, push the door open, leaning into the knob with my shoulder. A cold knob in the roundness of my shoulder. The door opens to a flight of cement stairs. I go up the stairs into the stark daylight, out onto a sidewalk by a red brick apartment building. The air is hot, humid and summer hot, I am wearing blue shorts and a sleeveless blue shirt. The apartment building is right by the walk, and just a few feet from the walk there's a metal fence. But this was not where I live. I recognize nothing. I see my mother talking to another woman, someone who apparently knows me, because she waves and calls me by name. My mother seems relieved to have "found" me. She takes me through a screened back door into a dingy kitchen. There is the little yellow table I remember from our kitchen at home, with our little red chairs. I ask my mother where my

father is. My mother says, somewhat crossly, "You know Daddy died."
That night my sister crawls under our twin bed (it seems we will sleep in
one bed now) and kicks the floor, crying because she "misses Daddy." I sit
by the side of the bed and watch her in wonder. Daddy is gone, to wher-
ever the people who are "dead" go. Wherever it is, he isn't coming back,
and it seems that we live now in this dark, small apartment. For my part,
I am relieved that Daddy will not be coming home tonight.

I open my eyes, recollecting myself, drawing myself back to my
desk and my index cards, and say to myself again and again,
"Write. Put this into words!" But, instead of writing, I walk
through my apartment to my bed, pull my blue quilt over me, and
drift into the oblivion of sleep.

I dream of myself as many, in pieces. When I waken, I want to call
Blumenfeld, but the phone is gone. It has completely disappeared!

When I waken from this dream of waking, I am fearful that I
am still dreaming. I pull back the blue quilt, climb out of bed and
try to call Blumenfeld. During the daytime, the only access I have
to him is through his answering service, and now it is late afternoon. When someone crisply rattles off the names of the doctors
she serves, I find that I can't say anything. I try to speak and can't
get one word out. I start to cough and choke. I put the phone down.

I tell myself sternly, "This is silly, this is all in your head. Of
course you can talk." But I am afraid that I will open something
up I can't bear to know or to reveal, and then get caught, tied up,
locked up, even put in the hospital again. I unplug my phone, creating the isolation I dread. I sit at my table in the heat of the summer and shiver.

I make a cup of hot tea and crawl back into bed.

The wind picks up outside, blows the white paper shade against
the window sash. It snaps against the wood, white on white.

I see a man holding a small girl up against his shoulder.

The wind dies down a little, and rain begins to fall. The rain
smells like wet pennies—sharp, metallic.

I feel myself held up in my father's arms, throwing pennies into a
fountain.

A lump rises in my throat. It is hard to swallow my tea, now getting cold. I could cry, but crying would make this worse, I know. I remember the sound of my sister crying under the bed among the clumps of dust and the thumping of her feet as she kicked the bare wood floor. Her cry is a poetry older than speech. It runs over my whole skin, and I want to cry out for her to stop.

I slouch down against the pillows, pull up the quilt. I fall asleep and dream again.

I am taken by the Nazis as a child—to be burned, hanged. But worse than that, a man wearing a uniform jabs at my stomach and vagina with his finger. He lifts up my dress, and he laughs. I am held from behind. I begin to cry, but already know that my crying won't matter. The person who is holding me says something gentle, and I realize she is a woman. I turn abruptly and bury my face against her, terrified. Someone behind me pulls down my underpants. Cold air and eyes upon me. Exposed, ashamed, I want to disappear. Someone gives me a shot while the woman holds me. I scream, struggling and wondering if she, too, is one of the Nazis.

Suddenly I am sitting at a dinner table. My legs dangle above the floor. I can't choke down the food, but know that I must eat or face some punishment. Someone asks me where I have been, and this question makes no sense. I ask, "What?" to buy myself a little time, to cover the knowledge that I don't know.

I am awake or asleep and dreaming again, I can't tell which. I am lying in a bed on my stomach, not sleeping, or sleeping lightly, or dreaming, I can't tell.

A man comes into the room and sits on my bed. He runs his hands under the covers along my back and bottom. I am paralyzed, powerless. I hear the sound of a zipper opening. I cry out my sister's name and startle myself awake.

I am lying facedown in my own bed, bathed in sweat. The night air stirs on my skin, chills me. I lie in bed shivering, and wonder if I am awake or sleeping. My beloved rabbit "sleeps" next to me, her soft belly against the sheet.

I see myself taking her into the kitchen and ripping into her belly with a knife. I see her bleeding all over the linoleum.

I take her into the kitchen, open my drawer with utensils, and realize then that my only knife is in the box I put in Blumenfeld's closet. Sobbing, I realize that I do not want to "kill" my rabbit. I look at the clock and see that it is 3:00 A.M. I go to the phone and call Blumenfeld.

"Hello. This is Dr. Blumenfeld," he says, sounding fully awake.

"Were you asleep?" I ask, choking back my tears.

"Yes, but now I will be able to go to sleep twice," he replies, instantly recognizing my voice.

"Huh?" I ask, surprised. I am ready with my apology for waking him up.

"Don't you remember, Annie? I told you that if you called me in the middle of the night, I would get to fall asleep twice, and I love going to sleep."

"Now I remember," and I smile despite my fear and the circumstances of this phone call. "I tried to call your answering service earlier, but I couldn't talk," I explain. "I've had a nightmare. I'm not sure what are waking dreams and what are dreams. Just now, I wanted to rip my rabbit into pieces. Then I realized you have my only knife in that box in your closet."

"Yes, I have your knife, and all the other things in that box, and the missing things too. But, Annie, you could tear your rabbit apart in many other ways, and you have called me instead. So you must know that she is already in pieces."

"The little pieces?" I ask.

"Yes. Did you dream about them?"

I tell Blumenfeld my dream about being taken by the Nazis and my dream about a man coming into my room at night.

I listen to Blumenfeld's breathing, steady and even. His breath is a heartbeat in my ear. He could be holding me close as I tell him these dreams, he is so near me. He does not interrupt my telling, so I go on and tell him about entering, earlier that day, the scene of being in the basement when I was five years old, and also about the man with gray hair moving away from me in his office.

"Do you remember when he was there in the office?" Blumenfeld asks.

"When I was on the floor and you said, 'Use your words,' or something like that."

"You saw a man going away, moving toward the door?"

"Yes. And he wasn't you. Your hair isn't so gray, and you were behind me."

"Like the woman in your dream?"

"Yes. But when I turned around in my dream, you weren't like that."

"I didn't allow someone to attack you from behind. But, Annie, you started to scream in my office as if I had done something just as terrible to you."

"No. I didn't."

"Don't you remember? When I said, 'Use your words,' you screamed and really fought me."

"I don't remember," I say, and the stupidity and shame of it wash over me.

"The little pieces remember," Blumenfeld comments.

"I'm confused," I tell him. "I can't tell in what dreams I'm sleeping and in what dreams I'm awake. I can't tell what is real."

Blumenfeld laughs. "Annie, you are trying to make some funny distinctions here. Everything you dream is real. What is confusing you?"

"I don't know. Something about words."

"What was most real in your life, Annie, perhaps most real of all, was the injunction not to use words, not to speak."

"Yes, as if, as if, if what?" I ask, struggling to know.

"If to speak is to risk irrevocably hurting someone, hurting someone so much that they will be lost to you forever, then you had better not use words."

I am crying. "How do you know that?" I ask him.

"When I said, 'Use words,' your father left the room."

"And then I remember lying on the couch crying. And you put your hand on my forehead, right?"

"Yes. And now I see how that might have confused you. Which father was which? Was this the father who put his hands under the covers? Was this the one who paid no heed to your cries and jabbed at you from the front and from the back? Or was this the father who held you while you threw pennies into a fountain? Your dreams are all about what was real, all about this very real confusion. Which father was which?"

As Blumenfeld asks me these questions, he asks them slowly, pausing between each one. What has been wordless now is coming into words. The room tilts, then holds steady. I reach for greater clarity.

"I don't understand why I would want to rip up my rabbit. I didn't imagine stuffing coming out either; I imagined blood and guts."

"Your beloved rabbit," Blumenfeld says.

"When I woke up the last time, I was lying on my stomach and my rabbit was lying next to me, sleeping in the same position," I offer. "I felt suddenly as if the rabbit was in the wrong position. And that made me feel terrible, terribly wrong."

"That does make sense to me," Blumenfeld says. "You dreamed that your father came into your bedroom at night and touched you on your bottom and unzipped his pants. You were lying on your stomach then, yes?"

"Yes," I say in a whisper.

"Annie, it is so much worse for a little child, well, really for anyone, to feel helpless terror than to feel that he or she is at fault, somehow wrong. Especially if that child feels helpless terror with someone she loves and has to go on loving, it is so much easier to bear a terrible guilt than to feel helpless terror."

I move from my chair to the floor and brace myself against the wall. What Blumenfeld is saying makes so much sense that it turns my inner world upside down. It makes me dizzy to listen.

He continues: "So you had to hurt the rabbit, who was at fault for sleeping in the wrong position."

"Yes. But just for a moment I wanted to cut my own stomach."

"But you didn't do that?" Blumenfeld asks.

"No. I have cut myself other times, my stomach, and my arms and legs, but I didn't tonight. I was *in* the rabbit. I was the rabbit."

"Yes, when you were very young, you were the rabbit. You were in pieces and the rabbit wasn't in pieces. And, when you were very young, you couldn't figure out which father was which. You must have felt that your life depended on figuring that out."

"My life," I say, stretching out my bare feet on the floor where I have been sitting.

"And in all your short, little life with your father, he did not really recognize you, Annie," Blumenfeld says. I start to protest, but he continues, "He did not really see you, or he could never have hurt you as he did. And then he left you."

I sit and cry for a long time and Blumenfeld is quiet, except for the sound of his soft breathing. Suddenly I am limp with relief and very sleepy. It is almost four in the morning. I thank Blumenfeld for talking to me and say goodnight to him.

In the predawn darkness, I sit on my back sunporch and watch the sky turn gray and the branches of the backyard tree go from black to brown. At daybreak, I crawl back into bed and sleep late into the morning, grateful that it is a Saturday.

65

As the pieces of this experience begin to come together, I write, just as I write about my sessions with Ben. I write furiously and quickly, because I realize these connections depend upon my getting them on paper. I write with a new sense of wholeness, I suppose, as Saint Augustine wrote to God in *Confessions*: "You hear what we speak by the fleshly sense, and you do not want the syllables to stand where they are; rather you want them to fly away so that others may come and you may hear a whole sentence."

I am trying to hear Blumenfeld as Saint Augustine believes God hears him. Words drop into me as wooden clothespins drop into a milk bottle. Some drop in with a resounding clink; others bounce off the rim. If Blumenfeld slows his speech, each word clinks into the bottle—"Are you wondering, Annie, how someone who doesn't see you, really doesn't recognize you, could possibly say goodbye to you?" I want to hear this as a "whole sentence," but I hear it word by word first. Then, as the syllables fly away and the words begin to form a whole sentence, I find that I can't listen without speaking.

Unconsciously working against an injunction not to speak, I burst into speech without words—kicking Blumenfeld in the shins. This act is followed by a gap in memory within the session itself. This gap in memory marks what withdraws from me, both literally and figuratively—my father and my speech.

The philosopher Heidegger writes, "What withdraws from us, draws us along by its very withdrawal, whether or not we become aware of it," in *What Is Called Thinking*. He goes on to explain how drawing toward withdrawal can shape who we are: "Once we are drawn into the withdrawal, we are drawing toward what attracts us by its withdrawal. And once we, being so attracted, are drawing toward what withdraws, our essential nature already bears the stamp of 'drawing toward.'" Another way of saying this is that the gaps in memory draw us into memory, whether we know it or not. So time is "interrupted" and "runs backwards" for me, and I am continually remembering things I don't recognize as memories. As Ben does in his playing.

What is clear to me now, as I think about myself at five (as if I were my own patient, just Ben's age), is that when my father died without saying goodbye (leaving me with an injunction not to speak, as Blumenfeld explained), then this death not only drew me to him, it also left me with the impossible task of trying to find him and memories of him without words. As I pursue this task now, shocking moments of memory draw me to my father. I remember being held in my father's arms; I also dream of waiting to be tortured. "And what withdraws in such a manner," Heidegger writes, "keeps and develops its own, incomparable nearness." Withdrawing when I want to speak, my father is with me; dying without saying goodbye, he is incomparably near. And Ben's first foster mother, the "mama bear" who left him forever without saying goodbye, is incomparably near him too. It is little wonder that I know how to play these scenes with him!

During the day and far into the night, as acts of terror on my body are being borne into words, a process of remembering that can be symbolized and shaped by the mind is under way. But the process itself is confusing and terrifying for me.

I distance myself a little from the terror by thinking about it abstractly. As I am a psychologist and a therapist, the way my own mind shapes an unbearable trauma interests me enormously.

It is impossible for me to know at what age my father started abusing me, and therefore impossible to know what memories might never have been preserved in words. Is it possible to recover memories that were never symbolized, I wonder? Or is the most common phenomenon of early childhood, amnesia about our earliest months of life, itself a result of speechlessness? I know from my reading that repeatedly abused children who have already learned to talk suffer partial or full amnesia about their ordeal. There may be a great part of their felt experience that can't be preserved in words, but can be preserved in some other way. I wonder. Whatever the child's age at the time of the original trauma, it seems that the process of remembering trauma in adulthood involves a psychological backtracking—going back through the barriers of amnesia that protected the child effectively against overwhelming feelings. Experiences in early childhood that could not be spoken are shaped by the adult's mind, perhaps for the first time. Whatever is left that can't be known, much less spoken, then would need to be endlessly relived. How does this ever end, I wonder. It appears that the process of giving words to unremembered experience involves returning to the feelings of unreality and horror that must have accompanied the original trauma. I say "must have" because we are in that gray area between memory and invention. I realize, even as I write these words, that this has been happening to me.

My weekend is marked with feelings of unreality and listlessness. Ordinary objects appear and disappear. I don't know when I am asleep and when I am dreaming. There are gaps, or amnesias, both in my waking life and in my dreams, which shift from scene to scene, and are incomplete. Some of the scenes I am reliving are so powerful and dreamlike that I call this state "being awake and dreaming." Time slows down and speeds up. The camera of my mind stops, freezes a scene, and sends me the sensations and sounds to go with it.

Throughout the day I feel as if I am caught up in a horror movie that's not of my own making. I am compelled to find words, to write, but sometimes I can't write. Then I read. Not psychology, but Saint Augustine, Martin Heidegger, Virginia Woolf. I can't put her down.

She records in her diary on the first day of March in 1937, "I wish I could write out my sensations at this moment." She goes on to try to find words for what she does not yet have memory for:

> A physical feeling as if I were drumming slightly in the veins; very cold: impotent and terrified. As if I were exposed on a high ledge in full light. Very lonely . . . Very useless. No atmosphere around me. No words. Very apprehensive. As if something cold and horrible—a roar of laughter at my expense—were about to happen. And I am powerless to ward it off: I have no protection. And this anxiety and nothingness surround me with a vacuum. It affects my thighs chiefly. And I want to burst into tears, but have nothing to cry for. Then a great restlessness seizes me . . . the exposed moments are terrifying. I looked at my eyes in the glass and saw them positively terrified.

When she wrote this passage in her diary, I notice, she had not yet written out, in "A Sketch of the Past," the memory of Gerald Duckworth molesting her on the ledge in the dining room at Talland House when she was six. In the diary passage, she is seeking the memory—as the memory itself tears through her consciousness. Entwined with physical sensations ("exposed on a ledge in full light"; "something cold and horrible"; "it affects my thighs chiefly") are suggestions of the ways that she was effectively rendered speechless ("a roar of laughter at my expense"; "I am powerless to ward it off and have no protection"; "I want to burst into tears, but have nothing to cry for"). These are the fractured pieces that she cannot yet assemble into a coherent story. The writing itself is cryptic. And when Woolf summarized her life in "A Sketch of the Past," she said that as a child, and even in the present, she felt her life "contained a large proportion of this cotton wool, this non-being."

Like Virginia Woolf, I experienced many times "this cotton wool, this non-being." Like Virginia Woolf, I feel compelled to write. I struggle for words against the "cotton wool." I record, as accurately as I can, the fractured pieces of memory that I cannot tell as a complete and coherent story, even now.

In the midst of this process of remembering and writing and

reading in earnest, I have Blumenfeld nearby, a man who wakes up fully in the middle of the night, to help me bring into words what has been unknowable because it was unspeakable.

His presence in my life makes Ben's story clearer to me too, and this shows me something new—a shimmering pool of light on a dark street, where our two stories overlap.

66

During this period I am seeing Blumenfeld three times a week, working at Glenwood full-time again, seeing my three supervisors weekly, and in the evenings also studying for my comprehensive examinations. It would seem that the process of remembering my own trauma would make all this very difficult, if not impossible. It is difficult sometimes. But what is most vivid about this time is that in the interludes between intensive and disturbing bouts of memory, I feel an enormous sense of freedom, the same soaring sense I felt when I first learned to balance myself on a bicycle. My voices are strangely quiet during these interludes. After their steady company all my life, I miss them. For the first time, I am experiencing loneliness.

In early June, I sit outside on the front steps with my gray-and-white cat, Murphy. It is dusk as I listen to a chorus of crickets and watch the washed light fade from the sky over the red slate rooftops. I notice that I am alive and can often remember details of daily events vividly. The periods of feeling unreal or numb or lost stand out now in clear contrast. In the past, moments of feeling alive blended almost imperceptibly back into the strong sense that I was not really alive. I could remember details then too, but it was as if they were not connected to events, to whole time sequences.

Now my dreaming time is vivid and memorable, and whole too—whether I am awake or asleep. Time begins to create a stream of impressions, rather than to pass in interrupted chunks. How odd.

• • •

I dream of a little girl who is vaguely familiar, but I do not know her. In the dream, I am dreaming her dream. There is a mug of milk, untouched. She leans against a wall. "Take me out, get me out of here," she whispers to me. I am standing by a screened door. It creaks as I open it, but the child does not move. The milk in her blue mug is tepid and she does not want to drink it when I give it to her. Outside a storm is brewing, seashell sounds loud in the trees, their green leaves white underneath, the sky white-gray, milk-light on leaves. Soon it will rain, and I want her to leave with me before it does. I feel quite urgent about this. Then it is night and we are put in the backseat of a car by a man who drives away. I pull the child toward me, bringing her head against my chest. In her stillness, I feel her terror. I take her completely onto my lap. She's too frightened to cry, but she pulls her legs up, so that I can hold all of her. We are going God knows where, and I remind myself that this is her dream, not my dream, to still my own heart's terror.

I waken and remember vividly that this little girl was in the examination room the night I was admitted into the hospital. She wanted to know why I was crying. I have the impression that I am a mother to her, or an older sister, someone related, somehow.

I dream of an old woman who sews Ben's shadow to his heels, and then she stitches my shadow to my heels too, and then she tells us that we are related—he is my own child, come back to me. Someone at a little distance is playing a piano and his fingers come down on the keys like a summer rain. Doors fling themselves open into a wide green field. Ben and I are unbelievably happy.

67

Ben knows he is to see me. When I spot him in the hall, he shouts,

"You see me today. You come get me at nine, 'member?"

As I hand him the playroom door keys, he asserts, "I remember the right key."

Inside the playroom, he is tense. He walks around in a stiff, bouncing gait, stopping now and then to touch something briefly.

Then he picks up the baby bottle on the sink and fills it. "Let's play baby," he says, turning toward me.

"You would like to be my baby?" I ask.

He lies down on the rug, with a bataka as a pillow, and covers himself with my sweater. He puts the bottle in his mouth and starts to suck, then pulls it out. He holds it out to me.

"Would you like me to feed you?"

He nods. "Where's that other blanket?"

I retrieve the old blue blanket and tuck it around him. I encircle him with one arm and offer him the bottle. He sucks greedily, looking off into space. When he stops sucking, I take the bottle from his mouth. He is very still. In his stillness, he reminds me of the little girl in my dream.

"'Member the mama bear?" he asks.

"Yes, I do remember her," I reply.

But Ben does not go on and I wonder what he is trying to tell me or ask me.

"What about the mama bear?" I ask back.

"She went away," he says simply. Three words, but a whole world came to an end.

"Yes, she did go away," I tell him, feeling my way, groping for his meaning. "But sometimes a mama bear comes back, Ben."

He glances at me briefly and nods, and again meets my eyes. Ben, child of my childhood—he could have been my own son.

He rolls on his side and reaches over to the dollhouse and begins to sift the toys through his fingers. He picks up a small toy toilet, sits up, and hands it to me.

"Make me one of these out of clay," he says.

"You want me to make it, or do you want to?"

"You!" he says, smiling.

As I begin to work the clay, Ben dumps an entire box of assorted small toys onto the floor. He sifts through them and selects a broken handle to a jump rope.

"What's this?" he asks, holding it up.

"A handle," I reply matter-of-factly.

"No, this is a cigar!" he declares.

"A cigar?" I ask.

"Yep. A cigar for the baby," he says.

"Oh? Some baby poop to go into the toilet?" I ask, thinking all at once that Rachael has influenced me. God, I sound psychoanalytic! I expect Ben to reject this interpretation.

But Ben blushes and sifts around through the toys again, muttering to himself, "Poop, poop, poo," pushing out the sound in short spurts, while bouncing up and down lightly on his bottom against his tucked-in heels, as if to confirm this interpretation. He looks from the toys to me.

"What a fine mess, Ben. Look at the fine mess you made!"

He grins. "You know what? We could make a fishing pole!" he says, holding up the handle again. He sits back on his heels and puts several straws together, pushing one into the other. With my help, he attaches the handle, a string and a paper-clip fishhook. Searching for these parts, he scatters the toys about so that they cover about one-third of the rug. Then he sits among them and, handing me the fishing pole, says,

"I am the fish and you will fish for me."

"You are the fish in a lake of toys?"

He smiles and nods.

I stand back and cast the line into the "lake" and wait. Ben tugs at it and lets go.

"It hasn't got any bait on it!" he complains.

I go to my desk drawer and pull out the animal cracker box and carefully stick one animal cracker between the parts of the paper clip, a task that requires some effort, then return to my fishing.

Ben watches me carefully, and I cast out the line again. He tugs at it and swiftly takes the animal cracker off and pops it in his mouth. As I reel the empty line back in, he bounces on his heels and giggles. I try two more times before Ben holds on to the line and follows it out up to my chair, allowing himself to be "caught." He stands before me. I look him over, touching his hair, his arms, measuring his length with my eyes.

"Oh, what a beautiful big fish!" I say. "And such a smart fish." I pause for emphasis. "I think I'll eat him up!"

Ben laughs for joy, struggles halfheartedly, laughs again.

"No. That would be a shame. I guess I'll put him back in his lake."

I pick him up and put him down among the toys with a verbal "Splash!"

"Fish for me again!" Ben says with renewed excitement.

"Not today. It is about time to go," I tell him.

Spontaneously, he scoops up many but not all of the toys on the floor and puts them back into their box.

He leaves me easily, dragging his fishing pole behind him.

68

It is the end of the first week in June before I am able to see Rachael again. She has had hip surgery during my absence, and is still recovering.

Crossing the parking lot to the Psychoanalytic Institute, I find company enough: the voices of two analysts carry on the air and come down to me like water on leaves, a splashing of confidences and laughter. In their gray suits, they nod together. There are sparrows here too; brown-and-gray-feathered, they balance between tails and beaks, hop, skitter, hop, hop this way and that, skittish. And here's a pigeon, startlingly large, with big red feet; it chortles to itself and hobbles importantly and slowly over the granite wearing its own suit of gray and blue, quite at home here.

In the waiting room I find the same outdated magazines and the same buzzer with its little note: "Please ring when you arrive for your appointment." I remember hesitating, wondering if I was a patient. Now I know: I am a patient and I am a therapist. The wholeness of my life hangs together in one still moment. And of that moment I will tell Rachael nothing. I could more easily tell her about the resemblance of sparrows and pigeons to her analyst colleagues than about this realization.

And here she is—stooped and tall, with those intense dark eyes, her white-gray hair, leaning on two canes rather than one—an addition that makes her more herself, not less. I get up to follow her and know that she is very old, that she will not live on and on, at least not in this particular guise.

Like my other supervisors, Rachael assumes that I have been

depressed. I do not tell her anything more and she does not press for details. She offers me candy, and it is as if nothing has changed and no time has passed; and it is as if all the colors and sounds and smells of the world have changed and years have gone by. Rachael wants to know about Ben and the other children immediately, as if she has waited for this next installment for a long time.

I tell her that Ben's play in the first weeks of my return has centered around being a baby and coming to terms with my absence and return. He seems even more ready to include me in his play. I tell Rachael about Ben's "remember" statements. In the most recent session, it seems as though his reminder to me to come get him at the appointment time and his familiarity with the key lead up to the more central question: " 'Member the mama bear?"

Rachael smiles and nods, "Yes, Ben is reminding you of many levels of his experience. He is saying, 'Remember how we used to play together, remember how the mama bear left me, and remember how you also left me?' That mama bear is always an important cue in his play, isn't she?"

"Yes, and she also is so very real. He plays with a different intensity when she is around." I pause. "But, you know, since I've come back, he also plays with a different intensity with me. I'm not sure I can articulate how, or why this should be so."

Rachael's face lights up, her dark eyes crinkle. She likes this. She comes to life thinking about Ben and the others with me. I wonder if she has missed me.

She puts her glasses on and looks over the pages of notes I have handed to her, reading and nodding. She slips her glasses off and they hang from a light chain on her sagging breasts.

"The mama bear is symbolic of Ben's desertion and, of course, the cause of his rage."

I nod. "Do you remember, last February, how Ben played out hunting her and killing her, and then taking her and her baby bears home?" I assume Rachael does not remember, and try to remind her gracefully of this again.

"Yes, now I do," she says. "That mama bear is an internalized good and bad mama Ben took home." Rachael looks at me sharply. "And now he has to approach her again. Because you've been away, she overlaps with you too now. You have also left him."

I look down at my hands, wishing I could tell her how much I have gone through to return, how much was at stake in making it right for Ben again. But she has her head back in my notes.

She looks up, slides her glasses to the tip of her nose and peers at me over them, a familiar gesture. She smiles, a real and radiant smile. "Look, Annie, you use Ben's question as an opportunity to make a 'corrective' interpretation here. Do you know what that is?"

I nod.

"You are changing Ben's internalized story of his abandonment when you say to him, 'Yes, she did go away, but sometimes a mama bear comes back.' Oh, yes, you have good instincts, Annie!" She looks at me intently and again asks, "Do you know what I mean?"

For the first time with Rachael, I am near tears. I feel them in the edges of my eyes. Sheer relief? Gratitude? Longing? I don't know. I shake my head, and she goes on, slowly and gently.

"By 'corrective' I mean that you make an attempt to modify Ben's internalized representation of 'mama' figures—from those who are callous in their desertion of him to someone who is sensitive to his pain and does return to him. Of course such a modification doesn't happen instantaneously, and Ben will need to continue to work and rework these themes."

I already know this definition, but the sound of her voice, its inflections, softened now in response to my near tears, is a familiar comfort to me.

"There is something that is new with Ben that I don't yet understand," I tell her, finding a new focus. "In this last session he directs me to feed him and he allows me to sit close, to hold him and stroke his bangs. There is a new intensity and directness in him."

Rachael looks off into space. "Yes, you are right, Annie. Both the request and his ability to enjoy physical affection underscore his attachment to you. You are his therapist, and here you are also his mother, but you must always keep in mind that you are also not his mother."

I want to tell Rachael my dream. I want to describe the old woman who stitched our shadows to our heels and told us he was my lost child. I want to tell her of our intense happiness. But the moment passes. "Why is it important to keep in mind that I am not his mother?" I ask.

"That you are his mother and also not his mother," Rachael clarifies. "Because he is struggling with the matter of loss, he is now seeking physical nurturing, but at the end of the summer you will leave him. You are a surrogate, Annie, a mother but not really his mother." She looks at me.

I nod, again wishing I could tell her my dream.

"Ben doesn't just ask for nurturing from you either. He is testing you as a mother. Will you accept a new set of themes in his play, the toilet-poop-messy themes?" She laughs. "You were clever about interpreting that cigar!" I laugh too, remembering my thoughts about her during the session.

But I do not wish to be clever. I want to understand Ben and, if I can be, to be his mother, at least for now.

Rachael goes on. "What strikes me here is his ability to tease you. He takes 'bait' off the hook and returns it empty. He likes the way you tease him back, saying, 'Oh, what a beautiful big fish, I think I'll eat him up!'" She smiles to herself. "You know it is really remarkable how far he has come, and how quickly you have regained his trust."

We set up a new schedule of appointments, twice weekly, as before. I realize, as I am leaving, that this is a parallel arrangement, that at the end of the summer, when I am not seeing Ben, I won't be seeing Rachael either.

Walking down the stairs in the late sun, I suddenly feel very much alone with all the pieces of my experience. I don't talk about Ben in any detail with Blumenfeld, and I don't talk about Blumenfeld at all with Rachael or Mary Louise. Melanie is lost altogether and yet near. And they all live together, intimately, within me, alongside Emily and Erin and Telesporus and Galle and an unnamed little girl, and others, some of them angels.

I invented Rachael once, I remember. When was that? Was it last January? She was a grandmotherly crone who tucked in the strands of my braids, she was a fierce and feathered creature who flew through the night skies, she was a protector who settled me under her wing in a soft bed. If she was my supervisor still, and that certainly seemed the case, she was also really and fully this invented creature too. The limitations of who she could be in supervision couldn't undo that.

I fervently wish I could tell her how playing with Ben changed and expanded my understanding of myself, and of her too.

69

In early June, Ben began to sneak away from his class and explore the Glenwood grounds until someone came to find him. The phrase "Ben is on the loose again," passed on to me between my seeing other children and attending meetings, was becoming a common experience.

One memorable Friday, Ben was "on the loose" and no one came after him. In his frustration, he threw a stone at his classroom window and broke it, which certainly brought his teacher after him! By Monday morning he was tense and contrite. He came to school with his piggy bank full of pennies and presented it to Mrs. Engle to pay for the window.

I learned this from Mary Louise as she stood in the doorway of her office that morning, and she thoroughly enjoyed telling me this story.

Ben asks to go outside as soon as he enters the playroom. When I agree to this, he picks up Tea Bags and the baby bottle and goes back out the door, without hesitation. I follow.

Outside it is a warm day, the sky bright blue, angelica blue, the grass vibrant green and still a little damp from the rain the night before. Ben hands me Tea Bags and breaks into a run across a stretch of grass to a clump of bushes. There he stands and starts to pick raspberries, dropping them into his large bag. When I catch up with him, he turns to me and says, in a rather impatient tone,

"You pick all those berries high up, Annie."

"You want to be the boss of me today, hmm?" I ask, amused.

"I'll be the boss; that's how it will be," he says, but seeing me hesitate, adds, "No, I know what, Tea Bags can be the boss."

I have Tea Bags on my hand already and I animate the puppet, imitating Ben's bossy manner.

"Go pick some flowers for me, Ben," the puppet says.

"Nope. Nobody will be the boss today," Ben declares, ignoring Tea Bags and returning to his berry picking.

I sit down on the grass several feet away and wait for him to finish picking his berries. He adds several rocks and leaves to his bag, then comes over to me to show me. I peer into the large grocery bag and admire everything in it.

Ben decides he wants to go to "our hideout," and I am quite willing to go with him.

He walks a pace ahead of me, silent and somewhat tense. When he reaches this familiar place, he kneels down on the grass, sits back on his heels, and briefly sucks on the baby bottle. He looks up at me.

"You go get wood for our fire," he says. "I'll wait here."

I take note that he has returned to delivering imperatives, but I decide to follow them and see what he will play out.

I move away and begin to pick up small twigs and larger sticks too. Ben finds this irresistible and joins me. We return with two bundles of sticks. Again, he sits back with the baby bottle and sucks on it. Suddenly, he puts it down in the grass.

"You make the fire over there. A big fire," he says. I have done this many times on camping trips, and as I begin to arrange the wood, Ben wants to see what I am doing. In no time, he is helping me.

"Now you light it with a match," he directs.

I pretend to light the fire, even blowing on it to get it started.

"Now I will be a baby raccoon," he says.

"You are the baby raccoon and I have found you?" I ask, knowing variations on this play.

He nods solemnly, hands me the baby bottle, and finds a place to lie down in the grass on his back.

"Feed me?" he asks, very tentatively.

I offer him the bottle and he sucks on it noisily, putting his hands up to hold it with me.

"You want to hold it by yourself?" I ask him.

He nods, and I let him feed himself, but stay close by, keeping eye contact. When he finishes sucking, he matter-of-factly puts the bottle aside in the grass. He gets up and crawls down by the "fire." He looks back at me when I don't follow him.

"Get me away from the fire. The baby will get burned," he says.

I go to him quickly and physically pull him back, taking him by the hand and admonishing him, "No. That's fire. You may not play so close to the fire." He struggles a bit, but I do not let go. When he sits down in the grass where I have taken him, I let go of his hand. He sits for several minutes and then crawls away in another direction on all fours. A short distance away, he again turns and looks back at me.

"Stop me from running away," he says. "I could get lost."

I go to him and pull him back by the hand as he whines and pulls in the opposite direction. Again, when I release him, he pauses and waits. Then he runs off, this time to a mud puddle.

"Come get me out of this mud," he calls to me. I run to him and pull him out of the mud, getting my own shoes a little muddy in the process. "No. You stay out of the mud. Wipe off your shoes on the grass," I say sternly. He wipes his shoes. I hold fast to his little hand and do not release it as I add, "And now it is time to stop and go inside."

Ben wants me to intervene and set limits in his play, but he doesn't want to give up control to come inside. He tugs hard against me, telling me he has "something secret to show" me in the woods, that he has to "pick just those few leaves" and "climb that one little tree." But each time I say, "No, it is time to go in," and continue to pull him along. Finally, he falls silent and walks along beside me.

I hold his hand all the way to his classroom. Once there, he lets out a big sigh and says, "Bye, Annie," and goes in.

I settle into the playroom with my coffee and yellow pad to make notes. I have only thirty minutes before I see my next child.

Ben is struggling here with impulses which typically get him into trouble. His play is an extension of his "on the loose" behavior, an almost daily attempt to get adults to set limits, as well as to undo his feelings of being lost or unwanted. When he escapes, he is typically missed, and then someone comes and finds him and brings him back; thus he is found and wanted. When this expected sequence did not happen, he broke his classroom window.

He begins by testing me with his old bossiness. Since this behavior is now rare with me, I comment on it, "You want to be the boss of me today, hmm?" Ben confirms and then disconfirms this, handing over the boss role to Tea Bags. When he discovers he doesn't like to be bossed, he takes the role away from Tea Bags. Ben is seldom "oppositional" with me, but here he stands and picks berries for a long time, as if to defy Tea Bags's (and my) request to do otherwise. I choose not to pick berries "high up" for him because I am curious about his response to my refusal. He simply ignores it, but it sets a stage for us, because my refusal is also a limit.

When he plays at the hideout place, giving me "bossy" directives, I follow them because I want to know what he will play out. Interestingly, he joins me in a collaborative effort to do the task he has just ordered me to do! In this context of our relationship, his bossy behavior is so uncharacteristic that he cannot maintain it. But he is certainly struggling with the issue of who controls whom. This is also clear in his ambivalence about my holding the bottle to feed him. He wants me to nurture him, but he wants to control it. For my part, I want him to feel in control of his own feeding, but I don't want to break emotional contact as he does so.

Then he is ready to get down to the major work of the session.

This child, who has been labeled as having "oppositional personality disorder," plays out the possibility of giving over control of himself to me. He not only wants outside controls, he wants protection from fire and from getting lost, as well as from his "naughty" impulse to get muddy.

By telling me how I am to intervene, he controls his fear of giving up control. More important, perhaps, he asks me to play a new part with him, one he senses I am ready to play—to stop him, to set limits he wants set for himself. I push him one step further, a step I sense he is ready for. When he does not want to go inside, he is no longer playing an "as if" situation, and I am no longer following his "orders" to control him. My behavior parallels what he has just shown me he needs and wants from me, including to be allowed to test me and struggle against the imposed limit. His behavior parallels his play of trying to get away from me. He is able to accept my limit and come inside. This is a huge step for the little boy who flies into temper tantrums when he doesn't get his way.

I pause in my notes, knowing I will go back and fill in the details of our dialogue later. I feel something is missing in these notes— I don't let the full range of my experience into them. I run my yellow pencil under my nose and let the pause grow into a silence, a stillness in the day's work.

I remember, just the other day, waiting outside a cafe for Sarah to meet me. A small boy in corduroy overalls was wandering about, scuffing up a few scattered leaves. He looked up suddenly and I saw—"lost," that terrible feeling of everything toppling. He scanned the crowd, holding his face perfectly still, as boys learn to do so uncannily well at a young age, and then his whole face lit up. I followed his eyes and saw a woman's face, her eyes alight too, looking at him and waving.

Ben. Of course you want to look up, to find that face, those shining eyes, in the midst of feeling so lost and abandoned. Beyond whatever issues of control Ben may need to work out with me now, I feel his need to be found—in a face that lights up to see him.

Telesporus found me in the hospital when I was lost like that, coming in to ask for lemonade in the winter, something he knew would catch my attention, I suppose. I smile to myself, remembering.

Ben is a little boy, human in his willfulness and his pain, but like Telesporus, he brings me more fully back to myself. Ben is giving me back my life.

A shiver runs down my spine as I realize this is not something I imagine. There is a sympathy outside ourselves that knows, carries, and protects a message sometimes long enough for it to be delivered successfully. I file my notes, brushing tears aside to go and meet my next child.

70

During these weeks in June I do not lie down on Blumenfeld's couch. I need to sit up in a chair, feet firmly on the ground, to sort through the intensity of my memories and dreams, going over and over the same things. I feel the need to find Blumenfeld's eyes, like pools of deep water, to drink deep from them.

The process of going over the same material reminds me of playing with Ben and the other children—going over their plays, overturning time, drying tears, changing characters and point of view, sorting through yet again, preserving, discarding, until finally what has been so relentlessly fascinating and puzzling in their playing becomes ordinary.

Sometimes I sit by myself with a photograph of my father.

My father's ears are close to his head, like my sister's, but his lips and chin are mine. I am about nine months old, and he is holding me on one knee and my sister on the other. This black-and-white photograph, mostly white, contains a secret. I see my tiny hand resting on his arm, and the long arm, covered with hair, holds me under a white dress.

I see him in this photograph the way someone sees the world after a catastrophe, with the kind of sight you develop after being trapped in circumstances and implicated in actions beyond your own design and control. I see with my "blue lenses," as Blumenfeld would say—I see into essences.

There is a silence and sorrow in my father's face that is

indescribable. Some feeling surrounds him, comes up in me, that I can't bear. Seeing this, seeing something I know already that I can't let myself know, I look from my father's face to my mother's face.

A companion photograph, taken a month earlier in a professional studio. Also in black and white. Her hair and eyes are dark, her eyes deep pools, but utterly unlike Blumenfeld's. Her small, tight smile hardly covers her despair.

In my father's arms, my lips are parted slightly and my eyes open, alert.

In my mother's arms, I am pulling my upper lip over my lower lip; my face is tight, closed. Whatever it is I am feeling there, I recognize it, wordlessly. And I know I have avoided this recognition all my life.

I feel as though I know everything, even if I recall almost nothing of this time in my life. I hold a whole history in my body, mine and theirs. This history is enveloped in silence and sealed tight. So these photographs whisper rumors, because I cannot bear their truths, which are also my truths.

The snow collects overnight. It covers the metal fence, then melts in the noonday sun. The paintings she started she has left unfinished.

Erin picks up brushes, puts them down, touches her paints the way one touches a lover when one has gone a long, long time without making love. She lifts the brush in her small hands. It quivers with her longing to know.

She knows their faces, the blurred light on the windows at twilight, the lines of grass all over the world. And it is like going back, through the spring into winter, going back to not one thing, but everything, unstarted, unfinished.

The snow collects, it falls whitening all sound, it muffles her refusal to know and her lack of forgiveness and her many and real failings and mistakes. It falls thick and fast, She lifts up, puts down her box of

*watercolors while the snow covers time and mortality and the metal fence
and her father and mother.*

*Could color, light, line bloom under her hands, hands with their nails
bit back to nothing? No, Erin does not want to know; she does not want
to paint.*

And I do not want to consider the box I left in Blumenfeld's closet
either.

I sense that the things in the box belong together and that the
reason they belong together would be discovered.

I am afraid to open up any of this, either by myself or with Blumenfeld.

Then something happens that forces me to talk about the box.

One morning I wake with a searing pain in my lower abdomen
and find blood in my urine. A week later, when I finally go to see
a doctor, he informs me I have a kidney stone. Immediately I am
checked into the hospital for two days to have it removed. During
this time, and during the days that follow, I am afraid I will get
lost again, I am afraid the snow will cover the entire world, not
just what I didn't want to know, but me, myself, because I do not
seem to exist any longer—as me.

71

Entering Blumenfeld's office the Monday after leaving the hospital, I am profoundly numb. My arms and legs feel laden down with invisible little weights. Sounds come to me muffled and dim. The streets are washed gray and white. And the inner world of thoughts and feelings, that world which I find so endlessly interesting, is covered up in a thick, milky fog. I sit in my chair and lick my dry lips and try to speak.

Words elude me. My thoughts escape into the fog. I move my body over to the couch for the first time in weeks, and Blumenfeld takes up his place beside me, his foot firmly anchoring me in time and place.

"Watch what comes to you and what eludes you," he suggests. I close my eyes and hold my rabbit, by now a regular in my sessions, a bit tighter. Nothing. I lie still and begin to breathe more evenly and deeply, matching the rhythm of my breathing to Blumenfeld's. The air conditioner hums along softly. Nothing comes forward to claim my attention.

Lying on the couch, I feel as if I am lying in my hospital bed. The angle of my position is the same angle. I am tired and deeply numb. I can barely feel my arms and legs after a few minutes. I begin to talk to dispel this numbness.

"When I was in the hospital, I felt like I was not me, not really alive. As if I were buried in snow." I shake my head. "No, not buried—obliterated, completely crushed down. Not myself. I can't shake off this feeling."

"Why would you want to shake it off? That feeling is probably going to be very valuable to us," Blumenfeld comments.

"The worst part was throwing up," I say, brushing aside Blumenfeld's statement.

"No one told me a spinal block could make me that sick." I pause.

"No, actually, the worst was the numb feeling. I think it started when other people were making decisions about how much pain I was in, after the surgery. When they were deciding how much pain medication I needed or didn't need," I tell Blumenfeld.

"No, that's not it either. I really am very good at making pain go away. I count to myself and can make the pain go away. Sometimes I don't even have to count." I pause again and sigh with the unnatural heaviness of an unspoken truth.

"I was constipated from all the pain medication and I thought, I was afraid that they would, they would . . . maybe the worst was the sense of foreboding I had all the time—foreboding, and then the numbness got out of control."

"A foreboding?" Blumenfeld asks. "As if you knew something terrible would happen to you?"

My breathing becomes shallow. I am afraid that he will know what I almost know, what I can't bear to hear in words, so I rush into it, out of my fear. "Yes. A foreboding. And then what I was afraid of, it did happen. They gave me an, an . . ." I feel myself blushing and stop.

"I hate this word, I can't say it."

"An enema?" Blumenfeld asks.

I close my eyes and feel my hand playing with the green velveteen ribbon on my rabbit. "Yes," I whisper.

"And did the sense of foreboding go away then, Annie?" Blumenfeld asks.

"No, it got worse." I can't depict the unknown, for him or for myself. It fills me with all its possibilities.

"As if you knew something worse could happen?" Blumenfeld asks.

"Yes, like that," and I feel the electricity of a little bit of my knowledge shared.

"When you feel you know the future, you can be sure that you are reliving the past, Annie, because nobody knows the future."

As he says these words to me, I know he is right. I tell him, "That makes me think about the poem I wrote to Ben. There's a line that goes, 'What you fear most has happened already.'"

"Yes, that's right. And what has happened already, Annie?" he asks, his voice low and gentle.

I see the box on the top shelf of Blumenfeld's closet. I float inside vivid, faraway images—tiny, boxed images I can't make out. I feel myself suddenly light and rise up a little out of my body and float toward them. I grab the sides of the couch, lest I float up to the ceiling or fly out of the room.

"The box in your closet. I keep seeing it now," I tell Blumenfeld. "The things in it are in littler boxes. Graham crackers and grape juice, comfort foods. Graham, graham—Ma. I had grape juice and graham crackers in nursery school, away from my mother. Other foods I ate too, but I wasn't hungry. I choked them down, unable to swallow, maybe knowing if I didn't eat, I'd get tied up."

"Tied up? How?" Blumenfeld asks.

I want to take it back. Suck the air and the words back inside, like a vacuum cleaner, take them back. "Not tied up, tied up inside I mean, in knots, my insides taken out of me."

In how many ways do I use this technique, a little touching up of things I can't stand to know? Would it be worse to know?

I pause. "There was rope in the box at first, in my apartment, and then when I got it here, the rope was gone."

"Mmm-hmm," Blumenfeld says, and he waits for me.

"I keep seeing knots and knots I can't untie. This is not memory. This is nothing." I do not want to think about this.

"I have to disagree with you there, Annie," Blumenfeld says softly.

"My mother was always saying I had a wild imagination and

made up things that never happened to me," I counter, as if this is an argument on my behalf.

"Is that what you were given to believe?" Blumenfeld asks. I catch something new in his tone and open my eyes and look at him. His face is flushed with anger.

I look away. My God, he is angry for me, I think to myself. Perhaps there is some reason to be angry.

I feel the sensation of cold air on my legs and my bottom. Exposed. Terrified. Suddenly I am back in my mother's kitchen as a child, but not as myself.

In the kitchen, it is Galle, younger and smaller than I, lying on the little yellow table, facedown. The little red chairs are in the wrong places, at the four corners of the table, with ropes tied to them. I hear Galle beg to be let go and watch her struggle against her bonds in terror. Then I watch my mother part this child's buttocks and insert the black enema tip into her rectum.

Now my mother is sitting in her chair by the big table. I stand behind her. I raise my head and look over my mother's shoulder so that everything I see is framed on one side by the curves of my mother's shoulder and head. Everything in the kitchen seems to be in its place, and the back door is open to the morning light. My mother has a burn scar from knees to neck, and she does not sweat there. But in the heavy air of the kitchen, beads of sweat collect in the shadows of her white flesh beneath her knees and around the graying edges of her dark hair. Standing behind her, I am able to use the shade of her body as a shield from the hot sun streaming in from the screen door.

My mother stares straight out, past the mesh screen where the fence is covered with purple morning glories, to a dark horizon. I watch the morning glories in a light wind turn into tiny evil-looking human faces that laugh at me. I turn to go into the living room. My mother's voice stops me. "Bring me the Q-Tips," she says.

I go into the bathroom, climb up on the toilet and sink, and reach for the blue box in the medicine cabinet. As I hand my mother the Q-Tips, however, she reaches out and catches me by the arm. "You need to have those ears cleaned out," she says. She draws my head into her lap, one ear

against her thighs, the other ear exposed. There is darkness and a surpris-
ing breeze on the back of my head. It is hard to breathe. My throat aches
and tightens, then closes.

My mother pushes the Q-Tip gently into Galle's ear and twirls it
around. My mother turns the child's head to the other side. Galle's cheeks
brush against the soft cotton of my mother's skirt. Then my mother repeats
the same motions on the other ear and releases her. Galle stands straight
up and the room tilts and spins into vertical position again.

I stand in my own straight body. I push my nails hard into my palms
to be sure of it. "What are you imagining now?" my mother asks me. She
is often amused by what I imagine, and I like to amuse her, but this time
I say, "I'm just thinking about what to do today." And I smile for my
mother.

I dig my nails into my palms, and turn on the couch to look at
Blumenfeld, to be sure he is there and I am here. Minutes pass in
silence. I don't know how to tell him any of this.

"The box, the thing, what place does that thing have in the
box? I can't say it. The, the . . . I can't say it." The word itself terrifies me, and I need another name.

"The intruder," I whisper.

"The intruder? The enema?" Blumenfeld asks.

"Yes," I say. "I was tied." That's just how things are, I think, but
this is unthinkable.

"No, just held down. No, not tied, that couldn't be. My mother
loved me. She loved me. I must be making this up for some
twisted reason. I'm a liar. I *do* make things up."

Blumenfeld is quiet. Then he says, "There are no lies here. Even
what you would call 'making things up,' maybe those things especially, are truths in this room."

"Hot water and soap. I can't move, tied or not. Baby bottle and
en . . . I can't say it."

"Some things must go on and on. That is just how it is. Don't
expect life to be fair to you." I hear these words, but they are not
my words. My mother irons my first-grade school uniform, blue and
white, cleaned, pressed, ready for me. Her words cannot be true.

"Things were poked into me, one into my mouth, the other into . . . It was a kind of daily torture." I carry a feeling about this, a sense of recognition, even if I don't want to believe it. The room is shaking, as if we are in an earthquake.

I shiver and remember, "When I was an adolescent, I used to force myself to drink hot, soapy water, sometimes shampoo. I did it all the time."

"And did you throw up?" Blumenfeld asks softly.

"Yes, but I could never get the taste of soap out of my mouth. It seemed better than . . . I don't know . . . Soap and that thing pushed into me from behind."

My body feels tiny. I know all at once that this was happening to me when my father was alive.

"Make it stop! It's too hard, it's too hot, it burns, oh God it hurts, it hurts!"

I sit up abruptly, put my head in my hands and hold my breath. I feel a familiar choking sensation, but do not cry. Did I hope against hope that this would not happen again if I didn't cry, if I didn't acknowledge it?

"My mother loved me!" I tell Blumenfeld again. "This is not what happened to me. This could not be."

"Her love was mixed with something terribly poisonous, terribly dangerous. The enema must have felt like rape to you." Blumenfeld pauses.

"No," he says. "That is wrong, Annie, and my words are very important here. The enema *was* rape, over and over again."

I have been told I make things up, I imagine things, I don't know what is real. Here is someone telling me these things are real, and he is calling it rape. Hearing him, it is as if a truth, consigned to a dark cell in some corner of my mind, heaves a little groan.

"I felt so completely crushed," I say in a whisper, not looking at Blumenfeld. I feel his presence, too near, and I move away a little. The truths in me, denied yet still alive, seek his presence, but I am afraid of him.

"The worst part is that sometimes, sometimes with my mother, even though it hurt me, sometimes, I felt that this, this horrible ritual, was what made me most interesting, most worth my mother's time. Most of the time she was far away, pulled inside herself, and I wanted her time, her attention. Sometimes I felt, I felt kind of . . . excited about it."

"Aroused?" Blumenfeld asks. I nod, knowing he has found the right word for the helpless excitement I felt as a child.

"Terrified and aroused at the same time?" Blumenfeld asks.

I nod again, and slip a little farther away on the couch, feeling myself to be too despicable to be near him.

"Your body's response, which you couldn't help, couldn't stop, created a need you kept on feeling," Blumenfeld says softly. "What you felt was a kind of induced need for arousal, created by adults, that young children find absolutely overwhelming, Annie."

I nod, crying. "But even when I was big enough to fight back and I could have run away, I didn't."

"You did run away, Annie. You fled into yourself, into your mind, and you became dangerously numb in your body. And you keep right on doing that now—because the things that happened so long ago go on and on, don't they?"

As if in answer to his question, Margaret Mary, a little girl named for my mother, comes back to me.

Margaret Mary sits up in bed in the darkness that was never just dark, but always filled with low whispers and shadows. Although the night is hot, she pulls the bed covers up to her chin. She watches the leaf shapes flicker in the purple streetlight against the white paper shade.

The chair in the corner moved. She is sure of it. She caught it out of the corner of her eye and now she waits to see what will happen next. She hears a hum coming from the chair, like the hum of a refrigerator, from that corner. As it grows louder, the chair seems to get larger and larger, the chair back huge, its slats like great bars. When the hum becomes a high screeching in her ears, the chair explodes and breaks apart. The room suddenly fills up with animals—rabbits, wolves, snakes, bears, insects spinning and humming with the same menacing hum of the chair. The leaf shapes still dance against the purple-and-white paper shade. She pulls her head under the covers.

At six, Margaret Mary, the brown-haired, brown-eyed girl who looks just like her mother, tears off the covers and runs into the kitchen where her mother sits up reading a book. She runs to her mother and leans against her. Her mother puts her arm about the child's shoulders. Margaret Mary climbs right up into her mother's lap, closes her eyes, and whispers, "Tell me about how you used to float your Raggedy Ann and Andy dolls down the creek when you were little."

Her mother laughs, the finest low laugh in all the world. She pulls a chair up right in front of her for Margaret Mary to sit in and pulls the child's bare feet into her lap to keep them warm. She begins her story, and her soft, low voice goes on and on in the night until the child is sleeping in the chair.

The next day, and the day after, forever and ever, going out and into this happiness with her mother, Margaret Mary would float her dolls and stuffed animals down the creek, and whatever happened in the time between these sweet adventures with her mother would simply vanish for her.

I pull myself back from Margaret Mary, from that night of my childhood. I feel a strange sense of jealousy, of wanting this night with my mother, this night that wasn't really mine, and much, much more.

Blumenfeld is patiently waiting by the side of the couch.

"I wanted my mother's attention," I tell him. "And I was ashamed to want it, but I did. I wanted her time and attention. I was unreasonably jealous of anyone who took that from me."

"Of course you wanted that. And your wish made you feel so confused and ashamed—wanting her attention, feeling jealous." Blumenfeld pauses. "Because when she gave you her attention, it could come in so many unexpected ways, and some of them were devastating, weren't they, Annie?"

Shame covers my whole body, the shame of wanting, endlessly wanting, never being satisfied; then the sense of devastation—it washes over me and threatens to drench the rabbit too.

"Take my rabbit. Please hold her," I plead.

Blumenfeld takes the rabbit and puts her up on his shoulder. He walks the floor with her, saying soft things into her ears.

A middle-aged man in a dark suit and white shirt walks up and down the room. He holds a gray rabbit with a bedraggled green ribbon around its neck. He holds an infant, a toddler, a little girl. He holds me and Galle and Margaret Mary.

My tears begin to flow as I watch them.

"It wasn't going to stop, not ever," I tell Blumenfeld. "I didn't expect that it would stop. When I was older, maybe seven, I would watch my mother at the sink mixing up hot water and soap. I felt by then that I was completely trapped. I didn't even hope it would stop, because I couldn't imagine that. I just wanted to stay small so that I could have the hope that someone would comfort me, make me feel alive, pick me up and walk with me like that."

Blumenfeld, still holding the rabbit, opens one arm to me. I go to him, and he puts the rabbit into my arms. He holds us both close against his starched white shirt, and lightly touches the back of my head.

72

I sit outside in my backyard on a picnic bench after this, watching the shadows splash over the sun-drenched wood. I have carried out some books, good company. I don't want to be inside and I don't want to be alone, that is, alone and without words.

I am light, and not a little dizzy. I write on my familiar yellow pad, and go on writing, trying to sustain the lightness and dispel the dizziness.

Virginia Woolf describes an endless wanting toward her mother: "To want and want and never to have." Writing to her friend Violet Dickenson about her response to the statue of Venus de Milo, Woolf describes the same wistful longing and her feeling of hopelessness about it: "I weep tears of tenderness to think of that great heart of pity for Sparrow [a pet name for herself], for my mother was locked up in stone—never to throw her arms around me—as she would, if only she could."

Writer and French feminist Hélène Cixous describes a very different quality of love between mother and daughter as the basis for a unique love between women. In this love one is mother and mothered at the same moment, a moment that goes on in all directions without end. Cixous describes this love as, "Having. A having without limits, without restriction, a having without any 'deposit,' a having-love that sustains itself with loving; in the blood-rapport."

I recognize myself and the ways I have loved my mother (and

later, other women, including Melanie) in Woolf's terms: "To want and want and never to have," and also (often with the same person) in Cixous's terms: "Having . . . a love that sustains itself with loving."

What is clear now is that while these feelings about my mother were held separately by Galle and Margaret Mary, I myself escaped the worst of the terror. I lost the bliss and promise of maternal comfort too. It was Margaret Mary, the child named after my mother, who snuggled up to my mother and heard a story one night—and it was Margaret Mary who had the feeling that this mother was hers, the most beautiful woman in the world, with the finest low voice and laughter. And it was Margaret Mary, and not I, as she listened (I'd tune out my mother's voice, even as an adolescent and young woman, although my mother was a wonderful storyteller), who wanted to listen for hours.

I think now that this child must have been, in those moments, in a state of "having-love" with this particular mother, her mother. But she was also my mother, even if as a child I was not able to want her or to receive the love she had to offer me. I suppose I didn't know how to bring this mother to Blumenfeld because she hadn't really been my mother. I can see now how carefully as a child I kept her, this mother of "having-love," separate and apart from the mother who sometimes, when no one was around, performed rituals of bodily torture.

Even so, I didn't experience the most terrifying and painful things she did to me; Galle did, and Galle unabashedly hated her mother, feared and hated her.

But if, as a child, I was "in pieces," as Blumenfeld says, so too were the people I loved in pieces. I wonder if my own dissociation kept me alive. Whenever my father or mother could not take me in or recognize me, and in their ignorance did terrible things to me, I broke them up into pieces. I could not afford to respond truthfully to them, to show them anything real about their effect on me. So I lost the possibility of loving and being loved by them too.

But my own dissociative skills must have been limited, because I also remember clearly how my mother's simplest acts, such as preparing a meal, or touching my back to hurry me along, or handing me a bar of soap in my bath, could touch off a nameless terror.

Blumenfeld is making room for me to find feelings and experiences with my mother that have been inaccessible to me.

I haven't told him everything, but he understands my feelings as a child—terror, want, arousal, love, shame—feelings that go on in the present too. What he sees and knows is my confusion of love with intrusion, a confusion so deep that it takes me out of my own experience and out of my body.

73

In the weeks that followed this session, it became clear that I wanted to see the repeated experiences of entrapment and intrusion with my mother as a kind of love. I told Blumenfeld that my mother loved me, and I wanted to deny the fact that she also often terrified me. Sometimes I simply called the experience of intrusion itself love. But as I sat with Blumenfeld, who was increasingly horrified by what he was hearing and who did not save me from his horror, the picture of my life with my mother became very grim indeed. I forgot her, for a time, as the mother with whom I might have experienced "having-love" if only I'd dared to love her.

In retrospect, how quickly I was able to hold, know and name the most devastating events and distortions of my life! At the same time my "symptoms" were rapidly vanishing. I had struggled for years in therapy with several different women and men to know my past, to fill in missing time, and to bear the traumatic feelings associated with this process. This was the case with Melanie too. At times I'd experienced "flashbacks," those terrible short flicks the mind replays of terrifying experiences. Often this led directly to visual hallucinations, voices, disconcerting illusions, accidents with my car or bike, unbearable physical sensations, and deep confusion and disorientation. And sometimes, usually once or twice a year, these "symptoms" became so severe that I was briefly hospitalized.

With Blumenfeld this pattern ended. It ended suddenly, in the first three months of our relationship.

And this is a great mystery to me. He certainly wasn't perfect.

He would be aghast at the very idea. He was rather dense about some things, in fact. He and I did not always use the same metaphors or words, and because we were each sensitive to the poetry of spoken language, we sometimes argued about these words and metaphors, much to my frustration. Blumenfeld was a more lively and skilled storyteller than I. I would grow frustrated with his skill when he was definitely telling me a story that was his own story, complete with his own metaphors, as if it were about me. He could be remarkably dense about this. Yet once I showed him how he was making this interchange, he saw what he had been doing and usually laughed at himself.

He was also apt to play his own grandfather at times, taking on the persona of the wise old man, but often he was deeply wise. Sometimes, however, just when I had the feeling he was really quite extraordinary, I had the sense that he was pretending. I could tell because he would suddenly become philosophical and distant, just a little too wise, as if he were hovering somewhere above us. Then I'd tell him to come down "off the ceiling," or to "land the helicopter, please"—and he would.

Blumenfeld was, and is, perhaps the most defenseless person I know. This in itself made me gentle with him. And when his defenses did come into play in relationship with me, I saw with great relief that he was able to set them aside (with a little nudging on my part) gracefully and easily.

Not only was Blumenfeld not perfect, he was also not very magical. I complained to him often about this. He never had the aura of "magic" about him that Melanie had had for me. Of course, part of her magic was that she reminded me of the mother of "having-love" and held out to me the promise of becoming that mother in reality; that was part of her magic. Blumenfeld once commented, "With her magical aura, she burned you—and I, without any magic at all, show you things by flashlight." This was accurate too.

All my friends, and certainly Sarah, felt and believed in the magic of Blumenfeld. I never did. He was such an ordinary man

to me. Or rather, things that I'd never dreamed could be ordinary
were with Blumenfeld. For one thing, I'd never been in any relationship in which I was not, sooner or later, terrified of being abandoned. With him, this was not an obsession, not even much of a
fear, though it took me some time to notice that I came and went
from my sessions with him without the company of this particular
lifelong fear.

Unlike every other relationship in which I wanted to feel loved,
I did not doubt his love. Once when I asked (smiling, already sure
of the answer), "Do you love me?" he smiled back and said, "Don't
you know, Annie? Can't you tell love when you can take it completely for granted?" I did, and do, take his love completely for
granted. This gave me a freedom with him I'd never dreamed possible. Among many other things, it allowed me to complain to
him about him and know he still loved me.

74

June wilted into July, and as the days became consistently muggy and hot, Ben asked to spend more and more of his time with me indoors.

While I was actively recalling my terror with my mother with Blumenfeld, Ben did not play outside, and he did not play any of the variations on the "mama bear" with me either. I don't really understand why, but it was as if Ben wordlessly understood that I needed a little distance from that particular play with him.

Then I had a dream that made it possible for Ben to go on.

In the dream I see Ben's hands, very much like my hands as a child, small and bitten down to the cuticles and scratched on the back. We are visiting a firehouse, complete with red engine and dalmatian dog. Big men lift Ben up and slide him down the pole, their pole, and he plays that he is flying fast into fires with them.

But Ben has his own fires to contend with. Next, I see his small hands gripping an axe. I go after him, but he has disappeared. I search the entire firehouse and can't find him. In the process, it becomes an ordinary house. Then I hear breaking glass, a far-off sound, and follow the sound, calling out, "Where are you, Ben?"

I find him in an upstairs room with the axe in his hands, all the windows broken and his face unreadable. "What are you doing,

Ben?" I ask him, needing to understand. He cries, "Breaking out of everywhere!" and he flings the axe toward me, as if to kill me for asking. But he misses me by quite a distance, as if to protect me.

He begins to cry and reaches his arms up. "Carry me, carry me," he says.

75

One bright July morning, when I come to pick up Ben in his classroom for our session, I am told he is "on the loose." He threw his workbook on the floor and started to kick another child; when his teacher moved in to intervene, he ran out of the room.

I walk the grounds and search his familiar hiding places, but do not find him. As I come back, I see him struggling to open a heavy door at the back of the building. I offer my hand and he comes around to the front with me easily, saying, "Now can I come to see you?"

"I think you have some schoolwork to do first," I reply.

"That's right," he says. "And I don't want to do it."

We meet Mary Louise in the hall. Back in his classroom Ben retrieves his workbook and settles down to work. I go on with my meetings and appointments, saving time for him later in the day.

Within thirty minutes Ben comes knocking on my office door. I am with another child then, but I open the door.

He peers in and is immediately furious with me.

"It's my time!" he shouts, turning red.

"No. You spent your time running outside," I say slowly.

"I don't care," he shouts back.

"You do care, and I will see you a bit later today," I tell him.

He begins to cry, and turns and stomps off.

When I come to his classroom to pick him up later, Ben throws his workbook on the floor. He has been working with Mary

Louise, who comments on how much work he's finished and how well he's done it. Ben listens and slowly retrieves the workbook. He reads a little of it aloud to me, but he still seems very angry. He opens his desk top, puts his head in and pounds the metal interior with his fists. I try to ignore this, hard to do, and talk quietly with Mary Louise. Finally, he closes his desk and sits and stares at me.

"Are you ready to come, bear?" I ask gently. He nods and I hand him the playroom keys.

As Ben walks into the playroom, he reaches down and pulls something out of his pocket. I see that it is an old makeup kit. I wonder where in the world he got it.

"I found this outside. Would you fix me into a clown?" he asks me.

"I believe I could do that. Is that what you wanted earlier?"

"Yes. But I had to do the workbook first," he says.

"And then you had to wait while I was seeing someone else," I add, wanting him to take in the whole day.

He nods solemnly, studying me.

"It's a hard job to wait, isn't it?" I ask him.

He nods, then smiles. "But now it *is* our time. Hurry up and fix me!"

On his upturned face I paint a red nose, a smile, blue dots and big round red cheeks.

Then Ben gathers up Tea Bags and the baby bottle and leads me outside. He runs ahead of me to his hideout, where he sits back on his heels and sucks the baby bottle, waiting for me. When I arrive, he tosses the bottle into the grass. He looks all around him, then points to a tree.

"There's going to be a fire. There. In that house."

"There is?" I ask, startled by this, given my dream about visiting a firehouse with him.

"Yep, and I am the fireman going to put it out," he says.

This seems uncanny to me, but I trust it completely.

Ben runs across a stretch of grass to a huge tree, making the high whine of a fire siren.

"Bring Tea Bags," he shouts back to me. Still surprised, I bring the puppet to him, and Ben places Tea Bags up in the tree. Then Ben turns to me.

"There's children up there and they will burn," he says, pointing up and looking at me with wide eyes.

He bends down and picks up a long stick.

"This is the hose with the water gushing to put out the fire," he declares. He points it into the tree and makes a loud "shhh" sound for the water.

"Hand me my axe," he commands.

In a bit of a daze, I find a small, stout stick and hand it to him. He chops the air with it.

"Now the long rope," he says, and I pretend to give him lengths of a rope, which he tosses up into the tree.

Then he drops the rope and reaches up with his hands cupped around something small, and hands it down to me.

"Here's the baby," he cries. "He's on fire. Put it out!"

I beat off the "flames" and hold the "baby" close while Ben watches.

"Here's the sister and brother," he says, handing them down.

I take them from him and comfort each one.

"Oh look, Tea Bags is on fire, too!" he shouts.

I take the puppet in my arms too, beat off the flames, and hold him close.

"Is he all right?" Ben asks.

"I think he is, but he is very frightened," I answer.

Ben comes straight to me and reaches out for Tea Bags. He folds the puppet in his arms and rocks. "Are you all right?" he asks softly. Then he looks up at me and points to the burning house.

"My imaginary mommy is still up there," he says, eyes wide. I wonder who she is, this "imaginary mommy."

"Who is she, Ben?"

"She is a sorceress. She will get me!" And he turns and runs up a long slope.

He hides behind another tree, and when I come up to him, he is crying.

"She'll get me! Hide me!" he says.

"She can get out of the fire all by herself?" I ask, seeing that she isn't really trapped, as Ben himself once was.

"Yes. She can, and she will get me!" he cries.

"For leaving her in the fire and wishing she'd burn up?" I ask him slowly.

A startled, puzzled look comes over Ben's face.

"It is only a wish," I tell him. "And she is your *imaginary* mommy." I emphasize his own word.

"Yeah," he says, looking relieved. "And it's just a tree."

"It's a tree now," I tell him. "But it *really was* a burning house and you really had to get the baby out and leave the mommy in."

He is still crying, but softly now. I pick him up.

"You're so brave," I whisper to him. He is still, just listening.

I put him down and take his hand and we walk back to the classroom building.

Inside it is dark in contrast to the brightness out of doors. Ben wants to go to the boys' bathroom and asks if I will come with him. I listen to him peeing, then help him scrub his grubby hands and painted, sweating face.

"Wash my arms, too," he says in a small voice.

I wash his arms with a brown paper towel and cool water.

"You dry me off, please, too," he asks, and stands limply.

I dry him, taking my time about it.

He appears calm now, but drained and somehow vulnerable. I take his hand again and walk him all the way back to his classroom.

When Ben chooses to escape and run around outside during the time of our session he is implicitly testing my reaction. He has also literally run out on his responsibility for his schoolwork. When I finally find him, he asks if he can have his session. I, however, have spent most of our usual session time searching for him, and do not want to support him in running away. As soon as I remind him that he has schoolwork to do, he remembers this. It might have been better if I'd thought to add that I would see another child and then see him later, and given him a specific time. My guess is that he worked hard and efficiently to get to see me sooner, then was disappointed as well as furious that I was seeing someone else. But, in reality, he had responsibilities for his schoolwork, and I had the responsibility of seeing other children at their regular appointment times. To use a therapy session to brush aside those constraints would be to deceive Ben about the world he and I lived in.

When I come to pick him up, he is angry, and though he is provocative, he does not lose control. When he shows me his makeup and requests to be "fixed" into a clown, I guess that he wanted that earlier, and use it as an opportunity to comment on how hard it was for him to wait: "It's a hard job to wait, isn't it?" He nods, and immediately decides to make full use of his time: "But now *is* our time. Hurry up and fix me!"

The clown makeup isn't part of his outdoor play. It is something he wants from me, but had to wait for, and as such it is part of the work of the session. Outdoors, he has a different piece of work to do.

I wonder how Ben knows that I am ready to play out this fire scene with him. My dream is no coincidence; it prepares me for Ben's play as perhaps nothing else can.

In his play about being a fireman saving the baby and children in the burning house, Ben reenacts the old trauma he cannot consciously remember (he had been less than fifteen months old). In his play he reverses roles in two crucial ways: he is the competent person who was the rescuer, not the helpless baby who needed rescuing, and he also rescues the baby first and "forgets" the mother.

In his play, he realizes his fear—the baby is actually burning and so is Tea Bags. What is different now? Now Ben is not alone.

He has come back to this scene with me. He wants me to play a part, asking me to put out the flames. I also give comfort, and Ben mimics my comforting with Tea Bags, showing his compassion both in his cradling and rocking, and in his anxious question, "Are you all right?"

The mother in his play frightens him, however. When he calls her "my imaginary mommy," he implicitly distinguishes fantasy from reality; but his other label for her is "sorceress," a magical, powerful figure, and his emotional response to her is fear. So he teeters there behind the tree, balancing fact and fantasy, reality and wish. I ask Ben if the imaginary mommy can get out of the fire, and he says, "Yes, she can. And she will get me!" He is so afraid of her revenge that he is crying by now. The missing connection is an answer to the question, "Why should she want revenge?" I don't ask Ben this, since I doubt he could know why, and instead I offer an interpretation, "For leaving her in the fire and wishing she'd burn up?" The look on Ben's face confirms that there may be some kernel of truth in my guess. But my guess also frightens him. When I interpret again, "It is only a wish," Ben looks immediately relieved. Here the world of fantasy shifts to reality. "Yeah, and it's only a tree," he says. I do not want him to dismantle entirely the powerful piece of playing he has done, to undermine his accomplishment, so I remind him that just a few minutes ago it really was a burning house.

Ben is shaken, but not overwhelmed by this experience. He calms down immediately when I pick him up. He takes my hand in a gesture of simultaneous reaching. In the boys' bathroom he sounds very vulnerable and wants me to take care of him in a physical, tangible way.

What has happened here?

When a child can't remember events he continues to react to emotionally, they control him and haunt him. Cut off from him, his own fears and wishes, belonging to the forgotten events, come back in fantasy, play, or dreams. Here Ben reenacts a haunting scene, reversing roles, and projects his own wish for revenge onto the imaginary mommy, she who left him shut up in a burning house so long ago he can't remember it—yet it haunts him. When I show him his wish and his own construction of this frightening figure as "imaginary," he shifts from a fearful reaction to a startled acknowledgment of reality. Once Ben knows his own wish, the imaginary mommy cannot haunt him and he is freer; but he is also now vulnerable to his feelings of hate and revenge.

I am beginning to know more fully how Ben's trauma and mine overlap. This is incomplete knowledge, as it must be, since it is continually revealed in vivo. I am playing with Ben and Blumenfeld by moving toward and away from my own story of trauma.

Ben and I play more intensely now and with greater freedom. We play from within our two distinct and overlapping stories. But when I am with Ben, the focus of our playing is Ben's story. I carefully follow his cues, his feelings, and wait to see his responses to my interpretations. Perhaps this is an illusion on my part, however, for Ben did not play any mother scenes with me for those weeks while I was intensely remembering my terror with my own mother, and he played out this crucial fire reenactment scene just after I dreamed of our visiting the firehouse.

How this unconscious knowing passes from one human being to another is a mystery to me. I sometimes wonder if it depends upon messengers. Are we surrounded by angels as we play together?

But Ben and I are not playing within a single story. In order for our playing to take place at all, in fact, there must be two stories and two perspectives. When each person is emotionally alive and distinct in the process of playing, she or he notices and responds to the other. Both are filled with one another's words and feelings, one another's truths (even if some truths are denials), and the unnecessary distinctions vanish. The two create a world together and a new story. When this happens, it seems to me that each person playing, no matter how conscious or unconscious the process might be, participates in a new story and is healed within it.

What has been wounded in a relationship must be, after all, healed in a relationship.

76

I begin to paint again. I paint the light on the windows. Not any light, but light reflected on glass. I paint the gray of dawn and the golden light of late afternoon and the blue-and-periwinkle light of dusk. The shapes of these colors reflected in the watery glass catch and hold my attention even when I am not painting. I hardly ever have time to paint midday, so I paint the bright light I imagine on the windows then. I paint yellow light that fades into whiteness. It is the most beautiful light I can imagine, yet it fills me with anxiety.

What is it, then, now when shaken and stunned, in the paucity of anything that might help me to know, or even understand what I do not know, that makes me create these illusions of beautiful light?

I dream of windows breaking, the sound of glass falling, that breaking and crashing a great relief, a big sea breeze of relief. I dream of breaking windows and standing by them to get air.

I remember the firehouse dream, its sound. Ben was, he said, "breaking out of everywhere."

But in his own playing, he didn't use his axe to break glass. A sense of fear sweeps through my body.

He cried and said, "Carry me, carry me." Was that in his play or in my dream of him?

It was in my dream of him.
In our play, he cried and I picked him up.

I look up Ben's record and realize that the little room he stayed in for the first fifteen months of his life had no window. Someone must have told me that months ago. There it is, plain as day, clear as light, written in the record. That little room he lived in must have been dark, not light.

Why have I so often imagined Ben bathed in light?

I paint the light at midday as if it comes from no identifiable source. Glaring. Electric. Yellow into blinding white. This is the realm of speculation and dream. Everything vanishes into that whiteness. Now you see it, now you don't.

People vanish and return, people vanish and never return. "Carry me, carry me," the chant of a child's terror of vanishing. People vanish and then turn up again to love and to torment. A child wishes they would vanish again.

The white light is sweeping all my family away, as if by violence. But there is no violence in this light, nothing but my wish for air.

And, meanwhile, I am talking to Rachael about how to tell Ben I will be leaving him at the end of the summer, the end of my internship. All the gestures of my painting and all the breaking of glass in my dreams seeps into and changes me, so that I feel my loss alongside Ben's, even before I tell him that I will soon be vanishing.

77

Ben has one shoe off when he comes to see me on a rainy day in mid-July. He comes into the playroom and immediately picks up Tea Bags.

"I'm gonna paint inside today, Tea Bags," he announces. "We will stay inside today," he adds, turning to me.

"I see you have decided that," I say. "But where is your other shoe?"

"In the classroom. I hurt my foot and it feels better this way," he says.

"How did you hurt it, Ben?"

"I tripped and stubbed my toe," he says absently, looking around the playroom. "Where's the skirt?" he asks, opening a drawer to look for the painting apron.

"I'll show you where it is, but first I want to show you something else," I answer, pulling down the calendar from the bulletin board above my desk.

Ben comes and stands by my side, bringing Tea Bags. I knew this moment would have to come, a vanishing point in a painting, and now we are moving toward it and into it.

"At the end of the summer I will be leaving Glenwood," I tell him slowly. "And then, you won't be seeing me, Ben." I keep my voice steady as I tell him this.

Ben stands and looks down at the calendar.

I circle the last day of the first week in August with a red pen. "This will be our goodbye day," I tell him.

Ben continues to stand still. I cannot tell what he is thinking and feeling, and I do not want to press him into feelings he isn't ready for or ask him to respond to such an important event before he has had time to take it in.

I put a large red X on each day I will see him. "There will be time to say goodbye," I tell him softly. "You will see me eight more times."

"Eight more weeks?" Ben asks, glancing at me.

"No, eight more times," I clarify. "Four weeks." Now the point of vanishing is clear to both of us.

Again, he stands very still, silent. As if staring into a night-mare, or a white mist. I don't know how to reach him.

"I want to paint today," he finally says without looking at me. But he does nothing. The most ordinary request is tinged with the unbelievable enormity of this leaving.

"Where's the skirt?" he asks, opening a drawer.

I show him where it is and help him to tie it on.

He stands very still again, as if in a daze. It is as if his mind has emptied itself of everything to take this in, yet he cannot take it in.

I wait, but Ben does nothing, says nothing. I cannot find the words I am searching for and my mind stumbles for them, franti-cally. Soon I stop searching and we enter a circle of silence that seems to exist outside of time.

"You don't know quite what to think or feel, do you?" I fi-nally ask.

He doesn't answer me, but with my words he begins to move again, setting up the plastic mat, the water and brushes and paints. He selects a piece of white paper and paints a blue border all around it. As he works, he gradually grows more animated. It is as if the sun rises slowly out of a white mist into which we are al-ready vanishing.

"I'm gonna use every color," Ben declares. "Is this magic? Is it?" he asks.

"Are all the different colors magic? What do *you* think, Ben?"

"No, I don't think so anymore." His observation resounds with time slipping away, a time he has already begun to remember.

He paints in silence for a while, bent over the page intently. Then he stirs the brush vigorously in the clear water, turning it blue.

"Ooh, look, Annie. Tea Bags, look. It *is* magic!"

I smile at him. "Maybe it is and maybe it isn't, hmm?"

"No, it really isn't," he says, his voice low, and then with energy, "but it could be!"

He stirs the brush in the red paint. "It needs some water," he announces and begins to tilt the large container of water, then decides to try another way. He runs and fills the baby bottle, then dumps a little into the paint jar.

"That's enough, Ben," I say, as the paint fills the jar to the brim, but he ignores me and pours in a little more. Expectedly, it overflows. Ben mops it up with a towel, then turns toward me.

"Are you mad at me?" he asks. What is he asking, I wonder.

"Am I mad at you for not listening?" I guess.

He nods.

"I am exasperated. Do you know what that means?"

"No."

"It means angry with a big sigh in it, and a smile right behind it. Get it?"

"Yeah," he says, but he still seems anxious.

"Look, Ben, you wanted to find out if it would spill. You found out and you wiped it up."

He turns and smiles. "Yep. I did!"

He paints a birthday cake in red, with six candles on it, and six tiny yellow flames.

"This is a present for Tea Bags," he says solemnly. He looks at the yellow puppet. "How old is he? Is he six?"

"He could be six, that seems about right," I answer. "That seems just right for Tea Bags."

"He's my friend. Look, Tea Bags! I'm making you a cake. Annie will put Happy Birthday Tea Bags on it."

"I will? Yes, you know I will." I take the brush and paint as he requests.

"Let Tea Bags paint?" Ben asks.

I put the puppet on my hand and carefully put a brush in its mouth. I have the puppet paint another cake, as close to Ben's as I can make it, while Ben looks on.

"Now, a big tall hat for me. A shiny hat with stars and dots," Ben says, his eyebrows characteristically arched high in excitement.

"A magician hat or a birthday hat?" I ask.

Ben is puzzled about this. "Both!" he exclaims suddenly.

Together we glue red and blue paper together and add yellow stars and pink dots. He leads me down the hall to the main office to have it laminated, running ahead of me and then back to me to urge me on.

In the office, he introduces Tea Bags to the two familiar secretaries, Jill and Karen. "This is my friend Tea Bags." He talks about his hat and asks them to have it "made all shiny." When the paper goes into the laminator, Ben stands still and watches the clock, counting the seconds aloud with Nancy.

"Boy, it's hot in there! It's getting all shiny!" he breaks out.

I staple the high, wizardlike hat together for him and place it on his head. It covers his dark head so only his face shows, whimsical and serious.

"I got to show this to Mrs. Engle," he shouts and runs out. I have the sense that he is already leaving me.

He reappears at the door. "C'mon, Annie, you come with me."

I've been searching all my life to play with a child as Ben invites me to play with him. Ben has found in me an adult who has the capacity to play with him and enter the drama he needed to play out in order to know that he has survived, a drama about abandonment. Yet Ben and I continue to search for one another, perhaps most intently, as we begin to say goodbye.

But this ending is not Ben's choice. I am the one leaving, and Ben has been left in devastating ways before. So I worry. Over the year, as Ben played with me, he has changed. He has changed me, too, as we played together. I can now hurt him and he can also hurt me, simply because we have become attached to one another. Harm is possible in our play, as well as healing.

I am worried about how my leaving will affect him. I run a terrible risk if I deny that I can hurt him. But if I wait and watch for his moments of hurt, if I can sustain the courage to accept these moments as part of loving him, then perhaps we might heal one another, most poignantly touch one another, in saying goodbye.

But saying goodbye is a risk to each of us, because love is fragile and cannot withstand any degree of hurt. So to deny the possibility of damage on both sides of this therapeutic relationship is also to deny the fragility of human love.

Upon first hearing of my leaving, Ben seems almost in shock, standing so still and silent, listening and trying to absorb what I am saying. Knowing his history, I read his silent gestures. But I don't know how to reach him, what words to bring to him. He is concerned only with the number of times he will see me, but does not approach the emotional experience of leaving me.

For the next several sessions, each time he returns, we look at the calendar and mark off another red X and Ben counts the days left. I sometimes suggest, "You might feel sad," or, "You have spent a lot of time here, and now it is ending," or simply, "It's hard to say goodbye." Ben ignores me, as if he hasn't heard my words. But we mark off the Xs and I make these tentative remarks anyway.

Today Ben uses the baby bottle to carry water. During the time left with me, never again does he use it as a baby bottle. Though it is not his birthday, he points out his age and Tea Bags's age, solidifying his relationship to the puppet as peer and friend. Over the next four consecutive sessions Ben relates to me as a six-year-old boy—struggling to understand what is magic and what is not, trying to do things by himself, but including Tea Bags and me, and occasionally asking for help. Ben does not play the mama-baby games again with me, perhaps because to do so would make the leaving too difficult, perhaps because he has played out what he needed to, culminating in this awareness of the wish to leave the imaginary mommy in the fire. I do not really know.

Ben begins to take more than a casual interest in the Glenwood staff, using his time with me to extend those contacts, even to the gardener. And he begins also to extend himself in gift-giving, first to Tea Bags. He returns in the next several sessions to paint pictures for his teacher, his mother, and for a little boy in his class, an autistic child who is far less social than he is now, as well as for himself.

While Ben is preparing to say goodbye to me, he is also preparing to make a transition into the Glenwood residential program. His psychiatrist, the Glenwood staff and I all agree that he needs a more consistent therapeutic milieu than we can offer six hours a day. Ben has made enormous gains this year, especially in his capacity to form new relationships. But he has regressed at times too, and his adoptive parents still feel often overwhelmed by his behavior. This is a period of waiting for all of us—waiting for a confirmation of admission and for an open bed.

One rainy day late in July, as I walk from the cafeteria back to my office, I see Ben outside by the cottages, bent over something, tugging at it. I go to him and see it is a child's jacket, muddy and wet.

"Hello, Ben. What have you found?" I begin.

"A jacket. Can I keep it? We could wash it and dry it," he says, still tugging at it and lifting it slightly off the ground.

"I think it belongs to a child who lives here, Ben, and he has left it out there in the rain."

"I will live here. Then it can belong to me," Ben insists.

"Perhaps you will live here. But then you will bring your own jacket," I tell him.

"No. I know."

"What do you know?" I ask.

"I will live here."

As he says this, he releases the jacket and takes my hand and we walk back to the school building together. I sense that he knows he needs Glenwood, but something is still troubling him.

Later that day, Ben asks Mary Louise to wash something for him—not the jacket—and she takes him to a washing machine in one of the children's cottages. There Ben spots a suitcase in a child's room. He asks what it is for, and she tells him the children who live at Glenwood put their clothes and toothbrush in it when they go home to visit and take the clothes out again when they come back. Ben is fascinated. He pulls Mary Louise into the room and plays with putting things in and out of the suitcase. He carries it around. Mary Louise tells him about weekend visits and coming back. She describes a daily schedule of waking, dressing, getting breakfast, a school day, playtime, supper, study or play time, a nighttime story read and lights out. She gives him a grand tour.

Hearing Mary Louise's simple description of the daily agenda and exploring the suitcase, the sinks, toilets, bathtub, and recreation area, Ben rehearses the experience of living among the children. He discovers that each child has his or her own bed, clothes, stuffed animal and cubby of toys. The suitcase is a concrete, visible piece of evidence that he can still see his family. The unspoken fears of owning nothing, and hence of anonymity, and of losing his home, are allayed in that sensitive, spontaneous tour of the cottage with Mary Louise.

Mary Louise tells me about this the next day, and I put it away in my store of ideas of how to help young children make difficult transitions. I also realize that Ben tried, first with me, and more successfully with Mary Louise, to go into a cottage to wash something. Without knowing why, he set the stage for that dramatic rehearsal. And I wonder how to make my leaving more concrete and more real for him.

78

I sit under bright lights on a hard wooden bench in an ice-cream parlor where they have homemade ice cream of all flavors. I wonder what it would be like to find Ben in such a place, after I am no longer seeing him. Heartbreak to see him again and not to go on seeing him.

At night, the light reflects everything within as if it were outside, and I wonder if history will record this bit of trivia about late-twentieth-century America—this obsession so many of us had with ice cream.

In my dream two women walk, one behind the other and far apart, across a lake that is only partly frozen. Melanie and I, walking. We wear bright orange vests to protect us from the men, the hunters, and stay carefully apart. If we walk too close together, we will break the ice and go down into the dark water. What is the ice I walk with Melanie? Blumenfeld tells me nothing of their talks these days. Into that nothingness, I invent the rehearsed responses to my fear that she is not coming back to me after all. We walk the ice, glancing at one another, inventing and reinventing one another. We find each other's eyes, keep the distance, knowing we might sink and freeze, lost to time and love. But already we are lost, rehearsing our far-reaching fear (what you fear most has already happened) and inventing, each by herself, her own memory. Soft green feathers of ducks and soft white feathers of geese drift over to us, carried by the wind to tell us that once these birds walked here. We walk in their three-pronged footprints, keeping carefully apart. How hard it is to read one another's eyes. We read the world we remember there, and this invention stamps something like hopelessness, a remembered despair, into the body's cells. If we could turn away from this, whisper across the distance, listen without words, in pure communion with one another, our despair might be redeemed. This I know from Ben.

79

The last time I see Melanie, she is wearing a navy-blue suit and matching blue high-heel shoes. In this outfit, with her long auburn hair drawn back, I hardly recognize her.

Melanie has agreed to meet with me in Blumenfeld's office after meeting with him alone for weeks. She is afraid and does not want to be alone with me in the waiting room, she's told Blumenfeld, so she will come a few minutes later than I. I might have guessed that the line between myself, Annie, and her fear of me, has not faded with time. I should have guessed this, but I didn't.

As she walks into the office, I wonder where she will choose to sit. I sit on the couch, leaving "my" chair at the head of the couch open, near me, hoping she will want to sit there. She does not. She chooses a chair next to Blumenfeld's desk, across the room from me. Blumenfeld is ensconced in the same chair he always sits in, by the lamp, nearer to me.

I have waited for nearly five months, since late February, to see Melanie, hoping to see her, unsure that I would ever see her again. Yet, once in her presence, I cannot connect this Melanie with the therapist I have loved. The silence between us grows, and Blumenfeld is quiet too. This silence has a dangerous tremor.

Finally, he speaks to Melanie, saying, "Annie has some questions about what to expect from you now. Probably her biggest question is about her hope that you will be able to see her again."

"No," Melanie says, "I will not see her again. I came to say goodbye."

Blumenfeld looks startled, but she is perfectly clear. There is something in this unflinching clarity that chills me. I sense how much it has cost her to be able to say this. She seems not entirely alive, as if this line has been memorized or rehearsed. I see that there will be no shortening of the distance we have been walking; it will become infinitely wider.

And since Blumenfeld and Melanie have begun to talk about me in the third person, as if I were not there, I leave them to it.

Most of the time Emily was used to disappointment. Still, when the stars fell from the sky, it startled her. She schooled herself against all expectations, but went right on wildly jumping into the arms of hope, then jumping back into herself—rocking herself alone in the night while the leaves spoke summer words and cars went by. Their tires made a splashing sound on the empty street and little bugs splashed on the screen. Emily was used to bitter disappointment, and knew already, even before her wish was formed into words, it was no use to wish for what she wanted. Emily remembered walking in her bare feet in the park one day. The wet grass under her feet hid a shard of broken glass, well no, not really, she saw it before she stepped on it, and then, pain, of course, but also her wish—that someone would look a look of kindness upon her today, because of the glass—an accident. But she knew better, and bandaged the foot by herself, then huddled over the pain, savored it for herself. It was of no use, to wish, forget it! she was used to it, before her wish shaped itself, the leaves whispered, stars fell, little bugs splashed—rocking, she sought the wish itself— no, it was not going to happen.

I come back into a silent room. Perhaps they, either one, have asked me something and are patiently waiting for my response. I want to say something suddenly. It is a grasping gesture, this speech I want to make. A lump rises in my throat, a sudden yearning to deceive. I would tell Melanie that I have betrayed her, that I was "sick" and "wrong," that it has all been my fault. Through this "confession," perhaps she would be able to find me again, to forgive me. I have done this before. The very words come up into my throat, but not out into the room. To say them would mean to sacrifice everything, every part of myself, the Annie who held the gun and the others behind her, including the voices, the ones I never met directly. They had been trying, as Blumenfeld said, to heal Melanie so that I could be free to love her again.

I fight for words, but the words that come out into the room to Melanie are not the words I have planned:

"You know, I could make a confession now, I know how to do it, I've done it many times in the past with you. But what's the use? It would be a lie. What happened between us was *not* entirely my fault." In each moment in every life, there is a gesture hovering, to move toward or away from a truth.

Melanie doesn't answer me. We sit in silence again.

Emily's words bleed into her own body. She'd rather not speak. She fingers her own pulse against her child's soul (at thirteen she still thinks of herself as a child), feeling the strength of her pulse beat against the smooth eye of her terror. Her mind empties out like a sieve—nothing stays, no words, just the intense look of pain on their faces when they found her bleeding, her wrists cut horizontally, because she didn't know how to do it properly. It was her fault, this pain she'd caused her mother. She couldn't forget that.

Melanie looks at me, and then at Blumenfeld. "I had a dream two nights ago," she says, "and in the dream it was clear to me that I had, in some way, I'm not sure how, preempted the gun and the knife." I sense the possibility of an opening.

"That does make sense to me," Blumenfeld says. "Can you tell Annie more about what was clear to you?"

But Melanie does not want to talk about her dream, after all. "This session," she tells Blumenfeld, "I assumed, was supposed to be about Annie, not about me."

And I feel, once again, the promise of an opening, the promise of a place to really begin a conversation with her, closed off to me, as she retreats from revealing herself any further. We walk the ice, farther and farther apart.

Emily stands apart. Despite all her promises to herself, the wish creates itself—not just within her, but in the real world that she shares with me.

Melanie, Emily knows, will actually hear herself and stand up at any moment. Melanie's going to see it all—the way she opens up a wish and then closes it off—she'll stand there fully within her own despair, and hold out her arms, and take Emily and me into her arms.

But that's not what happens, of course. Emily's wish does reach me, at least enough for me to wonder if Melanie could ever know again what she knew from the beginning: that she'd come to learn from me, and that I knew, better than she knew, exactly what I needed. I see suddenly, very clearly, that her trust in me changed as she acquired more and more clinical training and experience, until I felt, in the last year we met, that what I said to her hardly mattered. She had her interpretations all ready, and my words were fitted to them. Anything that did not fit could be attributed to my "denial" or "resistance."

In Blumenfeld's presence, however, and with Emily's wish vivid in the room with me, I insist that I know the details of my experience more fully than Melanie has ever known.

I speak angrily to Melanie, in a last-ditch hope: "I knew, from the beginning of our relationship, more clearly than you knew, what I needed. You thought so too, once. Don't you remember how you wanted to learn from me, how you wanted even to write with me?"

Again, she does not answer. But looking briefly into her eyes, I know that she knew this once. One can see such a recognition. But she looks toward Blumenfeld and away from me.

Once Emily sat with Melanie in the park nearby the Art Institute. It was a Saturday, time off, free time, endless time, and she was happy. Melanie bought them gyros and Emily chose a grape soda as her drink. She told Melanie about her writing. Someday, maybe, they would write a book together. But Melanie said, "No, you'll write your own book, and I, and a lot of other people, will learn from you."

Blumenfeld is asking Melanie a question. He is taking a while to get it formulated, and I wonder what else has happened. He has it: "I think that Annie needs to know if you think that you know what she needs better than she knows."

Under his question, the ice trembles beneath us.

Melanie, looking completely composed, answers his question: "Yes, I do think that. I was her therapist. I had to know."

Emily feels the cold pull of water gripping her legs and arms. She's drowning, going under, once, twice . . . Telesporus pulls her up and swims with her, tucked under his white wing. She wonders why he does not fly with her, then realizes that he wants her to feel the distance she has swum, to feel the danger she has put herself in. On the shore, he looks into her face, holding her face in his big hands.

"Have you ever—listen to me, Emily! Have you ever betrayed anyone yourself?" Emily nods, stupidly. She looks up from the sand to the waves to his face. "You," she says. "You, when I told them about you that time in the hospital, you know that." She sees the kindness in his eyes behind the white heat of his anger and fear, for her, mostly for her, not for himself this time. The darkness comes nearer, it's closing over her head, and he sees it coming. "I knew you didn't mean to endanger yourself and all of us," he says. "I knew you were trying to make a bargain with them, to get out, and you didn't mean to betray us. But now, you have to get this now, Emily." Against her wish (Mother and Father—they have to know what they have done to me. Melanie has to know too), the wish that also allows her to live, Telesporus goes on talking. His words keep pouring over her. "Listen to me! Melanie isn't going to be able to save you now, she doesn't even want to extend this torture any longer, she can't bear to watch you go under again and again. Let her go this time, Emily, let her go, without her knowing what she is doing to you."

And at that point, hearing the plea of the great guardian angel of my childhood, hearing his words right alongside Emily's, I watch Melanie go from the room—without any idea of whether or not I'll ever see her again. I know now that I can never have a relationship with her, not one I'd want anyway, since any relationship would mean having to know less than she knows, less about myself than I already know. So powerful is this knowing that I feel my life pulled in a new direction.

Not a voice was raised. In fact, a great deal of the time in this fifty-minute hour passed in silence. Things were said that I was not present to hear, of course. But no one knew that, not even

Blumenfeld, in all probability. As for Melanie, I knew then that while she knew the facts of my abuse (it was she who introduced me to an incest survivors' group), she did not understand the inner life of the child who had lived that abuse. I discovered nothing I did not know in some sense already. I feel an endless chill descending.

I sit on the couch, very still, unable to cry. Blumenfeld comes to me of his own accord and sits beside me. He, too, is quiet. He reminds me a little of Telesporus, but older, and not so big—and then there are the black shoes, the gray suit, no wings. Nevertheless, something in his demeanor reminds me of Telesporus with Emily, as he sits with me.

"Like your father," he says quietly, "Melanie is really blind to you. She left you without ever recognizing you. That's not a good-bye, Annie; it's just leaving."

What can I add? Only that I must have been terrified that Blumenfeld would gang up on me with Melanie, join her in her version of our relationship, and forget everything he knew about me. I refer to him as if he has joined with her already, as a "them." Yet he is still himself, and is very distinct from Melanie. He keeps asking the key questions which, I think, he hopes will allow me to see who Melanie has become.

And Melanie herself? Blumenfeld never told me anything about their talks together. Those were confidential. I doubt that he ever loved her, certainly not in the ways that I did. And without loving her, what could he ever know about her? No, I don't think he ever knew her very well. And during this session, I couldn't step into her soul, I didn't know what she knew, and she told me so little that it would be rash to speculate, worse to judge her. I trust my dream of her walking with me on the lake, more than anything I might know about her from this session.

And Emily and Telesporus, what can I say about them? Very little, but something. I know them, you might say, intimately. But they also have their own existence, and their own relationship with one another, which they choose to let me in on at times like this— when I might have been pushed back into madness without their presence and clarity.

Emily is a musician, a talented cellist with long red hair, a thirteen-year-old girl whose whole being is finely tuned to sounds. She came to me when I was an adolescent, when I was just a little older than she. She embodies my wish to kill myself—ironically in order to be missed, wanted, loved, and she brings to that wish the capacity to act on it. She's aware of hypocrisy, the treachery of words, in the way that perhaps only adolescents are—with the hope that someone can be and will be always truthful with her, will meet her in her own truths. When she cannot speak truthfully herself, she withholds speech, she stops thinking altogether, she stops all sound in the world. Yet she, more than anyone I have ever known, is attuned to all sound, all speech, including the speech of leaves, the different languages of the universe very few can hear. Her nemesis, if I can name just one, is her tendency to wish for things that can't ever be. In this session, she saves me from unbearable longing by forming a wish like this—for something apparently impossible—and then she saves me again by wanting to die as she takes in Melanie's response. Who is Emily really? It would be tempting to say that she is I, or that she is not, but neither is quite true. She's still alive, that much I know.

Which brings me to Telesporus himself. He was my protector as a child, my right-hand guardian angel in the flesh, and later, when I was an adolescent, he also became a poetic presence, a guide, and now you might say even he is a psychotherapist of sorts, when he speaks with Emily. Telesporus knows more than anyone, just about everything. When I brought Blumenfeld my paintings and my box, he hovered over Blumenfeld (was he crying that day?) to comfort him. He also steps in and saves Emily when Blumenfeld does not even seem to know that she exists. Telesporus is an angel, a mythic being, the one who came to me as if in response to Rainer Maria Rilke's first elegy: "Who, if I cried, would hear me among the angelic orders?" He was, in a way, Blumenfeld's precursor, and before Blumenfeld's arrival in my life, the one I counted on most for my sanity.

I leave this particular session less intact and yet stronger. My suffering does not pass unnoticed. My connections to Emily and Telesporus, and to Blumenfeld himself, ensure that this time my suffering will not pass without meaning.

But it is by now the third week in July, and Blumenfeld will soon be going away for his vacation in August.

80

At home, I enter Macbeth's world, where night and darkness are inseparable from the hauntings of battle on the wild Scottish moors, and the dreams that abuse sleep are indistinguishable from the lives of the characters who dream these dreams:

> *Now o'er the one half-world*
> *Nature seems dead, and wicked dreams abuse*
> *The curtain'd sleep.*

I try to sleep in the humid July heat. When I drift off, Melanie comes and looms over me, as animal as the unbearable longing for succor, for comfort. I remember the soft flannel of her shirt against my cheek. I hear her voice in my ears, her full laughter. Her hand stroked my hair. When she seemed most dead, most hopelessly lost from my life, it had always seemed to me that in my despair she would come to comfort me. I wake up, unable to shake off the dream of her: more a presence than a dream.

It occurs to me that the dream is an omen that Melanie will call me or she will come back fully, as herself.

After hours of waiting, I am stunned into recognizing that she might be gone from my life forever. The hours pass, and nothing enters my wordless longing except the desire for escape, death, oblivion. I remain wide-eyed awake—restless and exhausted. Everywhere I turn it seems as though there is no way out of the terror of loss (which persists, as if I have not lost the person I most loved

already), except through death. Emily is alive within me, and I feel
her presence vividly.

Telesporus is nowhere to be found.

Late in the night, I sit up on my little green sofa in shorts and
a gray T-shirt, making my death plans and writing out my hand-
written will. These acts of finality will finally, I imagine, bring
Melanie back into my life.

But what would it mean to Ben to have me leave him forever
without any goodbye? I promised him that there would be time
to say goodbye.

The phone rings, a wrong number. I thought it would be Melanie calling. I lie down, still waiting for her phone call.

*Gloved hands come into a place enclosed by glass. The hands are huge.
They drive needles under my skin. Cold, I am so cold. Yet I am burning
under bright lights. The hands come into the glass where my skin burns to
be soothed, where my body trembles to be held. The hands are cold and they
hurt. I lie naked and exposed, my skin burning, watching light reflected
on glass.*

I get out of bed and draw a warm bath, climb into the tub and
slide under the water's surface, trying to sooth the burning on my
skin. I lie in the water by the soft light of a single candle and listen
to Handel's *Water Music*. Finally, my skin stops burning. I towel
dry myself and move under the cool, smooth sheets, naked. Any
layer of clothing would hurt my skin too much to sleep. The cool
sheets soothe me just enough to fall asleep.

81

The following day I see Blumenfeld. Waiting for him for just a few minutes in the waiting room is extraordinarily difficult. I wonder if he has moved away, gone away early on vacation, or if I have come at the wrong time. Then he pokes his head around the corner and says, "Hello, Annie."

I sit down in my chair. It lifts my feet lightly off the ground. "Last night I kept waiting for Melanie to call me, but she didn't. She's not going to call, is she?" I don't pause for an answer, but go on: "If only I had admitted that what happened, I mean my part, the gun and the knife and everything that followed, was really my fault, just mine, maybe she would have been different." I am willing to undo the knowledge of yesterday this quickly.

"Maybe she would, and maybe not, Annie," Blumenfeld says.

"That was not the woman I knew and loved all those years," I say, thinking of the Melanie in my dream.

"Yes, Annie, she was," Blumenfeld says. "And do you know how I know that?"

"How?"

"You've brought her to me, in your journals, a really remarkable record, Annie. You were constantly trying to make a particular woman appear, and trying to make another one disappear. Then, and right now too, Annie." My perception of this is hidden so deep, I can hardly find it, but I feel it as Blumenfeld speaks.

"Last night, very late, I had this terrible burning on my skin, when I was waiting for her to call. The phone rang and it wasn't her, and I wanted to die, to kill myself, thinking that then, no, being quite sure, that then she would love me again."

"Once you lived in a world where it felt as if everyone wanted you dead, and maybe they did sometimes," Blumenfeld muses. "If you fulfilled their wishes and died, then maybe they could love you. You've toyed with this way of being loved, very dangerously, for a long, long time. This isn't new, is it?" he asks.

Such a statement finds its way within as much by silence as by speech. I am quiet for a few minutes.

"Yes, I've always imagined dying when I was afraid of being hated, or worse, of just being forgotten. You know, if I was dead, Melanie would miss me, then maybe she would realize . . ." I look at Blumenfeld.

"No, Annie," he interrupts. "The moment you feel your life depends upon what someone else does or does not do, that very moment, you get catapulted into another world, another time. It's not accurate to call it the past, because it's here, with you. And you've lived with this devastating, life-threatened feeling all your life. It's hard to see into it. The pain of it is so unbearable that it surrounds you. When there are no words for this, no thoughts, then it can only be lived out."

Listening to Blumenfeld is like driving through a very dense fog. Shapes appear only within a few feet of the headlights, and then go past. I feel Blumenfeld's words reverberate all through me, but I can't hold on to them.

"I don't understand a word of what you're saying. Not really." I look at him as if he is far, far away—because his words are so close to my unspoken knowing.

"Sometimes words get in the way," he remarks gently, but I am not interested in this line of thinking. I feel a grief beginning deep within and rising up over me. I want to stop it from flooding me, or at least to put up a levy, to allay it.

"Right now," I tell him, "I just want to find Melanie again, in any way I can, and if I can't, I'm going to die."

"Annie, you are looking in the wrong direction," Blumenfeld says.

"What do you mean?" I ask.

"When you turn your eyes out, looking for a particular response from Melanie, looking for Melanie to come back to you in a particular way right now (it's Melanie right now, but it's been many people), you don't notice the ghosts dancing behind you. Turn around slowly and look." Blumenfeld points behind me.

"Look for what? I am not going to live through this. I am going to die." I am yelling at him as the waters rise.

"You are in a real dilemma right now, Annie. You can keep looking for Melanie, or you can know that it's not really Melanie you are looking for. But then you would have to turn away from looking to find her, just for a moment, and if you stop this terrible vigilance, then you feel you'll die—you'll turn away from looking and you'll die."

I look wildly around the room and my eyes find a statue of a little girl, a red clay statue. Behind her, the blinds on the window are opened slightly so that I can see the glass pane of the window, which I've never seen in this room before. The sun on the glass rivets my attention.

"I am going to die. The glass, the lights, the hands coming at me, poking things into me, and sticking needles under my skin. I'm so cold, and I'm waiting and waiting for something, for someone."

"This is good, Annie. Your mind is starting to shape something you really must know right now," Blumenfeld says quietly. As he says this, I feel the electricity of new connections.

"Ben. In the poem I wrote to him, there's a line, 'Outside the glass,' and I was seeing him at a window, but there wasn't a window. And now I'm seeing him in his bubble bed, but it's all glass, he's a baby, and the light is intense—my God, it's an incubator."

I get up and move toward the window, as if this would resolve my confusion, and sit down again. "The light burns my skin. That's the feeling of waiting now. I'm going to die."

I am thinking of a baby's body—curled and sucking, her skin the finest silk. Eyes open and seeing everything. Her breath a little beating behind her belly button. Without secrets. Her whole life rests in that body of hers, in the hope of skin against skin—human warmth. She is freezing cold. She startles and cries, flails, startles and cries. She is burning.

I look up at Blumenfeld. "Do I matter so little that no one can remember me?"

Blumenfeld leans forward, "Tell me another way, Annie, if you can. Remember how dense I can be. Tell me another way."

"I can't remember exactly when, but my mother told me that I was hospitalized as a baby twice—I think the first time was at eleven months—for hemorrhaging diarrhea—or a virus—I don't remember. The second time, this is less clear, I was eighteen months old, but I have no idea why I was in the hospital then. When I came home after the first time, I couldn't let my mother out of my sight. She'd leave the room and I'd scream. She'd have to pick me up, carry me." I pause, remembering my dream of Ben saying, "Carry me, carry me," the child's chanted terror of someone vanishing.

"The second time," I go on, "my mother didn't say why I went back into the hospital, but when I came home the second time, I didn't recognize anyone, not even my family. My mother said that I didn't even recognize my toys."

I try to grasp that—that turning away from everything I knew and loved—that illusion of being able to turn from everything and everyone connected to me.

"And you almost died?" Blumenfeld asks.

I have tried to erase it. Even in daylight, I have erased it, and the tracks are now visible where I have left it.

"How do you know this? I'd forgotten all about it. I can't even tell you when she told me this now, but I did almost die. I was very sick the first time, and after the first time, my father wanted to take me back to the hospital and to leave me there. My mother was teasing me when she said to me, 'I told him babies aren't for sale; you can't just return them,' but I knew she was serious too. She said that he couldn't bear the sound of my crying and he wanted them to 'take you back.' I was in an intensive care nursery, my mother said, and they weren't allowed to visit that first time, for a whole month they were not allowed to visit."

This baby's body cannot belong to me. My parents could not have vanished like that.

I begin to sob. "I want Melanie, I want her voice, I want her to hold me, and it's hopeless, it's absolutely hopeless."

"Yes, they didn't come and didn't come, and out of your hopelessness you built yourself a little hope," Blumenfeld says, as if he is telling me a story. "But you could remember them, even if they had 'forgotten' you—and you would wait and wait and wait for them to come to you. And if they still did not come, you could make them appear in your imagination. But this was never really satisfying, no, not really. And so you are still waiting, Annie."

I pull my knees up to my chest and hold my rabbit and sob, feeling what Blumenfeld is saying to me, and beyond the endless present of waiting and waiting, an unspeakable grief opens itself to me and flows over my whole body.

I see the dark back of my father's coat retreating from me the last time I saw him alive; I feel myself disappearing in the wordless cab ride with a social worker, when I was ten and my sister eleven, taken from my mother for four long years to live in a children's home, seemingly forgotten; the film continues with friends who mysteriously left me for reasons I could never fully grasp; I see Galle and Margaret Mary move away from me; Emily goes under, a third time, and Telesporus turns away too, as he moves closer to the nameless others; and the film stops with the image of Melanie in her navy-blue suit.

"I've lost everyone, I've made them all go away," I whisper. "And it must be like this, looking out on a battlefield and seeing, no, knowing that everyone is dead. Or watching a trainload of your friends and family taken away to the camps."

"No, Annie, that's not quite true—you weren't able to make them come toward you, and you didn't make anyone go away either," Blumenfeld says. He moves his chair toward me a few inches. "And yes, it felt like the death of the whole world. But then there's little Annie; she's very much alive and with you. And that's remarkable, because you don't always treat her very well."

"Yes, you're right, I don't," I admit.

"Little Annie, she's not going to be with you if you won't listen to her," Blumenfeld warns me.

I raise my face from my wet hands and look up suddenly. This catches my attention. "What do you mean, if I won't listen?"

Blumenfeld smiles at me. "She's right here with us. She's been right here in the room listening to us the whole time. The experiences you keep having with Melanie (or whomever), little Annie just hates them. She's exhausted from staying on this treadmill—if you had done this, if only you hadn't done that. She wants the future, yours and hers together, to be unknowable."

"I know the future is unknowable," I counter.

"Do you really? Or do you believe, if only I could be this way or that way, Melanie would come to me as I want her, as I desperately want her?"

"The second way, you know that," I reply, feeling a bit defensive.

"You bet you do! And do you know what? When your father is tearing your insides apart and your mother is attacking you from behind, you'd better be able to imagine that you can get them to do what you want. You'd better be able to believe that you can do the right thing and that it will make all the difference!"

I think of the extraordinary power of that illusion.

"Yes, and sometimes I could. Then my mother would come to me and she'd hold me, she'd comfort me. I'd actually feel like a child for a moment or so. But most of the time, she didn't seem to know I was there. And my father, he played with me. He played as no one else ever played with me—I'd hold onto his hands and ride his shoe up and down; we'd go out and gather flowers in the big field behind the house, and once we found kittens and brought them home to surprise my sister; we played Mr. Potato Man on the floor and made the potato characters talk; and my father would sweep me up off my feet and dance with me sometimes too."

"If only you could repeat, Annie, remember exactly and repeat exactly the steps of your part of that dance, somehow you might be able to magically make him turn into that father, the one who played and danced—when he came into your room at night and unzipped his pants and you felt terrified?"

"Yes. How do you know this?"

"Little Annie, she tells me, and I listen. She wants you to start to really listen to her. She just wants to feel and be whatever—happy, sad, mischievous, frightened, mad—whatever—and for you to let her be, and to let the people you love be—whatever—because the future is really unknowable."

As Blumenfeld says this to me, I realize that it is barely imaginable. The future has already been laid down in the vanishing tracks of the past. It is as though I have forgotten that those tracks were laid down someplace within my child's body. This child could already foretell the future through the past.

"You know this poem, I'm sure," I tell Blumenfeld. "It's from Shakespeare—Our revels now are ended?"

"Yes, but tell me what you are thinking now, Annie."

I recite:

> *Our revels now are ended. These our actors,*
> *As I foretold you, were all spirits, and*
> *Are melted into air, into thin air;*
> *And, like the baseless fabric of this vision,*
> *The cloud-capp'd towers, the gorgeous palaces,*
> *The solemn temples, the great globe itself,*
> *Yea, all which it inherit, shall dissolve,*
> *And, like this insubstantial pageant faded,*
> *Leave not a rack behind. We are such stuff*
> *As dreams are made on; and our little life*
> *Is rounded with a sleep.*

I imagine a child's body before words, before plays and illusions and deceptions, before she was broken. Bathed in a passionate sweetness, she is sleeping and alive. And, because death is so near, she radiates her own beauty.

"Yes, little Annie wants you to be with her and listen to her like that," Blumenfeld says, "just exactly like that."

I lean back in the black chair and close my eyes and listen to the soft rhythm of Blumenfeld's breathing.

In Blumenfeld's company, the revels in "Our revels now are ended" become the plays of my life, on which my survival has depended. All my life, it becomes clear, I've been living within a particular play in the endless past, which becomes most vivid when, in Blumenfeld's words, "you feel your life depends upon what someone else does or does not do." Then, "catapulted into another world, another time," I play the scenes which are reenactments of trauma. Ben and I are alike in this. This kind of play is monotonous and grim, as Lenore Terr tells us in her invaluable book on children's experiences of trauma, *Too Scared to Cry*. Unlike other forms of play, traumatic play creates more anxiety than it dispels. Blumenfeld describes it in this way: "The pain of it is so unbearable that it surrounds you. When there are no words for this, no thoughts, then it can only be lived out."

It is as if Blumenfeld is saying to me, "These our actors, as I foretold you, were all spirits." The spirits of my play are indeed ghosts—missing parents who loomed over me, even as I waited for them to return. My fear of being abandoned, a terror in my body like the terror of imminent death, is the play I have lived all my life trying to escape. Just as Ben has fled his terror of abandonment and burning all his life. Fleeing my own terror, I created a play of vigilance and waiting—waiting for the appearance of my (remembered) mother and father, or waiting for their surrogates in later years. But, as Blumenfeld notes, to stop this vigilance is to know the terror of "I will die."

Later in my childhood and in my adolescence, apparently there were elaborations on this little play of terror: if I died, if I actively chose to die, I might be missed and loved then. Or, if I could not manage to die, perhaps if I could play my part just right (as Blumenfeld points out to me), I could magically find the feelings and gestures that would conjure up the mother who sometimes comforted me, the father who swept me up off the floor and sometimes danced with me. Who has ever loved and not learned to do this— to conjure oneself and others with the most loving gestures?

But for me, this play of conjuring became a haunting obsession. Waiting for Melanie to call me, I conjured her up and then felt as if I would die if I could not be in her presence. And when I saw she did not call, I wanted to die. Probably, had I dared to feel my rage that night, I would also have wanted to kill her for instilling that kind of fear in me. But the fear was in me long before I met Melanie. In fact, in my attempts to avoid the fear of death, to dim the life within my child's body that knew the nearness of death, I was living into tragic possibilities.

Lenore Terr describes the terror of trauma as the overwhelming, unexpected fear of death. It is human to fear death, but what marks a traumatic fear of dying is the victim's close acquaintance with death. A child will reconstruct his or her life under and around and behind this fear of dying, anything to avoid facing straight into it, ever again, as Ben did, and as I did.

I wonder if the basic tragedy of trauma is not so much the fear of dying as it is the denial of death itself. Ironically, this denial does not work, because it sits beside the grindingly repetitious (and sometimes dangerous) plays we create to transform mortality into invulnerability. The denial of death sits beside a repeated fear of unexpected annihilation for those among us who know fear much too intimately.

Blumenfeld gives me a way to know and reenter my experience of terror. When he says, "You are in a real dilemma . . . you can keep looking for Melanie, or you can know it's not really Melanie you are looking for," he isn't just pointing out that Melanie may be symbolic of someone else, he is also giving me a way out of the tragic endings to my play.

My grim little play needs another ending—one that is real, and therefore satisfying and healing. Blumenfeld reminds me that I've not lost "everyone." I still have a connection with "little Annie" (his name for the "little pieces" as one child), whom I admittedly "don't always treat very well." Through this relationship with her (a relationship within myself), he shows me how much I want to be able to be alive in my body and in all my feelings.

In this way, Blumenfeld poses another ending to ongoing play of my real life: I might learn to live with an unknowable future, unknowable in all ways except for the certainty of death. Knowing that "our little life is rounded with a sleep," I might be free to live fully and to love again.

82

Acorns, green in my hands; I pick them up from my yard. And yearn for a lost life, a lost self. I hold a little green breast in my hand, and desire has many doors.

I dream of little acorns popping down onto the roof; they touch me, here and here, on the small button, alive. Joan of Arc, courageous heretic, was burned for telling the truth about her voices, whom she insisted were substantial and touched her. How she yearned for them, missed them, at times.

I stand in the shower, a hot evening, weeping because I have not heard from or seen Telesporus in days.

With Blumenfeld's voice in my left ear (himself away in the land where analysts go to vacation in August), I watch a father with his two daughters outside a bookstore. The little girls sit on a brick wall, one four or five, the other maybe six, one in green overalls and a white undershirt, the other in a red and violet flowered dress. They sit side by side, blond-haired children, eating Skittles. Their feet, shod in red high-top sneakers, dangle and swing. The father, graying-blond and blue-eyed, tucks one under each arm and makes the chugging noises of an airplane starting and taking off. The two small girls giggle, find my eyes and burst into laughter. Whenever he stops and puts them back on the wall, "Daddy, Daddy, come here, once more, oh plllease!" And off he goes, one under each arm,

taking a turn around the building. They dangle, limp with laughter, one under each arm. I turn away, still laughing. Tears have
covered my face.

For the first time, I realize that Blumenfeld's eyes are brown, not
blue. My father's eyes were blue, blue-gray.

Behind the caverns of my soul's face, a blue eye is weeping again.
Whose eyes will light up to see Ben, when I am gone?

I find myself often in tears. Grief runs its fine rivulets down my
face at unexpected moments. I no longer paint the light on windows.

83

On a beautiful, bright morning the first week in August, Ben decides to play outside again.

He comes into the playroom and hops up and down.

"Let's go out, out, out today," he exclaims. "Oh, let's take Tea Bags, too!"

I smile at his antics. "You are all ready to go and we will go, but first we will mark off the calendar, OK?"

I pull down the calendar and give Ben a green Magic Marker to color over the red X. He counts the remaining X's until he comes to the circle.

"Two more times?" he asks in a small voice.

"Three more times including our goodbye day," I clarify, pointing to the circle.

He stands very still, all the liveliness gone now. He does not move or speak or cry. I know better now than to ask a direct question or make a remark. He will simply ignore me, as he has before. I feel his desolation and mine. What are the words, the sounds we might whisper to one another in this frozen frame? *Stay away fish for me I had a bad dream don't leave me please you are my mommy and now it is morning again I want a tall shining hat paint me a horse I don't want any turkey did I kill her? I am shot the baby bear is shot come to our hideout a house is on fire Tea Bags tell me what to say tell me.* Ben is remote, struggling alone. I ache for him.

Suddenly I have an idea. "How would you like to take a picture today, Ben? Jill can take a picture of you and me and Tea Bags."

"With a real camera?" he wonders.

"Yep. A real camera, and you can keep it," I tell him.

"I can keep it to remember you by," he says softly. Then the excitement he entered with comes back into his whole body.

"Put Tea Bags on your hand so I can talk to him!"

I put the puppet on my hand.

"You're gonna have your picture took, Tea Bags! You got to get your hair combed," he says, critically smoothing it down.

I offer him my pocket comb and he casually tugs a bit at Tea Bags' yellow fur. He combs his own hair too.

I planned to take pictures on the last day, so when we arrive at the main office, I cue Jill, one of the secretaries, into my change of plans. Ben dances from foot to foot, impatient, as he waits for us. We go outside, and Ben and I sit on the steps by the playground and have a picture there, and Jill takes another with Ben on a high swing and me standing beside him. She uses a Polaroid, so the pictures develop within minutes. I hand the pictures to Ben.

"You pick the one you like best. One for you and one for me," I tell him.

He picks the one with us sitting down, Tea Bags between us, my arm around him, and hands me the other.

"You look at me every day and you don't forget," he says solemnly.

"I won't forget," I say. "How could I ever forget?"

How can I ever forget you in this place of widening circles drawn into the air above us, this place we have come to, Ben, to witness wind leaves snow light leaving?

We walk along in silence. Ben bends down in the grass and lifts up a leaf with something on it.

"Look, a caterpillar! It got born from this leaf," he announces, extending it to me.

I bend over the leaf. "Yes, it is a caterpillar. Born from this leaf?" I ask skeptically.

"I got a whole bag of leaves and there was one of 'em in it. I didn't put him in there," Ben says, as if he has cracked a code.

"So the leaf did? Or all of them did?" I ask.

"Yep!"

"An egg was laid on a leaf perhaps," I suggest.

Ben looks at me as if I do not have good sense. "No, Annie. Eggs you eat for breakfast."

"So the leaf had him," I say tentatively.

Ben nods. I do not argue. To him the idea of an egg is outrageous.

We walk in silence again, along the garden and down a road lined with white morning glories. I carry Tea Bags along, and Ben looks up at the puppet.

"Will I ever get to visit you, Tea Bags?" he asks.

I give Tea Bags words. "Yes. I will still be here. Annie is leaving me in the playroom. Only she won't be here."

What is the vanishing point where buildings melt into air this detonation of doors windows toys signs Ben at the door?

"I'll miss you," he says to me, and reaches for my hand.

"And I will miss you, too, Ben. And I will not forget," I tell him. We walk, listening to the sound of bees and a lawn mower. The silence comes down on us again. We have gone so far beyond words.

"Who will I see when you are gone?" he asks.

"You will see someone else, but I don't know who that will be, for certain," I answer.

What are the sounds we will whisper to one another in this new territory where nothing is certain?

"No," he says suddenly. "I don't want anybody else." And he releases my hand and runs ahead of me.

We have come full circle back to the garden. Ben bends over the flowers to smell them. I catch up with him and squat down beside him. He looks longingly at the flowers, then at me, and again at the flowers.

"I wish I could have those!" he says, his eyes wide as he scans the array of red, yellow, orange and violet flowers.

I can see a man gardening just a short distance away.

"We can't just take these flowers," I tell Ben. "But we can ask that man for some of them."

Ben leads the way, but when he gets to the man, he stops and motions me forward.

"You ask," he whispers loudly.

"This is Ben," I tell the elderly gardener, "and he covets your beautiful flowers."

The man bends down to negotiate with Ben privately, and Ben comes away quite pleased. We return to the flower bed.

"He said I can have five. I want one of them, and that and that and that one," Ben says, pointing.

"Go ahead and pick them, but watch out for bees," I say.

He kneels and yanks up five flowers, one of each color and a white morning glory.

"Smell 'em, Tea Bags!" he says, offering the bunch to Tea Bags's nose. Ben puts his own face down in the bunch to smell it.

"This one gots a little bug in it," he notices, showing me the morning glory.

"Oh, so it has," I say, and I add, mischievously, "Do you think the flower made that bug?"

"No, Annie. Just leaves do that!"

Inside, we find a paper cup for his flowers and go back to the playroom to glue his picture of us on a sheet of sturdy construction paper. Ben looks at the picture, standing very still, and then at me.

I feel myself fade into the stillness of his brown eyes, as if Ben is photographing me—a span of time, consciousness, discovery, memory—coming together in that long look.

He smiles a small smile, waves to me and to Tea Bags and leaves us. Ready to go and reluctant to go, he stands at the door a moment, clinging to the doorjamb, then comes back to me.

"I believe you do know the lady I will see in the fall," he declares and runs off before I can comment.

Ben and I are each playing beside the shadow of our own perspective or story of loss as we anticipate leaving one another. As we listen to one another here, our shadows touch and the silence between us becomes very full. We go together into this silence— the territory of facing a goodbye, rather than being helplessly shattered by another loss.

I introduce the idea of taking pictures while Ben is immersed in his unvoiced inner struggle with my leaving. After he marks off the calendar, as we've been doing for three weeks now, he stands very still, remote in his feelings and thoughts. I have been making tentative remarks about saying goodbye during these moments previously, but Ben seemed not to hear me. Perhaps he would have heard me and responded this time, I do not know. I feel his desolation, and my own—wordless, beyond words. I hope that picture-taking will give him a concrete way to convey some of his thoughts and feelings about ending with me.

Ben knows immediately that the picture is meant as a keepsake. "I can keep it to remember you by," he says, and later, "You look at me every day and you don't forget." His words come into me and create a cryptic language that holds what is happening within me.

In the midst of our silence, laden with words and time and sorrow and rehearsed loss, Ben and I are not overwhelmed by our feelings. There is an underlying joy in this session that comes back to me as I write. Ben reminds me of the differences in our perspectives, he brings me new discoveries, he shows me beauty in the world we inhabit together as he picks his bunch of flowers from the gardener.

As we play between our silent walking we are light-headed, teasing. Ben finds a caterpillar on a leaf and says, "Look, a caterpillar! It got born from this leaf." I am a little skeptical because I hold a different view about categories of species in the world and about reproduction. Ben hears my skepticism, but he makes an effort to include me in his discovery: "I got a whole bag of leaves and there was one of 'em in it. I didn't put him in there." "So the leaf did? Or all of them did?" I ask. As I try to understand his view of birth,

I pose two alternatives: a birth by one leaf or by many. "Yep!" Ben answers, rejecting my categories by including both of them in his affirmation. I sense that to try to give Ben a lesson on how caterpillars come into the world will not only be lost on him, but I will also miss something here—for he brings me a bit of whimsy in his view of the world that is not unlike the wonder I feel in the presence of Telesporus. Nevertheless, I persist with my own point of view: "An egg was laid on a leaf perhaps." Now it is Ben who teaches me, "No, Annie. Eggs you eat for breakfast." Eating and birth have become separated for Ben, as they are not for a very young child, and he speaks to me as if I do not know this yet, with a tone of exasperated patience. We never understand one another wholly, because each of us lives and talks within the borders of a particular perspective. We are stitched to our own ways of knowing, "glued to our shadows," as the philosopher Hannah Arendt says. Yet, as we play, Ben and I understand one another well enough. Our shadows touch. Ben is full of discovery, then patiently exasperated; I am skeptical, then enchanted by another way of seeing.

As Ben and I face into the loss of our time together, the stakes of how we understand and respond to one another are very high. We are unable to escape the limits of our different perspectives, our own constraining and compelling stories. There is no place I can stand as a therapist outside and apart from my own shadow and understand Ben's and my play: I have no transcendent or omniscient view, no expert or foolproof understanding, and I am not and will never be entirely "cured" of my own suffering. We play.

I try to take seriously the old woman in my dream weeks ago who sewed my shadow onto my heels. I try to notice what should be obvious, but what I have to struggle to grasp in this year of my most intensive clinical training is that this story about Ben in all his suffering is also a story about my suffering; it contains all the ways I have worked to heal both myself and Ben, to heal myself and Melanie, and myself and Blumenfeld too.

Our playing also reveals how Ben has unwittingly healed me. His story fills the drama of our play, his feelings spill over into each scene; I respond to Ben when he comes to play with me where our shadows meet. I play with him, especially as we are saying goodbye, in the place of my deepest wounding and loss.

84

The last time I meet with Rachael, it is not at the Psychoanalytic Institute but a new office building in another part of Chicago, where she is consulting that day. I resent this breaking of tradition—the marble stairs unclimbed, the little note above the buzzer I would not read again, Rachael not sitting at her desk, not opening the bottom drawer for slippers, the piece of hard candy she would not offer to me today.

We meet in a conference room, at a long table of mostly empty chairs. I am leaving her in the wrong place and I resent it.

I take my notes and tapes from my briefcase. Her eyes catch the light. She wants to hear all the details of my work. We listen to parts of the tapes. She asks me to read my summary notes and the sketch of my own interpretations. She wants to read them herself. It is as if nothing has changed; I am not seeing her for the last time at all. But I am not so practiced at self-deception that I believe this. I watch her reading. The light glints off the frames of her bifocals. She seems very old today. I realize that she is two or even three generations older than I.

Rachael looks up from her reading and asks, "When Ben says to Tea Bags, 'Will I ever get to visit you, Tea Bags?', I wonder if he is also asking if he will ever get to visit you again."

"Oh, I hadn't thought of that. I must have missed that question in his play," I reply.

Rachael nods. "I don't know if he was asking you that, but he may have been."

I tell her that I plan to return to visit each of the children in the coming year. "I thought I'd say something to each one of them in the last session."

Rachael blinks and looks startled. "Continuity of interest and caring are not harmful to disturbed children," she says gently, gathering force, "but to offer, much less promise, future visits during the termination phase of treatment—that might be harmful." This is not what I want to hear. I look down at my fingers.

When I look up again, I see that Rachael is studying me. "Ah, Annie, you have come to love these children?"

"Yes, very much," I say, wondering how in the world this could be a problem.

"Of course you have," she says gently. "And you want to see them again—because you'll miss them—you, for yourself?"

"Yes," I admit, wondering if this is something I should not want.

She persists, "Can you imagine that to promise you will visit would allow the children to unrealistically cling to this relationship? Can you imagine that that would rob Ben of the real sadness, anger, and meaningful accomplishment of a clear ending?"

"I can imagine that, yes, but—"

"Annie, promises of visits are not for the child; they are for the therapist, if they are made at this time."

I myself did not know what would benefit Ben. But I wanted very badly to continue seeing him and the other children. So I treaded carefully answering her.

"Isn't it true that a crucial piece of the work of saying goodbye is a rehearsal of loss, but the loss has to be bearable?" I ask.

"Yes, and you have already begun the work of emotionally saying goodbye. There are other ways to make a loss bearable. Think about it, Annie. What emerged as significant to Ben in this session was the idea of remembering, despite the loss of contact with you. This is implied in the phrases "Don't forget" and "I'll miss you," as well as his fantasy that you know the person he will see in the fall."

I nod, listening.

"It is too difficult, just now, for Ben to anticipate the future without you. He has to reject the idea of a substitute, because he doesn't want to lose you. He breaks contact by running ahead of you after saying, 'No. I don't want anybody else.'"

"And, ideally, at some point, he will want to see someone else and not me?" I ask.

"Yes, that is absolutely necessary."

"And if I see him too soon, or if he holds on to my promise of visiting, maybe that won't happen?" I ask.

"I don't know, Annie," Rachael admits. "He believes you know the person he will be seeing already. That illusion will work for him as an internal bridge from you to that new person."

I sit in silence, rare with Rachael. I don't want to be here. I don't want to feel anything. I certainly don't know what to say. My sense of grief will not allow me to remain insulated from my feelings, however. I feel my eyes swimming.

"You could not have done the powerful work you've done with Ben, unless you loved him," Rachael says.

My tears brim over and I let them.

"It is just plain hard to say goodbye, isn't it?"

I feel the largeness of grief, how grief will not let you hide from the awareness of time passing and death, or from life itself, going on in all its unexpected ways. I look out the window, a little window next to the long table, into a rectangle of light.

How old she is. How fierce. How set in her ways. What authority she has. I don't agree with her on this. But how much I will miss her! I say none of this to Rachael.

"I will miss seeing you, too," she says, placing in front of me a package wrapped in white tissue paper with a blue bow. I open it and find a blue-and-white porcelain mug with a little blue-and-white top. All around it, blue fish swim in the same motion, around and around.

I brought nothing to give her. There is no promise of seeing her again. "I don't have anything to give you," I tell her.

"Yes, you have. Over and over again, every time we've met, you've given me something."

I wonder if she is being sentimental now.

"No," she says, as if reading my thoughts. "You are young, you are a new generation coming up. You will change this practice of ours and you will make a whole new world of it." She pauses, smiles, almost to herself. "It isn't often that the old get to learn from the young."

I go out into the afternoon sunlight. Maybe it isn't so terrible leaving her here. Who am I kidding? Yes, it is terrible. I sense that I won't ever see her again. And so, even as I am leaving, I continue to invent her, and her life within me goes on and on. Yes, I will change this practice. Yes, I feel her rising and billowing within me even as she lets me go from her.

85

The morning of my last session with Ben, I stand in the hallway talking to Mary Louise. I think of her now, that daily presence in my life and the lives of the children, and wonder if she has any idea of the power of her own presence—it is as unbroken as my own breathing to me, and one does not usually notice that one is breathing.

I see Ben out of the corner of my eye. He waves and I wave back. When I finish my conversation with Mary Louise, I look down the hallway and he is still standing there, looking at us. He turns and goes into his classroom.

Later, as we walk in silence down the hall to the playroom, Ben asks softly,

"Is this our 'last time' time today?"

"Yes. This is our last time and goodbye day," I answer simply.

"I want to do something special today," he tells me.

"Have you got something planned?" I wonder aloud.

He shakes his head no.

As we enter the playroom, he notices a stuffed rabbit on the toy shelves. He goes over and picks it up, then turns to me:

"Oh boy, a bunny. Did you buy this for me?" he asks. I wonder what yearning this last meeting stirs up for Ben.

"No, that rabbit has been here for quite a while, Ben," I tell him.

"I will play with him today," he decides, and carries the rabbit and Tea Bags over to my desk.

"Put Tea Bags on your hand," he says.

I do so, already recognizing Ben's request (how many times has he said this?), and my gesture, as a memory in the making.

Ben stands and looks at the puppet a long time, then cocks his head and smiles. What is he seeing?

"Let's do something special," Ben says.

"What would you like to do special with me today?" I ask.

"Make me into a Indian clown," he says seriously.

I lift his face and draw in soft oil crayon—violet eyebrows, a red nose and cheeks, a violet dot on his chin. Ben also wants hearts on the backs of his hands and war-paint stripes on his arms. An Indian clown. Fierce and magical.

I see that he is studying me as I draw.

"Are you feeling sad, Ben, or just standing still and watching?"

"Just standing still," he says. "Paint me a smile too."

I paint on a big smile, as a final touch, and then I gaze at him.

"I look pretty good, don't I?" he asks. I could not have spoken it, the ethereal beauty of this real child before me.

"Yes, you do, for a fact," I tell him.

Then he is off, gathering up Tea Bags and the rabbit, and in a few minutes we are walking across the field together in silence. The morning sun slants over the green and brown grass, throwing our shadows before us. Ben is quiet, subdued, walking beside me. Under the sharpening shadow of the minutes passing, we walk into our last session together.

We reach a large sandbox at the far edge of the field. Ben puts the rabbit and Tea Bags on the side ledge and climbs in. Then he climbs back out.

"We got to take off our shoes," he announces, tugging off shoes and socks and letting them drop on the grass. He swings his feet over the ledge of the sandbox and watches me remove my shoes and socks.

"Ooh, feel this sand on your feet, Annie! It's cold, and then it's hot!" he says, crossing from a shaded area of sand to an unshaded area.

He reaches over the side and tosses the pink bunny into the

sand, then begins to dig, throwing up the sand between his legs, and liberally scattering sand on me, not accidentally.

I move out of the way and wait.

Ben stops his digging and turns to me.

"But I want to throw sand on you," he complains.

"You want to, but the sand will get in my eyes. You can throw sand at the side of the sandbox, Ben."

So he does, attempting to make "sand balls" from wet sand. He digs around in the sand and finds a stick, a cup, and an old fishing bobber. He throws them at the side of the sandbox, too. Each object clanks against the wood. Then he sits still, his back to me.

"You are feeling mad because I am leaving today?" I ask slowly, wondering if his feelings can be put into words.

When he turns, his chin quivers briefly. "I don't want to," he says.

"You don't want to feel mad, bear?"

"I don't want to *be* mad," he says with determination. Now, under the sleeping shadow of this feeling, he moves in a new direction.

His eyes rove over the sand and he gets up and moves away. He spots a long piece of string alongside the sandbox, climbs out and picks it up, climbs back in and picks up the broken bobber.

"You could fish for me, like you usta!" he says, excited.

I take my cue. "And the sandbox will be our lake?" I ask.

Ben nods and squats down in the sand on the far edge of the sandbox. "Now fish for me! Throw out the line!" he shouts.

I stand outside the sandbox and tie the bobber to the string, then toss it in a high arc over to Ben. He examines the bobber and grimaces.

"No. It needs bait and a sinker!" he says in exasperation.

I tell him a bobber is supposed to float and bob, not sink, then I tie some weeds on and send it out to him again.

Ben snatches the "bait" off and gives me back an empty hook, laughing.

We repeat this sequence several times, and each time I respond in mock frustration and disappointment, fuming about the fish I want to catch.

Then Ben says, "Now let Tea Bags fish for me!"

I set up Tea Bags to fish, but I have Tea Bags be a more aggressive fisherman.

"There's a nice big fish in there, and I'm gonna get him!" the puppet declares loudly.

Ben giggles and squirms on the other side of the sandbox.

Tea Bags throws out the line and, of course, Ben rapidly unbaits it. Just as quickly, I crawl across the sandbox with Tea Bags on my arm and wind the big yellow puppet around Ben, lifting him onto my lap and tickling him. "We got you! We got you!" I chant, while Ben convulses into laughter, delighted with this ending.

Then we sit still in the sand, catching our breath. We are at the edge of a large field. What we know can't be seen easily, can't be spoken of carelessly. The big sunflowers off to our right nod in the wind.

Abruptly, Ben points beyond them and says, "Let's go back to those woods. I got something to show you."

He leads me to a place enclosed by fallen branches, with a small opening. He crawls inside and motions me in. I crawl in too and sit down beside him in a spacious, enclosed place where the sun falls through the branches, dappling the tall golden grasses. Here a child could sit, or lie down and dream. An idyllic spot, the kind of place I would have sought out myself as a child.

We sit together in silence. I am caught by the way the grass moves in the breeze, so that every color within it is distinct just before it bows and blurs with the wind. I can almost touch these colors, these moments, humming away.

I check my watch and tell Ben that our time is almost up and we need to head back.

He leads me out of his special place, and we pick up our shoes and socks and the other toys at the sandbox. Ben hands them all to me.

"Will you carry them so I can run barefoot?" he asks.

I nod and he loads up my arms.

I watch him dart and skim over the huge field, agile and fast. Then he sits in the grass and waits for me. As I walk toward him, I notice the gesture of his stillness. In the quiet recesses of consciousness, I wonder, does he hear music that plays over his earthbound body? It is not just the scope of the field and this tiny seated figure upon it that make me think this, but Ben himself, poised in that way, as if listening.

I catch up to him and we walk the rest of the way in silence together. Near the door, he asks,

"Will you take me tomorrow?"

"No, this is our last time," I tell him, and my voice cracks. I feel tears on my face.

Ben looks up at me.

"I feel very sad right now," I say. "I'm going to miss you, bear. I am already missing you."

Abruptly he hugs me and I hug him back.

He opens the door, brushing his eyes with the back of his hand.

"And you are sad, too," I state simply.

He shakes his head no. "I don't want to be sad," he says, not so much a denial, I sense, as a gritty determination to savor some elusive joy with me.

Inside, in the dim hallway, we sit down and put on our socks and shoes in silence. Then I walk Ben back to his classroom.

At lunch that day, the children I have seen all year eat with me and give me the cards they've made to surprise me. Ben's card is simple. A red heart with an I Love You message inside.

He stands by me, dazed, quiet, in the clamor and rattle of the cafeteria. Other children and adults speak to him, but he is in a trance, caught within himself, over and over, the way grass in all its colors can be caught for a second before a breeze that is repeated and repeated.

. . .

Outside on the play yard, I sit on a shady ledge and pat my lap. He comes and sits, first by me, leaning against me, then on my lap, saying nothing. He cries now, and again sits very still. He climbs down and stands a slight distance from me, smiles through his drying tears and waves.

What I see in these moments can be felt in the details, yet there is more in Ben's face than I can ever tell anyone.

He takes his place on the ball field and I watch him play for the remainder of recess, a small brown-headed boy with dark eyes among other boys and girls.

The loss of someone cherished and deeply loved is something every human being is confronted with sooner or later. But when an abandonment, a disastrous ending, imprints so much pain that life itself becomes a torment, as it had been for Ben, even as a baby, then the manner and meaning of leaving becomes vital. Such a leaving can be the shattering repetition of trauma, an ongoing nightmare from which a child tries in vain to awaken. It can also be a healing experience, even if saying goodbye is extraordinarily painful.

Almost from the beginning, Ben began the work of understanding his abandonment with me—in his fantasy play, he recreated his feelings of loss, rage and fear, and he replayed the scenes of his babyhood, discovering new feelings and new experiences. The process of therapy was incomplete by August a year later, and it was I, not Ben, who initiated this ending. It was not a fully resolved ending. At the end, Ben was still reacting with shock, and still reluctant to feel his anger and sadness.

I think it might have helped Ben to know that I would see him again for a visit in the coming year. Knowing that I was coming back, at least to visit him, might have helped him to make a transition to working with a new therapist. But I did not trust myself more than I trusted Rachael, so I did not tell Ben that I would return.

Yet I do not think this ending was traumatic for him. He was struggling with the loss still, but I did not become the bad deserting mama of his past, nor did he feel the need to become the bad little boy who caused my leaving. There were signs of potential healing. He could play with real joy even in our last session, even in the midst of his pain.

Mary Louise told me that Ben had stared into space after he made the card with her the day before, incredulously repeating, "I love her." So I knew that saying goodbye to me was not unbearable. "I love her" imprinted something new on the old story of abandonment, and it is this impression that marked our ending, and healed my loss of him as much as his loss of me.

Within any story, some things artfully repeat: a baby bear is lost and rescued, his heart stitched up; baby bears are called out of a drainpipe and taken home; a mama bear is killed and leaves, and sometimes a mama bear returns. These repetitions are themes that come back to a center, the inner sanctum and sanctuary of a story, its undisturbed mystery. For Ben and for me, this sanctuary, this central place of undisturbed mystery, had become deeply disturbing, but in the course of our relationship we played together and made a new sanctuary within each of our stories—a place where love survives unbearable loss.

86

I am sitting at my desk, reading a new book, a new author, Janet Frame—as a break from studying for my comprehensive examinations. "But it is too dark now, and the streetlights are switched on and the cats are lifting the lids of the dustbins and prowling secure and magnificent in their world, the narrow whisker-lane with smells sprouting in the hedgerows."

But it is too dark to see my book, the little black lines of print and magnificent words I love—"dustbins" and "hedgerows," not "garbage" or "bushes." Streetlights are yellow glass, thick glass atop black ornate columns, not the humming purple ones, those fluorescent curved ones, flimsy, made of aluminum rather than the noncrushable summer smells of childhood. The cats' whisker-lane was mine too, when my head didn't quite reach the top of the fence and my chin came just to the shelf on the bell-ringing Mr. Softee truck. I can see my sister in line in front of me, just a little taller, that blond, fine hair. We wait, while our guilty dimes (stolen from my mother's pocketbook) sweat in our palms, for the cold custard on our tongues. Then there were fireflies, also called lightning bugs, caught in a jar and released each night. Our mode of travel, anywhere, was running, not walking. Grown-ups were a lethargic lot in their brooding stillness and endless monotone porch-talk. We jumped, jiggled, fidgeted, turned and ran; we whispered, yelled, commanded, demanded, whimpered, taunted, sang—and kept the longest burning silence. I can see those raggedy cats with torn ears lifting the lids of the dustbins, metal lids that come off clattering and roll into the alley, where the evening's best drama takes place, before calling voices, bath time and bed, and the nightmare of the closet and under the bed and the chair coming to life, poking its long shadowy spokes right into my bed. Balanced carefully now, on the right and on the left between the hedgerows, unremembered details come back to me, the narrow whisker-lane of smells—pungent acrid sunflowers that hover above us in the dark, the sweet smell of Band-Aid on my finger, the tin-can smell as my nose presses into the screen door, the stale spun-out air, cooler than real air, that smelled of old newspapers— my mother insisted on air-conditioning us into hibernation each summer—and down I went, burrowing under three blankets, nose and all. Then there were the hedgerows—bushes, we called them, hedges or bushes, but not hedgerows, unless we were pretending to be English children, my sister and I, hovering over our plastic fine teacups under a sheet tent set up between two chairs and our beds. The hedges, they were dark, edgy, hedgy-edgy with fear. Their little leaves went from green to gray to black and stood in a tall mass, hedging me in, hiding something, someone. Any foot-fall, any shifting of leaves in the dark, the splash of night bugs on the screen window could be, but it could be—really, Mary, it could happen, really, it truly could, Mary—he would just step out of the bushes or come around the doorway or walk out of a field in daylight and take us, one by one. But it is too dark now, and the streetlights hum a little hum, a burning hum. I crawl into our bed, big sister, and feel your even breathing, a light breath in the night. I don't move so you won't waken and find me awake, yet in your sleep you move toward me and fling one skinny arm over me.

Above us, just above our heads, a circle of colored light particles spins in the darkness.

IV

EPILOGUE

Reading the bones, wetting a fingertip
to trace archaic characters, I feel
a breeze of silence flow up past my wrists,
icy. Can I speak here?
　　　　　—MARIE PONSOT, *In the Green Dark*

I have had such privilege and have wept . . .
　　　　　—STEPHEN DUNN, *Between Angels*

Terrible the rain, all night rain
that I love. So the weight of his leg
falls again like a huge tender wing
across my hipbone.
　　　　　—TESS GALLAGHER, *Moon Crossing Bridge*

Six years have now passed since I last saw Ben. I worked with Blumenfeld for another three years, and still have contact with him on occasion. I have not seen Melanie since the day we met in Blumenfeld's office. In the meantime, I finished my doctoral degree and moved to Cambridge, Massachusetts, to do postdoctoral research with Dr. Carol Gilligan on girls' and women's psychological development. Subsequently, I was hired as an assistant professor at Harvard and have begun a research project on children's experiences of trauma.

I have created a research and play therapy space, small, but complete with a child's table, shelves of toys and puppets, art materials, dollhouse and doll families. In addition to the two adolescent girls I have been seeing, Erika and Beth, more recently I began to work with Carrie, a six-year-old who is afraid to go to school, afraid of spiders, afraid of the dark; afraid, period. I have conversations with Fred, a floppy brown stuffed dog, as I hold her and listen to her raspy fearful stories. This practice is as big as it will get for now—three children, all girls.

I see Ben in this room, facing away from me, then turning around as he did in our first session. He would be twelve years old now. I have not seen him since he was six, when I returned to Glenwood to visit him. Mary Louise recently told me that he is attending a public school and living with his adoptive parents. He sees a psychiatrist, someone I do not know. I wonder if he remembers me. I find a blue-and-green marble in the side yard of my house and remember Ben spitting six marbles into my waiting hand. Of course he remembers.

I think often about Melanie. My thoughts drift around a core of lasting sadness, sometimes tinged with bitterness, sometimes with compassion. My relationship with Melanie deeply affects my understanding of myself and my questions about clinical relationships, particularly among women.

Carol Gilligan and I have often thought together about the particular difficulties women face in working in a traditional structure of psychotherapy—the desire by both patients and therapists for an authentic and enduring connection in a structure that upholds distance and teaches the necessity of giving up that desire. Precisely because Carol is not a clinician, she brings a unique view to psychotherapy. She and I speak the same language and react in similar ways to the various binds and facades of psychotherapy. I also have spoken at length about clinical relationships with Teresa Bernardez, who supervised my work with an adolescent girl and told me stunning stories of her own relationships with adolescent patients—relationships in which girls fought for a love that was trustworthy and enduring.

Tonight it is raining and I am inside, writing in a circle of light, with a cup of tea. Alice, a compassionate and careful therapist with considerable clinical experience, asked to speak with me about a patient who was abandoned by a therapist she loved because the therapist became frightened and overwhelmed. This patient now hopes for a different relationship with Alice. For the first time in years, I lay on my bed and wept for the loss of Melanie in my life.

As for Blumenfeld, he has not changed much, although he is older now. Last spring I went to see him, and that visit was like walking directly into my book. Blumenfeld is grayer and thinner, and most astonishing, he is much shorter! He said that he knew one day I would write a book, but he did not expect to be a character in it.

"Don't you recognize yourself?" I ask.

"Oh yes, I do."

"You have all the best lines, you know," I chide him.

We do not know if he is to remain Blumenfeld and go on having phone conversations with me in Cambridge, or if we will go out to tea and develop a different kind of relationship. As we puzzle over these possibilities, he remarks that my voice is stronger, my face more alive, and we don't know what will happen next because . . . I join in unison, "The future really is unknowable." "Otherwise, it is only a play of the past," he says. Then he laughs that great deep laugh, a man who loves to wake up in the middle of the night and who sees with his heart.

I have not seen or heard from Telesporus, or Emily, or Galle, or Margaret Mary, or Erin, or any of the others, except in my dreams. I am now taking a watercolor class with a wonderful Japanese man who points out light and shadows. "Look at autumn light. Paint the light." I see light on apples and bark, on the sidewalk, under a single twig. I have had to learn skills that once came to me without effort, those gifts from others within me lent to me during the time of a shining affliction. I feel their steady presence in my life and I am grateful to them for all that is alive in me.

Afterword

The people who come to see us bring us their stories.
They hope they tell them well enough so that we
understand the truths of their lives.
                    —ROBERT COLES, *The Call of Stories*

Take care when you speak to me
I might listen.
                    —TESS GALLAGHER, *Moon Crossing Bridge*

Afterward
I found under my left shoulder
the most curious wound.
As though I had leaned against
some whirring thing,
it bleeds secretly.
Nobody knows its name.
                        —MARY OLIVER, *Dreamwork*

To My Clinical Colleagues:

A Shining Affliction began simply as a lengthy case study about my relationship with the child Ben, drawn from tapes of our sessions and from my extensive notes. For a long time I was reluctant to bring the story of my own failed psychotherapy and subsequent breakdown into this book. What made this addition almost un-thinkable was my observation that clinicians did not reveal the details of their personal histories. Those who wrote most elo-quently about their cases, such as Freud, Winnicott, and Seche-haye, revealed themselves indirectly in the telling. But they focused on their patients and, when speaking about themselves, used an abstract language that often obscured direct access to the inner life of the writer. As therapists, we are acculturated not to disclose the details of our lives. Yet I felt dishonest as I continued to write about Ben without revealing my own experience. To write with any integrity, I had to say clearly how I was wounded and healed in my personal psychotherapy, or my book would not be able to sustain the emotional truths at the heart of my relationship with Ben.

What were those emotional truths? As a novice therapist, I treated an "untreatable" child. Given the enormity of my own psy-chological struggle at the time, I should not have been able to treat him at all, much less work as an effective therapist. Faced with this enigma, I read my own words for the psychology of relationship they contained, sketching out a fragile trace of love and knowledge that runs all through this story. I wrote to Ben, "What you fear most has already happened." But Ben did not know this about himself, and I did not know this about myself either. Both of us, in different ways, had to reexperience or reenact a devastating loss, in order to see that we had survived. What finally became clear, in my overlapping relationships with Ben and with Blumenfeld, was that Ben and I were each the fighting survivors of our own worst nightmares. In our short relationship, we were able to play with one another, to love one another, and to say goodbye. I know that in the process we were each healed in some crucial way.

It has taken several years and many conversations with other patients and therapists for me to realize that the failure of my relationship with Melanie is a rather common story. It is ironic and heartbreaking to hear again and again how therapists took creative risks, which became seductive and false promises, and how, in the end, when they abandoned their patients, they used the language of clinical practice to step away from any real responsibility for those abandonments. When psychotherapy fails, we are accustomed to consider the shortcomings of patients and not the failure of the therapeutic relationship and our own part in it. Interestingly, many of the therapists whom I talked to initially tried to break with the structured distance of traditional psychotherapy because it was not working. At first, their patients were relieved and grateful. But it seems that these therapists had no conceptual structure that enabled them to think critically about the changes they made, and no supervisory relationship that could support the intention of what was, perhaps, their most courageous work. Because this story is relatively common, I think that it represents a systemic problem in clinical practice.

If we consider carefully the possibility that an individual's failed psychotherapy may center around a systemic corruption of a relationship that should be basically trustworthy, then our current practice of psychotherapy becomes suspect, or open to questions. Sometime in the distant future, I wonder if readers will see what seems so obvious that it is hardly worth mentioning in the current moment: that our language is suffused with an us/them split, so that we, the therapists, appear to have no serious psychological difficulties, while our patients clearly reveal whatever pathology fascinates us at any given time. If we are affected in a psychotherapy relationship, this influence is called "countertransference." It is clear that we think we should eliminate such an influence as quickly and painlessly as possible, primarily by thinking about it with colleagues. These false beliefs and distinctions are maintained through clinical training, supervision, and clinical practice. In clinical training, often we are reticent to reveal our own lives for fear that we might be judged as pathological. In supervision, we sometimes do not describe what we actually do in practice, especially if what we do deviates from established norms and if we have serious questions and doubts about it. In practice, if we are uncomfortable, or truly frightened, we have a tendency to blame our patients, and we have concepts readily at hand to effectively squelch any doubts about our assessment. Yet, in the act of defending ourselves, we are most likely to pass on our deepest wounding to our patients. If this seems like a parody, an exaggeration that distorts the current state of affairs, consider these observations at your next conference or public case presentation.

I hope it is apparent from reading *A Shining Affliction* that I love the work of psychotherapy and do not want to turn away from it. I wish that I had the answers to the enigmas of psychotherapy, beyond the story itself. I do not. I have some ideas, however, about how possibilities for harm and healing arise within our current structure of practice.

The psychotherapy relationship is two-sided, whether we acknowledge it is or not. Each person brings to that relationship whatever is unrecognized, unknown, and unapproachable in her or his life, and a wish for knowledge of truths and wholeness. Since one cannot thrive on memories, on a relationship with projections, what keeps alive the hope of wholeness is an interchange of love, longing, frustration, and anger in the vicissitudes of a real relationship. Such an interchange is part of the fragility of this relationship; with openness, one is vulnerable to hurt and to loss, on both sides of the relationship. However, the therapist must, of necessity, understand the vulnerability of both persons involved. This necessity is sometimes very frightening. Yet if it is possible to remain open to our fears and make reparations for our mistakes, our vulnerability can be used in the service of healing. On the other hand, perhaps this terrible vulnerability explains why we sometimes speak as if we know (speaking in some combination of condescension and beneficent authority) what patients need when we do not know, when we cannot possibly know.

In any treatment situation, it is the therapist who is responsible for holding two stories, or two plays, together. The work of sustaining a therapeutic relationship demands a two-sided perspective in order to understand both stories. And the deepening of this relationship over time demands honesty and intimacy and sometimes extraordinary courage. Knowing that we are human, and therefore limited in our understanding and courage, we can be overwhelmed by these responsibilities. We can then create a greater distance to protect ourselves, and even appear to be unmoved by our patients' responses to that distance. But the effect on our patients is deadening whenever we show them that they do not affect us. Or, alternatively, we can create an illusion of intimacy by making false promises, unwittingly seducing patients to reveal their deepest and oldest wishes, as if we could somehow mete out the right responses and withhold what would be harmful, as if we really knew that difference. But neither of these strategies really protects us from the terrible responsibility of holding another's heart in our hands, at least for a time, while not forsaking ourselves.

As I write this sketch of my observations about clinical practice, I see that, rather obviously, they carry the story of the book as a whole. I hope that others—parents, teachers, patients of every age, but clinicians especially—will read this story as if standing outside a house at a window at night, peering into a room at once familiar and unfamiliar, and watching an unfolding drama that adumbrates their own knowledge of relationships in psychotherapy.

Acknowledgments

Five people deserve particular thanks for accompanying me over several years in the writing of this book. Louis Smith got me started writing it and responded extensively to the first draft. Carol Gilligan asked me crucial questions and gave me the gift of her sensitive and perceptive readings. Dorothy Austin challenged me to understand and forgive the characters in this book. Meg Turner read several drafts of the manuscript with knowledge and love. Mary Mullens Rogers, my oldest friend and sister, was a wise critic and steady support throughout the years of writing and revising this book.

Many friends who read and commented on drafts of this book helped me to shape its final form: Teresa Bernardez, Mary Casey, Nancy Coyne, Kathleen Curtis, Joan Erikson, Kathryn Geismar, Cynthia Hazen, Judy Jordon, Ruthellen Josselson, Jane Loevinger, Laura Maciuika, Vicki Magee, Joe Maxwell, JoAnn Miller, Kitty Moore, Normi Noel, Kate O'Neill, Arthur Rosenthal, Marilyn Southard, Catherine Steiner-Adair, and Karen Theilman.

This book is most deeply indebted to the characters in it: Charles and Kate Brinker, Helen Hoeltzman, Mary Rogers, Michael Connelly, Rachael Sachs and Mary Louise Sweeney. I also want to acknowledge my friends Sarah and Patricia, as well as friends within: Emily, Galle, Margaret Mary and Erin. This book would not exist without my mother and father: Margaret Mary Mulvihill Rogers and Otis Benjamin Rogers. Telesporus, you are going to wing your way into many people's lives, I hope. I want to thank Melanie Sherman for teaching me so much about myself, and Sam Blumenfeld for a ground of sanity to walk upon. To Ben, I send my love.

I want to thank Carol Gilligan for sending me to my agent, Katinka Matson, and thank Katinka for finding Nan Graham and Courtney Hodell for me. Courtney Hodell, who became my editor, gave me excellent line edits, raised challenging questions, and cautioned me not to change this book too much. She has been a strong ally of the book throughout the publishing process.

Finally, I want to acknowledge Ide B. O'Carroll, grá mo chroí, for her sustaining love.